Databases:
From Relational to
Object-Oriented Systems

Databases:
From Relational to
Object-Oriented Systems

Claude Delobel
Christophe Lécluse
Philippe Richard

INTERNATIONAL THOMSON PUBLISHING

I(T)P An International Thomson Publishing Company

London • Bonn • Boston • Madrid • Melbourne • Mexico City • New York • Paris • Singapore
Tokyo • Toronto • Albany, NY • Belmont, CA • Cincinnati, OH • Detroit, MI

Databases:
From Relational to Object-Oriented Systems

Commissioning Editor:	Samantha Whittaker
Editorial Assistant:	Jonathan Simpson

The Publisher gratefully acknowledges the help of Dr Jack Howlett in the preparation of this edition.

Made in Logotechnics C.P.C. Ltd., Sheffield

Project Management:	Sandra M. Potestà
Production:	H.-D. Rauschner, O. Jackson + Team
Artistic Direction:	Stefano E. Potestà
Cover Illustration:	William Smith

First printed 1995

International Thomson Publishing
Berkshire House
168–173 High Holborn
London WC1V 7AA

ISBN   1-850-32124-8

British Library Cataloguing-in-Publication Data
A catalogue record for this book is available from the British Library

Bases de données: des systèmes
relationnels aux systèmes à objets
© 1991, InterEditions, Paris

Contents

Preface

The last decade has seen important progress as regards relational database management systems in professional environments. These are mostly the result of the research and development undertaken during the 1970s which was designed to provide new technology for databases. This technology evolved from the progress made in various domains:

- The definition of a query language which is independent of data organisation.

- The automatic translation of a declarative language into a procedural language.

- The efficient management of the disk for large amounts of data.

- Transactional management which guarantees secure and easy concurrent access for users.

From the beginning of the 1980s, this research has taken a new direction due to two factors in particular.

On the one hand, users are demanding new facilities which are not catered for by database systems on the market which were designed to satisfy the needs of application management. Since the mid-1980s, applications developed from new innovations where the design process is central (computer aided design, document design, developments in software, office and production technology, ...) have become much more important.

On the other hand, the use of relational systems has demonstrated certain limitations in application development. Most of the time, the latter necessitate the implementation of at least two languages: one language of the imperative type such as Cobol, PL/1, Pascal or C, and a relational language such as SQL. Errors, whose causes can be clearly identified, are brought about by the communication between the two languages. These errors cause problems, so much so that the data structures manipulated by the languages are more inaccessible.

Many areas of research have been considered. Persistant languages (languages which allow us to manipulate persistant data in a way which is more or less transparent) constitute one of these areas. Work on this area can be traced back to the beginning of the 1980s, when languages like PS-Algol and Pascal proposed the first basic techniques. However, one of the most important phenomena of the last few years has been the bringing together of object-oriented languages and databases. Concepts of abstract data type, of modularity and of software reuse, introduced by object-oriented languages, are major extensions for database systems. Numerous prototypes have been developed and products appear on the market. In this book, we focus on this approach in particular, taking into consideration the experience of the authors who, since 1986, have been part of the GIP Altaïr team, which has developed the object-oriented databases system O_2. This experience is recounted in the book *Building an Object-Oriented Database System: The Story of O_2*[1], which shows different aspects of the design and development of the O_2 system. In this study, our approach is complimentary. We do not offer a description of one system and its genesis, on the contrary, we have attempted to encapsulate and outline the different currents of evolution amongst database systems.

There are four distinct sections to this book. The first section describes the evolution of databases, out of relational systems, in response to the demands of new applications. In the second part, the fundamental principles behind data models and the type systems of programming languages is described. The key to understanding the new database systems lies with the integration of these two domains. The third section illustrates, by presenting the existing systems, the aspects which were expounded in section two. The principles behind the object-oriented systems and a detailed presentation of the O2 system constitute the bulk of this section. Finally, the fourth part presents the architecture of the systems when they are implemented.

---

1 *Building an Object-Oriented Database System: The Story of O_2*, F. Bancilhon, C. Delobel, P. Kanellakis, (Editors), Morgan-Kaufmann, 1991.

Acknowledgements

This book would never have seen the light of day, in all probability, had it not been for the creation, in September 1986, of GIP Altaïr[2], of which we were a part. We wish to thank, in particular, its Director, François Bancilhon, as well as all the staff at Altaïr whose scientific and technical support was indispensable and who enabled us to complete this work.

We also wish to thank Serge Abiteboul, Michel Adiba, Veronique Benzaken, Christine Collet, Anne Doucet, Jean-Marie Larcheveque, and Michel Scholl for their encouragement and comments which greatly helped to improve this work.

We also offer our thanks to those that gave us help on certain technical points. We are particularly thinking of Malcolm Atkinson, Dave DeWitt, Dave Maier and Patrick Valduriez.

Finally, we also wish to thank all the teams on the Esprit FIDE project, who supported us scientifically and helped us to clarify our ideas.

Claude Delobel   Université de Paris-Sud GIP Altaïr
Christophe Lécluse INRIA GIP Altaïr
Philippe Richard   INRIA GIP Altaïr

About the authors

Professor Claude Delobel is a lecturer at the University of Paris-Sud. Dr Christophe Lécluse was a researcher at INRIA in the Altaïr Project, and he is presently Technical Director of AIS, a company specialized in electronic publishing. Dr Philippe Richard was Director of Research at INRIA in the Altaïr Project and he is presently leading a research group in the Corporate Research Center Alcatel Alsthom.

---

2   GIP Altaïr is a non-profit making group founded by INRIA, IN2 Group Siemens, Bull and the LRI (Université de Paris-Sud and CNRS).

Part I

Towards a new generation of systems

The aim of this part is to summarize the evolution of databases up to and including the development of relational systems.

Chapter 1 defines the general principles of database management systems. Chapter 2 describes the main principles of the relational model and systems. In Chapter 3, we show the limitations of these systems and the need for a new generation of systems that can provide the specific functions required by the new database applications.

1

Database management systems

Any definition is a limit.
André Suarès
Variables

1.1 The concept of the database

In the past few years, and in particular because of the increased use of telematics, the general public has become relatively familiar with the concept of the database. Roughly speaking, a database can be seen as a collection of data managed by a computer which can be accessed by several users at the same time.

The idea of the database was in fact conceived in the 1960s. It was during that period that, as storage device technology evolved, applications for managing large quantities of data were developed. These first applications held their data in files and used the standard access methods via programming languages such as Fortran, PL/1, Pascal or Cobol. During this period considerable effort was put into improving the physical file supports and developing techniques for accessing files and records.

However, the data that needed to be held in order to manage a company, for example, was becoming increasingly complex and more and more interdependent. The users of various data files wanted to *integrate* files and

3

applications which had previously been used independently. They also wanted to be able to represent more complex links between the various records.

Thus the concept of the file was gradually replaced by that of the database. The latter can be defined as follows, taken from [DA82]:

> *A database is a structured set of data items which can be accessed by the computer in order to satisfy several users simultaneously, within an appropriate time.*

The database management system (DBMS) is the software package used to interact with the database. A user can use it to define data, to consult the database or to update it. An essential aspect of these systems is that they must allow users to specify the data they wish to find in abstract terms, while at the same time undertaking the search according to how the data is organized in the database. More specifically, the aims of a database management system are as follows:

- Links between data

- Data consistency

- Ease of access to data

- Data security

- Data sharing

- Data independence

- Performance

- Administration and control

Let us discuss these points one by one.

1.1.1 Links between data

Traditional file management systems are inadequate because they do not allow complex links between data items to be defined or handled. These links correspond to the associations you can identify between application *objects*, which you want to represent. A DBMS must be based on a *data model* whose specific aim is to define the way data items represented in the system are structured and the links that can be established between those data items.

1.1.2 Data consistency

When a set of data items containing a large amount of knowledge is stored, the stored data must be consistent with reality. This is why a DBMS must allow the user to define rules for maintaining the consistency of the database. These rules define properties that the data items must satisfy. Maintaining the consistency of a database also involves installing a system of permissions so that certain operations can be restricted to groups of responsible users.

1.1.3 Ease of access to data

A DBMS must allow any data item in the database to be accessed easily. More specifically, the system must allow data to be accessed using high-level declarative (non-procedural) languages called query languages. These languages contrast sharply with the classic file management operations which are limited and totally procedural.

Users can use query languages interactively to consult or modify a database. There are therefore two different ways of accessing a database: in an application connected to the DBMS (that is, a user program) or interactively, using a query language.

1.1.4 Data security

A DBMS must be capable of protecting the data it manages against any external aggression. Such aggression may be physical, such as the breakdown of a storage device or a software error, or it may be human, such as a deliberately destructive operation executed by a user. In order to protect the data against hardware and software faults, the DBMS must allow *checkpoints* to be set, so that the system can be restarted and restored to a satisfactory state. It must also *log* changes made to the data, so that any changes can be undone and/or redone.

1.1.5 Data sharing

Previously, we stated that the need to share data between several applications was one of the main reasons for the formulation of the database concept. Different applications working with the same data must be able to execute as if they were the only one working with that data. The DBMS must provide the means for managing data sharing and for detecting any access conflicts that may arise between several users or applications and provide the tools for resolving them.

1.1.6 Data independence

Data independence is one of the major advantages provided by a database management system. An application that handles data using a file system is strongly *dependent* on its data. The application must know how the files are structured and the methods for accessing them. If, for some reason, the way the files are structured or the access methods have to be changed, this cannot be done without requiring modifications to the application. In contrast, a DBMS should allow applications to be written without the programmer having to worry about the physical structure of the data and the associated access methods. Thus the system can evolve to take account of new needs without disturbing applications that have already been written.

Data independence is a concept linked with the evolution and maintenance of an application. You should realize that the cost of maintaining traditional applications is often far higher than the cost of writing them in the first place. For this very reason, any factors that make it easier to develop future versions of an application, and particularly data independence, represent possible large-scale savings. This is one of the major reasons for using a DBMS.

We can distinguish two levels of independence: physical independence and logical independence.

Physical independence should allow changes to be made to the storage structures or the data access methods without there being any repercussions at applications level. Thus an index can be added to a collection of data or deleted from it, the internal representation of numeric data can be changed or the sorting method altered. It is very important to be able to update the way data is represented physically, so that the system can adapt itself to deal with data belonging to specific applications whose performance criteria require different access methods. The performance of a system that does not allow the physical and logical representation of data to be clearly separated will *only* be good for the data configuration and the application the programmer initially had in mind.

Logical independence should allow the way data is organized to be changed without it affecting the users. The purpose of this level of independence is to allow an existing database to be enriched by adapting to new structures, without disturbing those that already exist. Therefore, logical independence allows new needs to be accounted for, which is essential when you remember that a database is a model of the real world and that the real world, just like the users' needs, changes over time.

It is obvious that the principle of data independence is an ideal which is often very difficult to attain and that, depending on the system under consideration, we will find different levels of independence.

1.1.7 Performance

The above aims must be realized without detriment to the system's overall performance. A DBMS must be capable of managing a large volume of data and providing users with reasonable access times. This need for performance has meant that a large part of database technology has been, and still is, devoted to improving access techniques and optimization. The problems of performance and optimization underlie all the problems considered in the database domain.

1.1.8 Administration and control

System administrators play a prime role in the design and maintenance of a DBMS. As a database is used by several users at the same time, and those users have needs which may sometimes be incompatible, the control and administration of the database must be entrusted to someone who is independent. More specifically, the role of administrators is as follows:

- Deciding what data is to be stored in the database.
  Administrators are responsible for defining the structures of the data contained in the database and for making any subsequent changes to it to take new applications into account.

- Deciding on the physical structures and the access strategies.
  Administrators define how data is represented at the physical level as well as the various storage and access methods. Physical independence should make it possible to specify these in an entirely autonomous fashion.

- Defining the permissions granted to users.

- Defining the checkpoints and backups.

- Optimizing the physical organization in order to improve the system's overall performance or take new specifications into account.

To sum up, system administrators are responsible for managing all aspects of the DBMS that are not automated and must be transparent at user level. Their role is all the more important because an application using a database management system has a long life cycle and during that life cycle the application will often have to evolve in order to adapt to new specifications.

1.2 Levels of representation

We have seen that the concept of data independence is a fundamental aspect of a DBMS. Generally, in order to attain that independence, three levels of representation are considered: the physical level, the conceptual level and the external level. Figure 1.1 illustrates that architecture.

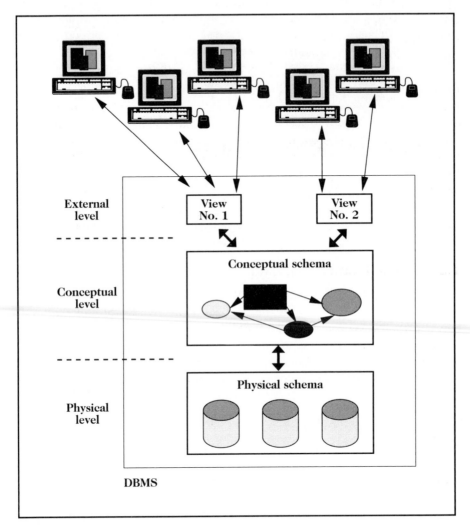

Figure 1.1 Levels of representation

1.2.1 The physical level

The physical level defines the database's physical schema, that is, how the data is represented on the storage device used by the computer system. The physical schema is defined in terms of files and records. The computer's file management system and operating system are responsible for the actual management of peripherals and devices.

1.2.2 The conceptual level

The role of the conceptual level is to define and manage the conceptual schema, which is the logical representation, inside the system, of the reality which the database is supposed to transcribe. You can see, therefore, that the conceptual level is the main part of the DBMS.

Defining the conceptual schema is a *modelling* process, because it involves translating real-world entities into abstract terms. The DBMS provides a *data model* for this process, with an associated *data definition language* which is used to specify the conceptual schema within that model.

The data model has very important repercussions on the type of applications a DBMS can support and on how those applications are built. In fact, the model defines the system's vision of the real-world. Applications have to use the possibilities the model provides and put up with its constraints.

Until now, three main models have been used in existing database management systems. They are the hierarchical, network and relational models.

1.2.2.1 The hierarchical model

In the hierarchical model data is organized in a tree structure. Each node in the tree corresponds to a class of entities in the real-world and the arcs between the nodes represent the links between the objects. Systems like IMS are based on this model. Numerous situations can thus be represented, but the tree structure of the graph of objects becomes limiting when you want to model the sharing of certain data items.

1.2.2.2 The network model

The network model is an extension of the hierarchical model in which the graph of objects is not limited. Amongst other things, it allows objects to be shared and cyclic links between objects to be represented. This is the model used by CODASYL systems. In the network model, a conceptual schema is composed of *record* definitions, which define the entities and the links between those entities, and of *set* definitions, which express the multivalued links between the records.

1.2.2.3 The relational model

The relational model is based on the mathematical idea of a relation. It allows data to be represented in the form of tables whose size is predefined. For example, a person is modelled as a row in a database table. Each element in the row represents one of the person's characteristics (his or her name, age, and so on). This model will be described in greater detail in Chapter 2.

1.2.3 The external level

A DBMS is used by several users at the same time. The conceptual schema represents all the data known by the system, but individually each user only uses a small fraction of that data. Therefore a DBMS provides, at external level, the concept of the view (or the sub-schema) which allows users to be shown the part of the conceptual schema that corresponds to their needs (or their access rights!).

The idea of a view is more than just a simple restriction of the conceptual schema. A view can also provide a user with data *synthesized* from the data actually represented in the database. For example, a view could give statistics about a set of people about whom the conceptual schema had detailed data.

The external level is the one that allows logical data independence to be achieved. The global schema of a database can evolve in order to take new needs into account without disturbing existing applications, as long as the views are preserved.

The problem in defining such general views lies in translating operations from the external level (the view) to the conceptual level (the database). The problem of updating view in relational systems, in particular, has not yet been resolved generally and there is probably no general solution. An important consequence of this is the fact that most systems do not provide complete logical independence.

1.3 Using a DBMS

Let us now describe the languages used at each level for building and manipulating a database.

1.3.1 Data definition language

The data definition language (DDL) is used to specify the database's conceptual schema. Naturally, it is very strongly linked to the data model used by the DBMS. It allows all the concepts whose representation is permitted by the model to be defined and modified.

This language should not contain any information about the physical organization of the data or the storage device. The conceptual schema describes the logical organization of the data and should not be affected by how the data is managed physically. This separation is directly dependent on the level of physical independence provided by the system.

Finally, the data definition language is used to specify the views, and therefore the external level. Even though *a priori* they could be specified using a language that is independent of the DDL, most systems use the same language to specify the views and the conceptual schema.

If, for example, you wanted to represent towns with their names and populations[1], you could do it in a network system in the following way:

```
area name is The_towns

record name is Town
   location mode is system default
   within The_towns;
   identifier is name in Town
   02 population; type is fixed decimal 10;
   02 name; type is character 30;
```

You could write the same definition, in a system that uses the relational model, thus:

```
create table The_towns (
                population integer,
                name char(30) )
```

As the data definition language is intimately linked to the underlying data model, there are very important differences between the data definition languages of existing systems. Porting an application from one system to another is a task that calls for a great deal of time and energy.

1.3.2 Physical description language

A DBMS also provides a language for specifying the physical organization of data. This physical organization involves describing the storage devices, the placing of data, the access methods and the file organization (inversion, chaining, B trees, and so on). System administrators, whose aim is to improve the overall performance of the system for which they are responsible, can choose from among these implementation options. Obviously, the ultimate aim is that the DBMS should take complete responsibility for physical organization, but existing systems are far from achieving this ideal.

---

[1]   The examples used in this book are based on a pilot application developed at GIP Altaïr which describes the business of a travel agency.

1.3.3 Data manipulation language

The data definition language is used to define the database schema. The DBMS also provides a language for searching, consulting and updating the data in the database.

The style of the data manipulation language is also very dependent on the model being used. In a system using a network model, the data manipulation language is composed of elementary commands such as **find**, **get**, **store**, **modify**. These are used to navigate the database by searching for data, either by direct access or by association (**find**), by reading data (**get**) or by modifying it (**modify**). The program below shows a sequence of commands used to display the names of towns with more than 100 000 inhabitants:

```
find first Person record
while not fail do begin
    get Town; name, population
    if population > 100000 then print name;
    find next Town record
end
```

It is important to note that data manipulation languages like the one above are simply lists of commands which must be embedded in host languages like Pascal or Cobol.

The data manipulation languages associated with the relational model are much more declarative because they are based on a logical language. In SQL (Structured Query Language), which is used by most relational systems, the above query is written as follows:

```
select name
from Town
where population > 100000
```

1.3.4 Application programs

Application programs that use the database are written at external level, that is to say they only need the knowledge of the system that is available to a user. The application is written in a normal programming language and communicates with the DBMS by sending commands written in the data manipulation language. Actual transfers of data between the application and the DBMS are done using a buffer memory area into which data is written and from which it is read. This mechanism is shown in Figure 1.2.

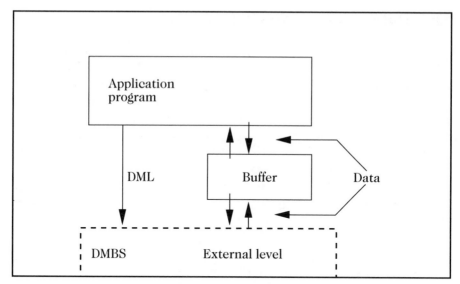

Figure 1.2 Communication between a DBMS and an application.

The way in which the applications that use the DBMS are programmed, and therefore the way in which the DBMS is coupled with a general programming language, has important repercussions, firstly on the level of logical independence provided by the system and secondly on its overall performance. In reality, an application is not simply a conceptual schema manipulated using a data manipulation language; it also includes a large amount of general programming that uses data extracted from the database by means of the data manipulation language. When the system administrator wants to change the logical organization of the data, those changes may have effects not only on the data manipulation commands but also on the Pascal, Cobol or PL1 programs. As far as performance goes, the way in which data is transferred between the general programming language and the DBMS is the determining factor in system performance. We will come back to this point later in Chapters 2 and 11.

Bibliographical notes

This chapter's contents have been derived, in the main, from [DA82]. You can also find a general introduction to database management systems in [Ull89] and in [Dat86].

A DBMS's three-level architecture is described in the report [Gro75]. The essential concepts behind databases, and particularly the concept of the data model, have been described using examples that correspond to the network and relational models.

Exercises

1. Define the eight aims of a database management system.

2. Data independence is an essential part of a DBMS. What are the two types of data independence and why are they so important?

3. What advantages does a DBMS have for the applications programmer over traditional file management systems?

4. Describe the role of a database administrator.

5. Generally, databases are divided into three levels. How would you distinguish between those levels?

6. What is the importance of the data model?

7. Until now, most commercial systems have used one of three data models. What are they and how do they differ?

8. A DBMS usually provides two different languages. What are they and to which of the levels do they correspond?

9. What is the difference between a data manipulation language program for a network model DBMS and one for a relational DBMS?

10. In what languages are application programs written and how do they communicate with the DBMS?

2

Relational systems

Everything has already been said; but as no one ever listens,
it has to be said over and over again.
André Gide
Traité du Narcisse

2.1 Towards the relational model

The relational model was not the first to be proposed as a definition of a database's conceptual schema. However, ever since Codd first proposed it in 1970, its popularity and its use in prototypes and commercial systems has gone from strength to strength. Today, it is true to say that the relational model and the systems that use it dominate the database market.

We must therefore ask ourselves why relational systems have achieved this dominance and what are this model's essential advantages over previous models, and in particular over the network model, which was the most widely used for a long time.

The function of a data model is to represent the real-world inside the system. In most applications the model must represent entities (like people, historic buildings, and so on.) and the associations between those entities. The differences between the various models lie essentially in the place (preponderant or not) that they assign to one of those categories in relation to the other.

Let us take as an example a simple application that manages data about the famous historic buildings in a country's main towns. The conceptual schema must define, in particular, the concepts of historic building, town and country and the links between those entities: a town has several historic buildings but a historic building can only belong to one town.

2.1.1 Using the network model

2.1.1.1 Defining the schema

In a system using the network model, the application's conceptual schema will be represented in the following way:

```
1   schema name is Historic_building_management

2   area name is The_Towns
3   area name is The_Historic_buildings
4   area name is The_Countries

5   record name is Towns
6         location mode is system default;
7         within The_Towns
8         identifier is town_no in Towns
9         02 town_no; type is character 5
10        02 name; type is character 30
11        02 population; type is fixed decimal 10
12        02 country_no; type is character 5

13  record name is Countries
14        location mode is system default;
15        within The_Countries
16        identifier is country_no in Countries
17        02 country_no; type is character 5
18        02 name; type is character 30

19  record name is Historic_buildings
20        location mode is system default;
21        within The_Historic_buildings
22        identifier is hb_no in Historic_buildings
23        02 hb_no; type is character 5
24        02 name; type is character 30
25        02 entrance_fee; type is fixed decimal 4
26        02 address
27              03 number; type is fixed decimal 3
28              03 road; type is character 30
29              03 town_no; type is character 5
```

```
30 set name is Countries_towns;
31       owner is Countries
32       order is permanent sorted by defined keys
33       member is Towns
34             insertion is automatic
35             retention is fixed
36             key is ascending name in Countries
37             duplicates are not allowed
38             nulls are not allowed
39       set selection is thru Countries_towns owner
40             identified by identifier country_no in Countries

41 set name is Towns_historic_buildings;
42       owner is Towns
43       order is permanent sorted by defined keys
44       member is Historic_buildings
45             insertion is automatic
46             retention is fixed
47             key is ascending name in Towns
48             duplicates are not allowed
49             nulls are not allowed
50       set selection is thru Towns_historic_buildings owner
51             identified by identifier town_no in Towns
```

The three **record** clauses define the entities representing the towns, countries and historic buildings. The **set** clauses define the (multi-valued) links between the countries and the towns on the one hand, and the towns and the historic buildings on the other. These clauses express the facts that a country contains several towns and a town contains several historic buildings. The **insertion** and **retention** clauses describe the required system behaviour when the link's **owner** or **member** entities are updated.

We should make several comments at this point. Firstly, it is quite obvious that describing a very simple conceptual schema, such as the one we have chosen, entails relatively long-winded counter-intuitive definitions. Furthermore, those definitions intermix quite intimately the descriptions of the conceptual schema and the physical data. The clauses in lines 6, 14, 20, 32, 36, 43 and 47 are descriptions of access paths and storage. The fact that you have to specify the schema and its implementation *at the same time* goes against the principle of physical independence described in the previous chapter.

2.1.1.2 Data manipulation

In this example of data manipulation, we assume that we know the name of a town and that we want to display the names of all the historic buildings whose entrance fee is more than the average entrance fee for that town.

In order to do this in a CODASYL system, the data manipulation commands must be used inside a program written in a programming language such as Pascal, C or Cobol. For example, we could use the Pascal code below:

```
Towns.name:= "Town";
average:= 0;
number:= 0;
find Towns record
find first Historic_buildings record in current
Towns_historic_buildings set
while not fail do begin
    get Historic_buildings; entrance_fee
    average:= average + entrance_fee
    number:= number + 1
    find next Historic_buildings record in current
Towns_historic_buildings set
end
average:= average / number;

find first Historic_buildings record in current
Towns_historic_buildings set
while not fail do begin
    get Historic_buildings; entrance_fee name
    if entrance_fee > average then
        print name
    find next Historic_buildings record in current
Towns_historic_buildings set
end
```

Once again, it is clear that expressing something very simple in the data manipulation language is extremely complex. The first part of the program initializes temporary variables. Then the Town_historic_buildings set is processed sequentially in order to calculate the average entrance fee. The set is processed using a pointer manipulated by the **find first** and **find next** commands. The last part of the program is a second sequential run-through of the *same* set to select the historic buildings with an entrance fee greater than the average and display their names.

The data manipulation language is entirely procedural because it is simply a series of commands (**find**, **get**, and so on) integrated into imperative code.

2.1.2 Using the relational model

Now let us look at how the same conceptual schema and the same data manipulation can be expressed in the relational model. We gave a brief account of this model's concepts in the previous chapter. The next section will give a fuller definition.

2.1.2.1 Schema definition

When we use the SQL relational schema definition language, we get the following definition:

```
create table Countries (
    country_no char(5),
    name char(30) )

create table Towns (
    town_no char(5),
    name char(30),
    population integer,
    country_no char(5) )

create table Historic_buildings (
    hb_no char(5),
    name char(30),
    entrance_fee integer,
    add_no integer,
    add_road char(30),
    add_town char(5) )

create table Towns_in_countries (
    town_no char(5),
    country_no char(5) )

create table Historic_buildings_in_towns (
    town_no char(5),
    hb_no char(5) )
```

You can see that the relational model represents the entities (Countries, Towns, Historic buildings) and the links between those entities (Towns_in_countries, Historic_buildings_in_towns) in the same way. Also notice that the address of a historic building, which was represented in the network model as a sub-record of a Historic_buildings record, must here be broken up inside the Historic_buildings relation. We will see a little later on that this corresponds to a basic hypothesis of the relational model. Finally, notice that this description of the application's conceptual schema contains no information about the physical storage of the data. Separate commands are used to define indices on one or more attributes of a relation.

2.1.2.2 Data manipulation

In SQL, you can write the program for searching for those historic buildings whose entrance fee is higher than the average as follows:

```
select name
from Historic_buildings
where entrance_fee > select avg(entrance_fee)
                     from Historic_buildings
                     where add_town = select town_no
                                      from Towns
                                      where name = "Town"
```

You can see from this example that data manipulation can be done in a purely declarative way in the relational model; you can use the SQL language **select...from...where** construct to express complex filtering operations in a compact syntax. The most deeply nested filter selects the town (the town number) with the required name. The filter one level above calculates the average entrance fee of the historic buildings in that town, using the **avg** operation. Finally, the first filter extracts the names of the historic buildings whose entrance fee is higher than the average. The SQL language is described in greater detail in Section 2.3.

2.2 The relational model

2.2.1 The concept of a relation

The relational model is based on the mathematical concept of a relation. A relation is a subset of the Cartesian product of various domains. For obvious reasons, we are only interested in finite relations, even if the domains on which they are constructed are infinite (the domain of integers, for example).

1	2	3
Paris	2600000	France
Marseille	1000000	France
Brussels	1000000	Belgium
Berlin	1300000	Germany
Madrid	1200000	Spain

Figure 2.1 An example of a relation

The relation in Figure 2.1 is built on three domains: the domain of town names, the domain of integers and the domain of country names. Each element in the relation, that is, each elementary association, is called a tuple. To make the representation of relations more meaningful, the column numbers are replaced by names. These are called *attributes*. A *domain* is associated with each attribute. The use of named attributes makes the ordering of columns insignificant. The above example can be re-ordered, using the attributes name, population and country, as in Figure 2.2.

name	pop.	country	name	country	pop.
Paris	2600000	France	Paris	France	2600000
Marseille	1000000	France	Brussels	Belgium	1000000
Brussels	1000000	Belgium	Berlin	Germany	1300000
Berlin	1300000	Germany	Marseille	France	1000000
Madrid	1200000	Spain	Madrid	Spain	1200000

Figure 2.2 Two representations of the same relation

As suggested in [Ull89], a relation can actually be seen as a set of partial functions[1] which associate an attribute with an element in its domain. This definition is certainly more exact than that based on the mathematical idea of a relation. However, what is also evident is that tabular representation is the simplest and most intuitive, even if the order of rows and columns is not significant.

2.2.2 The relational schema

Relations are constructed on *relation* schemas. A relation schema is made up of a name for the relation and a list of its attributes together with their associated domains. The relation schema is thus the *intensional* part of the relation, whereas the list of tuples in the relation is the *extensional* part. As well as the relation schemas, a relational schema provides the means for specifying the intensional part of the database more precisely by introducing *integrity constraints*.

Integrity constraints are general rules whose role is to specify which instances of relations are meaningful[2]. Numerous classes of constraints have been proposed in the context of the relational model and a significant part of the theory of relational systems has consisted, and still consists, of the

---

1   Each function represents a tuple.

2   That is, consistent in terms of the real-world we are modelling.

study of these constraints from the point of view of their modelling power and the ways in which the system can verify them. A particularly important example of these dependencies is *functional dependency*.

The idea of a key is found in all the models that have been used to represent the conceptual schema. For example, the key of a CODASYL set is a value which is used to identify and/or find one or more records of a predetermined type. In the more formal context of the relational model we can give a precise definition of a key.

A set of attributes X is a key to the relation R if there are no two different tuples in R which have the same values for attributes X and if this property is not true for any subset of X.

Key definitions are integrity constraints which are defined at schema level. Thus we can define a relational schema representing the towns and historic buildings in our application in the manner shown in Figure 2.3, where the keys correspond to the attributes in bold.

```
Towns (name, population, country)
Historic_buildings (name, entrance_fee, number, road, town)
```

Figure 2.3 A relational schema

It is evident that the main part of the work involved in building a relational schema consists of choosing the set of relation schemas you are going to use. There are numerous possible choices for representing the same data. We could have chosen a different schema to that shown in Figure 2.3 to model our application, the one shown in Figure 2.4, for example.

```
Historic_buildings (name, entrance_fee, number, road, town,
population, country)
```

Figure 2.4 An alternative to the schema shown in Figure 2.3

In that solution, a single relation is considered adequate for containing all the data about the historic buildings, the towns and the countries. One of the essential contributions of the relational model has been to provide, by using a formal approach to the problem of integrity constraints, a theoretical basis for the problem of modelling. It has thus allowed us to define what constitutes good relational schemas and has provided methods and tools for designing them.

In the above example, relational theory shows us that the schema in Figure 2.4 is not well constructed, given the constraints that can be picked out in our application. We know that a town can only be in one country. On the other hand, a town can contain several historic buildings. In order to represent two historic buildings we will have to store two tuples, and therefore represent the information about a town being in a given country twice. It is therefore better to decompose the relation in Figure 2.4 into two relations and thus obtain the schema in Figure 2.3.

2.2.3 Null values

When DBMS users manipulate data and, in particular, when they introduce new data into the database, they do not always have complete information about that new data. If, for example, they wish to insert a new historic building into the database with the schema in Figure 2.3 without knowing the entrance fee, the fact that the data is structured into tuples does not allow them to do this immediately, because the Historic_buildings relation explicitly requires three values.

In order to resolve this incomplete information problem, which is a very common practical problem, you can use *null values*. They are represented by a special symbol, $\perp$, which can replace a value from any domain.

In order to define historic buildings without knowing their entrance fees or define towns without knowing their countries, you can use these null values. You will get relations like the ones below:

name	entrance_fee	town
Eiffel_tower	27.50	Paris
Louvre	$\perp$	Paris
Great_pyramid	$\perp$	$\perp$

Numerous theoretical works have been written about the semantic definition of these null values, and in particular about how they behave when the database is queried or updated.

We have defined the idea of a relation, which is at the heart of the relational model, and given an outline of how integrity constraints are used; in particular the definition and the use of keys to relations. Now we are going to consider the problem of manipulating those relations. The relational model provides two types of language for doing this: an algebraic language based on operators that combine relations, and a logical language that allows you to specify relations by using logical formulæ. An interesting point about relational theory is that these two languages of very different types have exactly the same powers of expression. We will come back to this point in Section 2.2.6.

2.2.4 The relational algebra

The relational algebra is a set of operators which are used to manipulate relations. We can isolate five primitive operators, from which the others can be derived; each of these operators generates a new relation.

- *Projection.*
  The projection operator, written π, is used to ignore certain columns from a relation. Figure 2.5 shows the projection of the Towns relation on the name attribute, written π_{name}(Towns). This projection returns the set of names of towns and ignores the rest of the information in the relation.

- *Selection.*
  The selection operator, written σ, is used to select a subset of a relation using a predicate. Figure 2.5 gives the relation $\sigma_{population>1\ 500\ 000}$(Towns), that is, the descriptions of towns with a population larger than one and a half million inhabitants.

- *Union.*
  The union operator takes as arguments two relations with the same attributes and unites the tuples of those relations. The domains of the respective attributes in the two relations must be the same.

- *Difference.*
  The difference operator is also applied to relations with the same attributes and the same domains. The difference between the two relations is the set of tuples in the first relation that are not in the second.

- *Cartesian product.*
  The Cartesian product takes two relations as arguments. Each n-tuple of the resulting relation is made up of a tuple from the first relation and a tuple from the second. Figure 2.6 shows the Cartesian product of the relations Towns and Historic_buildings.

Other operators can be built from these five primitive operators which, though they do not add to the power of the algebra, are very often useful short cuts.

- *Intersection.*
  The intersection of two relations can be obtained from the union and the difference.

- *Division.*
  If R and S are two relations built on the attributes $A_1... A_n – B_1... B_p$ and $B_1... B_p$ respectively, then the quotient relation $R \div S$ constructed on attributes $A_1... A_n$ is made up of those tuples $a_1... a_n$ such that for *every* tuple $b_1... b_p$ in S, the tuple $a_1... a_n b_1... b_p$ is in R.

Towns:	name	population	country
	Paris	2600000	France
	Marseille	1600000	France
	Caen	200000	France
	Lille	1000000	France

Cities:	name	population	country
	Brussels	1000000	Belgium
	Berlin	1300000	Germany
	Madrid	1200000	Spain
	Paris	2600000	France
	Lille	1000000	France

π_{name}(Towns):	name
	Paris
	Marseille
	Caen
	Lille

$\sigma_{population>1500000}$(Towns):	name	population	country
	Paris	2600000	France
	Marseille	1600000	France

Towns $\cup$ Cities:	name	population	country
	Paris	2600000	France
	Marseille	1600000	France
	Caen	200000	France
	Lille	1000000	France
	Brussels	1000000	Belgium
	Berlin	1300000	Germany
	Madrid	1200000	Spain

Towns – Cities:	name	population	country
	Marseille	1600000	France
	Caen	200000	France

Figure 2.5 The use of relational operators

Towns:	town_name	country		
	Paris	France		
	Marseille	France		
	Caen	France		
	Lille	France		

Historic_buildings:	hb_name	entrance_fee		
	Eiffel_tower	52.00		
	Museum	48.00		

Towns × Historic_buildings:	town_name	country	hb_name	entrance_fee
	Paris	France	Eiffel_tower	52.00
	Marseille	France	Eiffel_tower	52.00
	Caen	France	Eiffel_tower	52.00
	Lille	France	Eiffel_tower	52.00
	Paris	France	Museum	48.00
	Marseille	France	Museum	48.00
	Caen	France	Museum	48.00
	Lille	France	Museum	48.00

Figure 2.6 The Cartesian product of two relations

- *Join.*
  If R and S are two relations built on relation schemas with attributes $A_1... A_n$ in common, then the join of R and S is the relation R ∞ S constructed on the union of the attributes of R and of S containing all the tuples made up of a tuple of R and a tuple of S which match on $A_1...$ A_n. Figure 2.7 gives an example of a join.

You can use the operations in the relational algebra to specify the data you want to extract from the database. If, for example, you want to know the names of the countries containing towns with more than a million inhabitants, you can write the following expression:

$$\pi_{name}\sigma_{population>1\,000\,000}(\text{Towns})$$

However, as a language for expressing queries, the relational algebra is not easy to use because users have to have a thorough knowledge of the database's schema in order to find their way around the relations. Furthermore, such a language is not highly declarative, which we defined in Chapter 1 as one of the essential characteristics of a data manipulation language. It was to resolve this problem and allow queries to be expressed in a declarative manner that the relational calculus was introduced.

V1:	name	population
	Paris	2 600 000
	Marseille	1 600 000
	Caen	200 000
	Lille	1 000 000
	Brussels	1 000 000

V2:	name	country
	Paris	France
	Marseille	France
	Brussels	Belgium
	Berlin	Germany

V1 ∞ V2:	name	population	country
	Paris	2 600 000	France
	Marseille	1 600 000	France
	Brussels	1 000 000	Belgium

Figure 2.7 A join between two relations

2.2.5 The relational calculus

The relational calculus is a logical language upon which most relational query languages have been built. The principle of the relational calculus is to identify each relation in a database with a predicate and the tuples in that relation with values that satisfy that predicate.

To put it more precisely, we take as given an infinite set of variables that represent the values in different domains. The formulæ of the relational calculus are constructed in the following manner:

- The values in the domains and the variables are terms.

- If x_1... x_n are terms, then the expressions $R(x_1...x_n)$ and x_i θ x_j are formulæ. The θ symbol stands for any of the usual comparators (=, ≤ and so on) which can be used with the domains involved.

- If F_1 and F_2 are formulæ, then $F_1 \vee F_2$, $F_1 \wedge F_2$, $F_1 \Rightarrow F_2$ and $\neg F_1$ are formulæ.

- If F is a formula in which the variable x is a free variable, then ∀x F and ∃x F are formulæ.

The formulæ of the relational calculus are interpreted in the same way as those of a first-order logic language. For a given value assignment to variables, a formula $R(x_1...x_n)$ is true if and only if the corresponding tuple exists in the database's relation R. A query in the relational calculus is therefore an expression of the form:

$$\{ (x_1...x_k) / F(x_1...x_n) \}$$

where $x_1...x_k$ are free variables. The reply to the above query is the set of values in $(x_1...x_k)$ for which the formula F is true.

In reality, two relational calculi have been defined: the relational calculus with domain variables, where the terms designate elements in the attribute domains, and the relational calculus with tuple variables, where the terms designate tuples. The equivalence of these two calculi gives a classic result. The calculus we have described is the relational calculus with domain variables.

If we take the relational schema in Figure 2.3, we can express the following queries:

Return the names of the towns with a million inhabitants
{ x / ∃ y Towns (x, 1000000, y) }

Return the entrance fees for the historic buildings in Paris
{ x / ∃ m, n, r Historic_buildings (m, x, n, r, "Paris") }

2.2.6 The power of relational languages

One of the fundamental points of relational theory is that relational algebra and relational calculus are just as powerful as each other, that is, any set that can be described by a formula in the calculus can also be obtained using an algebraic expression, and vice versa.

Most of the query languages used in relational systems are based on the relational calculus. This is because it allows the data required to be specified in a non-procedural way. However, the systems themselves implement the operators in the relational algebra. Therefore the role of a query compiler is to transform expressions in the calculus into expressions in the algebra which can be used to manipulate the data in the database.

This transformation is at the heart of the optimization mechanism for relational systems because for any one expression in the calculus there are numerous equivalent algebraic expressions. Therefore, the optimizer's role is to choose the least costly of the various possible expressions, meaning those that use the schema's physical information in the best way.

The power of relational languages (algebra and calculus) is not however sufficient for expressing all possible manipulations. A simple example of an operation that cannot be expressed by a formula in the calculus (or an algebraic expression) is the transitive closure of a binary relation. If we take the Stage relation in Figure 2.8 we can write a formula in the calculus that represents the journeys made up of a *fixed* number of stages, but there is no formula that represents the set of all the voyages, whatever their lengths. In order to calculate the transitive closure of a relation we have to write a program, as we shall see in Section 2.3.6.

			Journeys:	departure	destination
				Paris	Orleans
Stage:	**departure**	**destination**		Paris	Lille
				Paris	Tours
	Paris	Orleans		Paris	Bordeaux
	Paris	Lille		Paris	Nancy
	Orleans	Tours		Paris	Metz
	Tours	Bordeaux		Orleans	Tours
	Lille	Nancy		Orleans	Bordeaux
	Nancy	Metz		Tours	Bordeaux
				Lille	Nancy
				Lille	Metz
				Nancy	Metz

Figure 2.8 Transitive closure of a relation

2.3 Using a relational system

Numerous prototypes of relational systems have been proposed in recent years. Among the main languages that correspond to those systems are QUEL, based directly on the relational calculus, QBE, a unique language which uses the concept of forms to describe queries in the form of tuples, and SQL which, having rapidly become the standard, is now supported by most commercial products. We will therefore use examples in SQL to illustrate the implementation of a relational system.

2.3.1 Data definition language

The main command used to create a relation is the **create table** command, which takes a relation name and a set of attribute definitions and their associated domains as parameters:

```
create table Countries (
    country_no char(5),
    name char(30) )

create table Towns (
    town_no char(5),
    name char(30),
    population integer,
    country_no char(5) )
```

In SQL the attribute domains can be integers (**integer**), floating point numbers (**float**) or long or short character strings (**char(n)** or **long char(n)**). By default, the values of attributes in a relation can be null values, but the designer of the schema can stipulate that the value of an attribute cannot be a null value:

```
create table Historic_buildings (
    hb_no char(5) not null,
    name char(30),
    entrance_fee float,
    add_no integer,
    add_road char(30),
    add_town char(5) not null)
```

Naturally, SQL provides a command for deleting a relation. This is the **drop table** command, which is used in the following way:

```
drop table Historic_buildings
```

2.3.2 Physical schema

The SQL language provides the option of defining indices in order to speed up access to certain relations. To create an index on the Towns relation we created above we would write:

```
create index Ind1
on Towns ( name )
```

An index can be created on several of the relation's attributes at the same time. You can also specify, using the keywords **asc** and **desc**, whether you want the data to be sorted in ascending or descending order. Finally, the **unique** clause allows you to specify that the index's attributes are a key for the relation. If you try to insert a tuple into a relation in which there is already another tuple with the same key, it will be rejected. Using the current example, we can define the following index:

```
create unique index Ind2
on Historic_buildings (hb_no)
```

Note that the choice made in SQL to associate the key constraint with the creation of indices goes against the principle of physical independence set out by the founders of the relational model. Evidently, in this specific case, the choice was based on implementation and efficiency considerations because it is much simpler and quicker to check a key constraint when there is an index.

2.3.3 Data manipulation language

Data manipulation in SQL is based on the **select...from...where** construct, which is a very general filter that allows you to build other relations from the relations in the database. You could, for example, search for the list of historic buildings whose entrance fees are higher than 50 francs:

```
select *
from Historic_buildings
where entrance_fee > 50.0
```

The **select** clause defines the attributes in the resulting relation. By convention the * character represents all the attributes in the relation involved. The **from** clause defines the relation or relations to be searched and the **where** clause defines the conditions for the selection. Notice that the above example is simply the SQL expression of the relational algebra's selection operator.

If you want to find all the names of the historic buildings in towns with more than 500 000 inhabitants whose entrance fee is less than 50 francs, you would write:

```
select Historic_buildings.name name_historic_building
from Towns, Historic_buildings
where entrance_fee < 50 and
      population > 500000 and
      Towns.town_no = Historic_buildings.add_town
```

In the relational algebra, this query can be implemented by joining the Towns and Historic_buildings relations and then creating projections and selections. In the above example we have used several SQL conventions concerning the naming of attributes. Firstly, attribute names can be qualified with the name of the relation when there are conflicts between different relations. Thus we have written Historic_buildings.name to designate the name attribute in a tuple of the Historic_buildings relation. You can also rename the attributes in the **select** clause.

2.3.3.1 Manipulating sets

The **where** clause's selection conditions may apply to atomic values, as in the previous examples, but they may also apply to sets. The above query can be reformulated as follows:

```
select name
from Historic_buildings
where entrance_fee < 50.0 and
      add_town in
              (select town_no
               from Towns
               where population > 500000)
```

You can also express the fact that a condition is true for all the elements in a set or for (at least) one element in a set. If you wanted to find the names of those towns where all the historic buildings can be visited for less than 50 francs, you would write:

```
select name
from Towns
where 50.0 > all
            (select entrance_fee
             from Historic_buildings
             where Town.name = add_town)
```

2.3.3.2 Aggregation operators

SQL provides aggregation operators for obtaining the sum, the average or the upper and lower bounds of a list of number and also the numbers of tuples in a relation. To find the number of historic buildings in Paris you can visit for 50 francs, you would write:

```
select count (*) number
from Historic_buildings
where add_town = '<town_no>' and entrance_fee < 50.0
```

This expression returns a relation with a single attribute, number, which contains the required number as its only tuple. The aggregation operators like **count** are at their most powerful when they are used with the grouping operator **group by**. This operator allows you to partition a relation according to certain criteria and to apply an aggregation operator to each of the blocks partitioned. If you want to find the number of historic buildings you can visit for less than 50 francs *for each town*, and not just for a particular town, you would write:

```
select count (*) number, add_town town
from Historic_buildings
where entrance_fee < 50.0
group by add_town
```

The **group by** clause can itself be combined with a selection condition, which allows only certain blocks in the partition to be selected. Thus if you only wanted the above results for large towns, you could write:

```
select count (*) number, add_town town
from Historic_buildings, Towns
where entrance_fee < 50.0 and add_town = '<town_no>'
group by add_town
having avg(population) > 100000
```

2.3.3.3 Insertions

To insert new data into a relation, we use the **insert into** command as follows:

```
insert into Countries
values (21, 'France')
```

```
insert into Towns
values (432, 'Paris', 2350000, 21)

insert into Towns
values (433, 'Lille', 870000, 21)
```

You can also use a **select...from...where** expression to insert new tuples into a relation. For example, if we have just created a relation Metropolises (name, population) to group together the large towns, we can populate that relation by writing:

```
insert into Metropolises
select name, population
from Towns
where population > 1000000
```

2.3.3.4 Deleting

In order to delete tuples from a relation we use the **delete from** command. If you wanted to delete all the towns that have a historic building with free entry, you would write:

```
delete from Towns
where town_no in
               (select add_town
                from Historic_buildings
                where entrance_fee = 0.0)
```

2.3.3.5 Updating

As well as providing the means for adding new tuples and deleting existing ones, SQL provides the means for changing the values in existing tuples. We use the **update** command for this. If you wanted to increase the entrance fees for the historic buildings in Paris by 20%, you would write:

```
update Historic_buildings
set entrance_fee = 1.2 * entrance_fee
where add_town = '<town_no>'
```

2.3.4 Defining views

Views are a mechanism for defining *virtual* relations which you can interrogate just like ordinary relations. Views are defined using the **create view** command. The following example creates a view that corresponds to the historic buildings in Paris:

```
create view Hb_paris as
select name, entrance_fee
from Historic_buildings
where add_town =
        (select town_no
         from Towns
         where name = 'Paris')
```

Using this view, you can ask for the list of all the historic buildings in Paris whose entrance fee is higher than 50 francs by simply writing:

```
select name
from Hb_paris
where entrance_fee > 50
```

By using views, each user can be given a different vision of the database. This is a step in the direction of logical independence, as defined in Chapter 1, because it allows the database's schema to be modified without the user, who is interrogating views, being aware of it.

The main limitation of the views mechanism concerns updates. Really, in order to offer complete logical independence, the database management system must allow the user to perform update operations via the views. Unfortunately, in the majority of cases, this problem has not been resolved.

To delete a view you use the **drop view** command, as in this example:

```
drop view Hb_paris
```

2.3.5 Permissions

In SQL, data security is provided by a permissions mechanism which uses the **grant** command. This command is used to acquire or to give other users rights in the database.

The owner of the Historic_buildings relation (the user who created it) can control access to the relation by writing:

```
grant select insert on Historic_buildings to Delobel
grant all on Towns to Delobel with grant option
```

The first command allows a user, Delobel, to interrogate the Historic_buildings relation and to add tuples to it. But he does not have the right to delete tuples or to update them. The keywords **delete** and **update** can also be used to give specific rights.

The second command gives user Delobel the right to perform any possible operation on the Towns relation. Furthermore, the **grant option** clause allows him to transmit this right to others by using the **grant** command himself. By default, a user who has received a right to a relation cannot transfer it to others.

The opposite of the **grant** command is the **revoke** command, which removes users' rights. The following command removes all user Delobel's rights to the database:

```
revoke all on Historic_buildings, Towns to Delobel
```

2.3.6 Applications development

We saw in Section 2.2.6 that the power of relational languages is limited and that, for example, they do not allow us to calculate the transitive closure of a binary relation representing a graph. Similarly, relational languages like SQL are relatively limited when it comes to defining input/output and more generally so when it comes to the dialog with the user.

The aim of database applications development is to provide end users with finished (and closed) systems which access the data via special interfaces.

In order to compensate for the lack of power of relational languages and to construct the special interfaces, a general programming language has to be used, with the relational data manipulation language integrated into it.

The following example shows how SQL can be integrated into C in order to calculate the transitive closure of the Stage relation from Figure 2.8.

```
1  exec sql begin declare section
2       int size;                 /*A C variable known to SQL*/
3  exec sql end declare section
4  int last_size;                 /*A C variable not known to SQL*/

5  exec sql execute immediate
```

```
6           create table Journeys (
7                   departure char(20),
8                   destination char(20))
9  exec sql execute immediate
10 insert into Journeys
11         select *
12         from Stages

13 exec sql prepare an_iteration from
14 insert into Journeys
15         select Journeys.departure, Stage.destination
16         from Journeys, Stages
17         where Journeys.destination = Stages.departure

18 exec sql prepare calc_size from
19         select count (distinct *)
20         from Journeys

21 size = 0;
22 last_size = 1;
23 while (size != last_size) {
24         last_size = size ;
25         exec sql execute an_iteration ;
26         exec sql declare cursor1 cursor for calc_size;
27         exec sql open cursor1;
28         /*We know the result contains a single tuple*/
29         exec sql fetch cursor1 into :size;
30         exec sql close cursor1;
31 }
```

In order to integrate the two languages, the SQL clauses have to be introduced by **exec sql**. The C variables used to communicate between C and SQL must be declared in a specific area delimited by **exec sql begin/end declare section**. The programmer can define SQL operations without executing them immediately. They must be named using the **exec sql prepare** clause as in lines 13 to 20 above. Operations thus prepared can be used several times later in the program. The example shows how a cursor is used to read the tuples in a relation sequentially. The relation in the example is simple because it is only made up of a single tuple with a single attribute, which is the product of an aggregation operation. In order to go through a more complex relation we would use the C language **while** iterator. In Section 2.4.2, we will see the problems that arise from integrating a data manipulation language (declarative) into a general (and procedural) programming language.

2.4 Advantages and limitations of relational systems

We can summarize the advantages of the relational model in the following seven points:

1. *The simplicity of the concepts and the schema.*
   We saw in previous examples that the network model puts the definition of the conceptual schema and the definition of the physical schema in the same schema. Furthermore, the resulting schemas are difficult to understand and therefore to modify, so they can only be created by expert programmers who know the system's technical details. In the relational model, the schema is made up of a list of tables and the physical data is defined separately.

2. *A good theoretical basis.*
   Until the relational system was invented, there was no formal theory for databases, such as there was for programming languages. This lack of theory prevented any significant advances in research in this area. The relational model fully fulfilled its role by proposing a simple theory which allowed database research to develop in the same way that programming language research had already done.

3. *A high degree of data independence.*
   This objective has been attained principally from the point of view of physical independence and represents very significant progress in relation to previous systems. However, we should note that the problem of logical independence has not been totally resolved. There are two main reasons for this. Firstly, the transition from conceptual schema to external schema is not always easy. There have been no satisfactory solutions to the problems of the definition of views and the repercussions of updates to views. Another problem arises from applications programming. Applications programs are specified independently of the data in the database. However, a large part of the application's semantics is coded in the program and not in the conceptual schema. The latter defines the data's logical structure but not its dynamic behaviour.

4. *High-level manipulation languages.*
   The network model's data manipulation languages are simply a collection of commands used in a host language. They are therefore totally procedural. By contrast, relational languages like SQL are declarative, because they define the data you want to extract from the database, and not the way it is retrieved.

5. *An improvement in integrity and security.*
   Systems that use a network or hierarchical model do not propose satisfying solutions to the problem of data security. Relational systems, by using

high-level languages and specifying integrity constraints, allow progress
to be made in this area.

6. *The possibility of optimizing accesses to the database.*
Optimization becomes a crucial factor in a relational context. This is
because the system itself has to find the optimization strategies and access
methods, which are no longer the user's responsibility. A large part of
relational technology has been devoted to improving optimization techniques; this is why relational systems have become the fastest systems.

7. *Manipulating data in sets.*
In contrast to first-generation systems, the relational model provides
data manipulation languages that allow sets to be manipulated globally.
The advantages of such an approach are obvious: it allows doubles to be
managed automatically and makes it possible to use parallel processing
to handle large sets. Unfortunately communication between SQL and
general programming languages is in terms of single tuples and not in
terms of sets. If a programmer wishes to perform an operation on relations
that cannot be directly expressed in SQL, he or she must use cursors to
go through the relations tuple by tuple. A major part of the benefits
derived from SQL set manipulation is therefore lost.

The main limitations of relational systems stem from the fact that they
provide an oversimplified data model and manipulation languages that are too
limited.

2.4.1 An oversimplified model

Traditional business management applications, as they existed at the time
the relational model was conceived, only used data with simple structures
built from atomic types such as integers, reals and character strings. The
relational approach matched these needs and the structure composed of
relations, sets of tuples with atomic type attributes, was adequate. However,
new applications, such as computer-aided design and office integration,
called for data structures with a richer expressive power. Therefore
relations in *first normal form*, that is, whose attributes take their values
from atomic types, quickly became inadequate. These new applications
required hierarchical data structures.

If we look at the example in Section 2.1.2, we can see that we have to
define five relations in order to model a set of towns and their historic
buildings. Apart from the fact that relations proliferate uselessly, this approach
also gives rise to the problem of loss of semantic data. The links between
towns and historic buildings are lost and have to be re-created by defining
integrity constraints. In this case, a referential integrity constraint must
explicitly state that the `add_town` attribute in the `Historic_buildings`

relation is a foreign key (it is the key to the `Towns` relation). This prevents there being a historic building without a corresponding town. The major disadvantages of this approach are that the data's semantics are split between the relations and that maintaining the integrity of such a schema is difficult.

Another problem presented by the relational model in this context involves data manipulation. In order to access the countries where the historic buildings are to be found we have to make two joins. These operations are costly, even though they are optimized, and, in the case of a CAD application where accessing an object can require several dozen joins, may prove prohibitive.

2.4.2 Limited manipulation languages

We have seen that relational data manipulation languages do not allow us to program an application in its entirety and that they have to be integrated into general programming languages. This encapsulation of one language in another gives rise to system malfunctions. These malfunctions can appear at various levels.

2.4.2.1 Programmer level

The programmer must handle two languages with very different paradigms at the same time because SQL is declarative and C is procedural. The typing systems of the two languages are not the same and in numerous cases the programmer must write data conversion procedures. The name spaces in C and SQL are different. The programmer must therefore declare the variables used for communication between the two languages in a special area, and sometimes prefix these variables with special characters. Finally, the reliability of such programs is low because most of the checks are carried out during execution. Debugging such applications is therefore long and difficult.

It is clear that an application programmer's productivity is considerably decreased by this malfunction problem and that the resulting applications are difficult to validate and maintain.

2.4.2.2 System level

We have already mentioned the problem of set manipulation, which is done by sets in the database and tuple by tuple, using cursors, in the programming language. In addition, the optimization mechanism, which is vital from the point of view of performance, only applies to those parts of the application written in SQL. All these factors make the connection between programming languages and the database uncomfortable and inefficient for the programmer.

2.4.3 Conclusion

Objectively, relational systems represented a considerable advance in the database area. They allowed a large amount of relational technology to be developed based on precise theoretical foundations. The general performance of relational systems has improved continuously compared with that of first-generation systems and today these systems dominate the database applications market.

Nevertheless these systems have proved to be inadequate for new applications. In particular, the relational model is too sparse to take easily into account the complex links that exist in CAD and office automation applications. However, the essential limitation remains the weakness of the data manipulation languages, which makes it necessary to encapsulate them in general programming languages, thus giving rise to malfunctions.

Bibliographical notes

The data models proposed as the bases for database management systems are certainly not limited to the three models we have discussed in this chapter, namely the hierarchical, network and relational models. However, these three models have been most widely used. The interested reader can find a more thorough description of the various data models in [Dat86] or [Ull85]. The article [Abr74] also greatly influenced the various models that have been proposed since it was written.

The hierarchical model is the basis of IMS systems whose description can be found in [IBM78]. Usually, the genesis of the definition of the network model is attributed to the proposition by [Gro71].

The relational model originated with the proposal by Codd in [Cod70]. It has since been extended several times, notably in [Cod79]. That said, the concepts behind the relational model already existed in fragmentary form in articles such as [Chi68]. Codd's contribution was to assemble these ideas into a unified framework.

The problem of null values and, more generally, of incomplete data was studied in [LP76], [Lip81] and [Rei86].

The problem of the repercussions at conceptual level of updates expressed on views defined as general expressions is complex. Propositions have however been made about how to resolve it in specific cases, like, for example, [BS81], [DB82], or [Kel85].

We have already described the implementation of the relational system using the SQL language, which is one of the languages most widely used today. This language, originally called SEQUEL, was first described in [Cha76]. SQL cannot be disassociated from the System R DBMS, which was the first to use it. This system represented a considerable effort on the part of IBM to develop relational technology. You can find a description of System R in [Cha81] and of SQL in [IBM81].

Today there are numerous relational DMBSs that are commercial products. As well as System R, we will cite Ingres [SWKH84] and Oracle from Oracle Corporation. You can find a comparative study of these products in [GV85].

Exercises

1. Write additional code for the network database schema on page 18, defining the concept of a painting. A painting has a number, a name, the name of the artist who painted it, and the year in which it was painted. It is housed in one historic building, referred to by its number. A historic building can contain more than one painting, so you will also have to define a set linking the historic building and the paintings in it.

2. Write the same additional code for the relational schema on page 22.

3. What is it about relational systems that made it easier to write the second than the first?

4. Define the relationship between a relation, a domain and an attribute.

5. Here are two relation schemas. Say which is the well-constructed one and why.

    a) Paintings (name, artist, date, historic_building, number, road, town)

    b) Paintings (name, artist, date, historic_building)
        Historic_building (name, number, road, town)

6. The relational model provides two data manipulation languages. What are they and how do they differ?

7. Using the addition to the schema you wrote in Exercise 2, how would you write the SQL code to search for the list of all the paintings painted in the years 1730 to 1770?

8. How would you create a view showing the paintings in the historic buildings in Paris?

9. List the advantages of the relational model.

10. The disadvantages of the relational model are said to spring from an oversimplified model and limited data manipulation languages. What exactly are the negative effects of these defects?

3

A new generation of systems

I like to feel time, stronger than memories of you,
Wiping out, step by step, the tracks of your fame.
Alphonse de Lamartine
Freedom or a night in Rome – New poetic meditations

In the previous chapters, we saw how database management systems evolved from the first-generation systems, which mainly used the hierarchical or network models, to the second-generation systems, which used the relational model.

We saw how that evolution, by the use of non-procedural languages, brought improvements in the physical data independence (and to a certain extent logical independence), improved data integrity and security, provided declarative query languages and allowed data access to be optimized. To these specific points we should add another which is much more difficult to measure but which is also an essential contribution of this approach. The relational model contributed a theoretical foundation for databases and made them into a research area in their own right.

Nevertheless, relational systems suffer from certain weaknesses that make their use for certain types of applications difficult or even impossible. Among these weaknesses we have emphasized the oversimplification implicit in the concept of a relation and the problem of the encapsulation of a data manipulation language in a general programming language.

These observations have led us to assert that a new generation of database management systems must succeed relational systems. This third generation must preserve the important advantages of relational systems as well as provide more elaborate semantic concepts than the relation and integrate database concepts with those of programming languages.

The purpose of this chapter is to describe the context in which those systems are going to develop and to set out the main objectives. The computing context in which network and then relational systems developed was in fact totally different from the computing context in which the new systems will develop. We will also take care to consider the evolution of databases in relation to convergent evolutions taking place in neighbouring areas, such as programming languages and operating systems.

3.1 A new computing context

3.1.1 Hardware developments

Relational systems first made their appearance when the use of magnetic disks was becoming widespread and disk capacity was increasing rapidly. The classic architecture of a computing system at the start of the 1980s was still a server (called a mainframe) connected to a number of alphanumeric terminals. This very centralized architecture probably contributed to the very centralized definition of the relational model, where a global conceptual schema is shared by several users via views. Furthermore, the high price and large size of central memory devices led to the development of very sophisticated techniques for optimizing the use of that memory.

By the start of the 1990s that context had changed radically, even if many applications are still running (and will continue to run) on old systems. Firstly the cost and size of computing systems have fallen continuously while performance has continued to improve. The most important change, from the point of view of database applications, is probably the emergence of graphics workstations interconnected by local networks. Each workstation now has the computing power and the performance that a mainframe server had in 1985.

The idea of the workstation, shown in Figure 3.1, will probably bring important changes in the classic architecture of a DBMS. The computing power which was concentrated in the mainframe server is now distributed to the workstations while the server's role is limited to managing the storage in secondary memory. New systems must take this decentralization of computing power into account in order to distribute processing more effectively. In the fourth part of this book, we will see how this decentralization of computing power influences the internal organization and architecture of a DBMS.

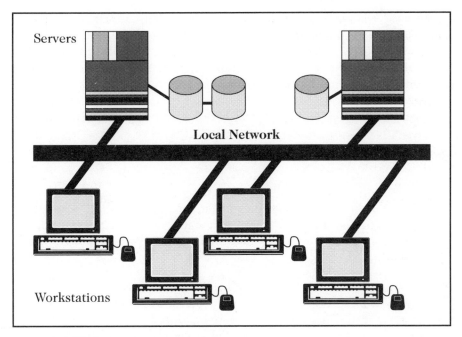

Figure 3.1 Workstation network architecture

3.1.2 Human–computer interfaces

One important consequence of the introduction of graphics workstations has been that human–computer interfaces have become more powerful and more user-friendly and therefore more important. These days it is not rare for a computer system to be judged mainly on the qualities and defects of its interface.

These interfaces have a considerable effect on the working lives of users and sometimes allow non-specialists to use very complex applications. The downside of this is that the amount of code needed to define these interfaces has increased dramatically to the point where experts now agree that 60% of an application's code is dedicated to managing the dialog with the user. However, relational systems were not designed either to manage graphical data or to support elaborate interfaces.

3.2 New applications

The relational systems were designed to satisfy the requirements of traditional business management systems. The way they describe data, in the form of tables, corresponds well to the type of data manipulated by these applications.

With the simultaneous decrease in the cost of hardware and increase in the power of machines, new applications which handle large amounts of data have appeared. Among the most significant we have already mentioned computer-aided design (CAD); others include software development environments and multimedia applications that handle, for example, geographical data.

3.2.1 Design applications

Design applications manage all the phases of product design. The data items handled are often very complex; they might, for example, be the descriptions of engine parts, and thus very interdependent. There is also a large amount of documentary data. We can pick out the following characteristics of design applications:

- *The data items in the database represent artefacts.*
  This means there is a direct (and sometimes explicit) link between certain entities managed by the application and objects in the real-world. A system for designing printed circuits manages both the idea of the circuit and that of connection between components and can be connected to a physical development system. In that case there is a direct link between the data managed by the application and electronic components manipulated by a robot. This is very different from a traditional application where the data items obviously represented real-world objects but where the link between, for example, a historic building and the data item representing that historic building was much weaker.

- *The data items are very often in hierarchies.*
  A CAD system handles links between components and sub-components, and therefore a hierarchy of assembly. This hierarchy plays a very important role in the manipulations that are carried out, and you could say that the efficiency of the manipulations that implement the hierarchy often conditions the performance of the whole system.

- *Design is an interactive process.*
  This interaction has several consequences for the system that has to support the application. First of all, as we have already said, the quality of the user interface is of prime importance. Secondly, the system must be capable of handling the modifications resulting from that interactivity. In order to be able to support a design application, the system must be able to modify not only the data in the database (the price of a transistor or the weight of a wheel), but also the meta-data, in other words the schema. This is a very different situation from the traditional one where the schema is, if not unchangeable, at least relatively stable and where any changes are the responsibility of system administrators,

that is, experts. In the case of a design application, the schema must be able to change often and without having to call on the services of an external expert. A final consequence of the interactivity of the design process is that the system must provide a version mechanism that allows alternative designs to be defined and manipulated and/or previous design choices to be traced. If we pushed this line of thought to the limit we might say that a design application *never* deletes data but saves the whole history of the design process in successive versions.

- *Several designers must be able to work at the same time.*
  It is this characteristic of design applications, along with the large volumes of data manipulated, that justifies the use of a DBMS as a support. Data sharing in a consistent manner is one of the essential functions of a DBMS. However, the nature of these applications is such that data sharing and concurrency control between designers may be totally different from data sharing and concurrency control in classical applications. This problem will be discussed in greater detail in Part IV.

3.2.2 Multimedia applications

The main characteristic of multimedia applications is that they manage unconventional data. The best-known examples are applications that handle images and sounds. There are actually commercial applications that handle such data. Meteorological applications are also examples of multimedia applications.

Firstly, applications are characterized by the volumes of data processed. Images are extremely large data items that require extremely powerful storage devices. Digital optical disk technology is particularly suited to these applications.

A DBMS, that supports multimedia applications, and in particular geographic ones, must be able to implement the classic operations on images and manage all sorts of links between them. You can imagine a meteorological application having to search through all the stored images for those on which a cyclone can be detected. An operation like that would have to implement traditional database search and access techniques and specific image processing techniques at the same time. Once again, good integration between several technologies is what these applications require.

3.2.3 Conclusion

All these design and multimedia applications exist and represent a very large potential market for database management systems. However, almost all these applications *do not* use a DBMS but are built on dedicated systems. The reason for this is that relational DBMSs do not provide the necessary functions.

These applications can be seen as challenges thrown down in front of database management systems, challenges that relational systems cannot take up. The new generation of systems must take into account not only the traditional business management applications but also these new applications. The use of a standard DBMS instead of a dedicated system should allow considerable savings to be made in the cost of implementing these new applications.

It is, however, entirely conceivable that more new types of applications will appear. Faced with them, the systems of the future must not find themselves in the position that relational systems find themselves in today, unable to cope. This is why the concept of extensibility will be a key concept in these new systems. They must be capable not only of managing all the applications identified at a given time but also of adapting to new applications which were not foreseen when they were designed. We will return to the concept of extensibility throughout this book.

3.3 Programming languages

Database applications programming is first and foremost a programming activity. However, ever since relational systems appeared, this programming aspect has been left to one side while the main efforts of the database community have been put into developing the technology of those systems.

Two languages have to be used to program relational applications, a data manipulation language and another language to program the rest! In the last chapter we saw the problems caused by integrating the two languages, both in terms of the programmer's convenience and productivity and in terms of application performance.

It is important to remember that this separation between programming languages and databases has not always existed, but only dates from the emergence of the relational model. We saw, in Chapters 1 and 2, that first-generation systems were closely linked to programming languages such as Cobol.

The return to a symbiosis between programming languages and databases has made certain experts say that the database programming languages constitute a historical and scientific return to CODASYL systems. Let us look at the arguments used in order to reject this approach [Ull89]:

1. It is very difficult to combine the declarative nature of relational languages with a traditional programming language.

2. An important aspect of relational query languages is that the results of queries are in the same form (a relation) as the database, which allows any queries required to be formulated.

3. The new systems give preference to certain links between data and certain access paths. Queries about other links or using access paths other than those defined would be difficult, if not impossible.

When talking about new systems, J. Ullman alludes to systems using the object-oriented approach. We will discuss this approach, and a certain number of systems that use it, in Part III.

The first argument does not solely concern object-oriented systems but rests on the fact that most existing database programming languages are based on an imperative paradigm. In Chapter 2, we saw how ponderous and inefficient set manipulation can be when it has to be implemented using an iterator and a cursor. Therefore, the new systems must combine general programming, which is essentially imperative, with the manipulation of collections of data, which is essentially declarative. In Chapters 5 and 6, we will see how a type system that reconciles these two tendencies can be defined.

The second argument is specific to the object-oriented approach in which the operations are attached to certain data types. In these systems it can be difficult to formulate a query when the result of a query is not of the same type as the data to which the operations are attached. We will come back to this problem in Chapters 9 and 10. The new systems must provide query languages that make it as easy to consult a database as it is with relational systems.

The third argument is the most important, because this is one of the major arguments that differentiated CODASYL systems from the relational systems of the 1980s. The new systems must not give preference to certain accesses to the data at the expense of others. It should be possible to define complex and non-directional links between data items simply. This is simple when handling relations but more difficult when you are handling records and attributes.

J. Ullman's arguments are not really an argument against database programming languages, they are a list of relational system functions that the new systems must preserve. In the second part we will see how to use programming language technology to define typing systems that satisfy these requirements and in the third part the extent to which the existing database programming languages lend themselves, or not, to these criticisms.

At the same time as the database community is once again becoming conscious of the importance of the programming aspect, the language community is feeling the need to store and handle large volumes of data using a more sophisticated system than a file management system. Their aim is to define languages called *persistent languages*, because the data they handle survives the termination of programs.

There is therefore a real meeting point between the new database management systems, which must provide a complete and integrated language, and the new programming languages, which are tending to manipulate more and more data in secondary memory.

No doubt, there will continue to be differences between these two currents of thought. Persistent languages, for example, take no account of the *serious* aspects of databases, that is, managing concurrency between users accessing data simultaneously, and fault tolerance. Nevertheless, the features and the concepts used are very similar.

3.4 Operating systems

In the same way as the database area is in the process of taking into account applications programming, the operating systems area is evolving towards features which are not dissimilar to those of a DBMS.

Operating systems are tending to make file management systems more and more abstract. In particular, the use of the NFS[1] protocol makes the use of local networks and workstations transparent to a file system user.

It is true that ever since DBMSs first appeared in the 1960s it has often been said that database functions would rapidly be integrated into operating systems and that this has not in fact happened. Notwithstanding, the new generation of database management systems must take important changes in operating systems into account and their design and architecture must take factors pertaining to operating systems such as memory, disk and network management and so on into account.

We can summarize this discussion by looking at Figure 3.2. This figure, which is based on [Atk90], shows in schematic form the changes in computing techniques that have occurred in the past few years.

In the 1960s, processing was seen in terms of processors, the data was stored on magnetic tape and communication between systems was expressed in terms of peripherals.

Technical evolution up to the 1980s consisted in defining increasingly abstract concepts, which were less and less dependent on the physical devices, for each of these three dimensions. The concept of the process replaced that of the processor. Files came into use and the network replaced the peripheral. The second diagram corresponds to the situation when relational systems were developed.

The last diagram describes the situation in the 1990s. The concept of the file is tending to be replaced by that of the database (or of persistence) and the concept of the network by that of distributed systems. Graphical user interfaces have made their appearance as a new dimension.

---

1 Network File System

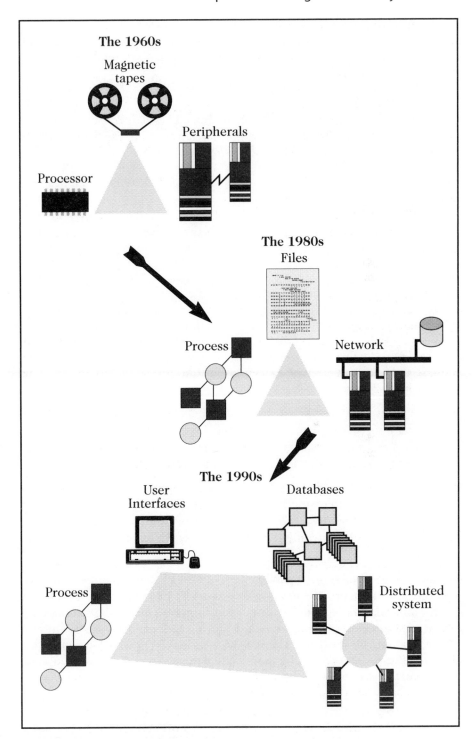

Figure 3.2 Evolution of system components

3.5 Aims

In the preceding chapters, we have discussed database management systems, and in particular relational systems. We have pointed out their strong points and their limitations. In this chapter we have tried to illustrate the context in which a new generation of database management systems will develop.

The concept that has appeared most frequently in this chapter is that of integration: integration of language technologies, of operating systems and of databases, integration of graphical user interface technologies and databases, and integration of dedicated tools for managing complex applications such as multimedia applications.

The DBMSs of the new generation will be both integrated systems and integrating (extensible) systems and we can summarize the aims assigned to them thus:

- They must have a new approach to applications programming, based on the integration of the DBMS and a programming language, that will resolve the problems encountered by relational systems in the context of traditional applications.

- They must manage data and meta-data (the schema) more flexibly so that they can implement extremely interactive applications, such as design applications.

- They must have a modern, integrated development environment that uses all the recent advances in graphical user interfaces. A consequence of this is that these systems will have to be able to handle the data needed for implementing such an environment, particularly graphic data.

- They must be adapted to the new hardware architectures, and in particular to workstations interconnected via local networks. The new systems must be designed so that they take into account the fact that computing power and storage are distributed between different machines (distributed databases).

- They must have an extensibility that allows them to take new applications into account. The new systems must be not only integrated better but also extensible, which means open to new domains. For example, it should be possible simply to couple an image management system to a DBMS in order to develop a meteorological system at a low cost. This extensibility will make them into building blocks that can be used directly in widely differing applications.

But in order to satisfy these aims completely, we must not entirely wipe out the past, and especially the relational approach. Among the major aspects that the new systems must preserve, we should mention:

- A declarative way of manipulating a collection of data.

- The possibility of representing complex and non-directional links between data items simply.

- The independence of data and programs.

- A solid theoretical basis.

Exercises

1. How has the hardware in computer systems changed since the relational model was introduced?

2. The development of the new graphical user interfaces, which users are coming to expect, has implications for databases. In what particular ways are relational systems unable to meet those expectations?

3. Four aspects of design applications are mentioned in the text as presenting specific challenges to the new generation of DBMSs. Explain exactly what is involved.

4. In our historic buildings database, it might be interesting to attach scanned images of the paintings as data items. Why would this be impossible using the relational model and what must new systems do in order to make this possible?

5. Explain the concept of extensibility and why it will allow the new generation of systems to avoid one of the pitfalls of relational systems.

6. It is said that database research and programming language research are converging. What particular problem of relational systems has led to this convergence?

7. Why do defenders of relational systems see these developments as a step backwards?

8. Which key DBMS concepts are now being applied in the new generation of operating systems?

9. A set of aims for the next generation of DBMSs is outlined at the end of this chapter. Summarize them.

10. Finally, which aspects of relational systems should system designers seek to preserve?

Part II

Fundamental Aspects

The purpose of this part is to highlight the basic principles of the new database management systems. We said previously that these systems must have richer modelling powers than relational systems and that they must be better integrated with the world of programming languages.

In Chapter 4, we will discuss the main ideas about data models, on the whole very rich, which have been proposed as aids in specifying database applications. These models help the application designer to describe the data stored in the database and the interactions between data items. In most cases, however, these models have remained abstract and have not been integrated into a DBMS.

The world of programming languages is vast. In Chapter 5, we have tried to isolate those aspects pertinent to the design of a database management system. We will show, in particular, how the ideas of typing and data abstraction, which are very important in the new programming languages, have become central in the context of databases.

The new database management systems will be integrated systems. After discussing the principles of data models and typing systems it is incumbent upon us to show how these concepts, which come from different worlds, can be integrated into a coherent whole. That is the aim of Chapter 6.

Data models

Count your riches by counting the means
you have for satisfying your desires.
Abbé Antoine François Prévost
The story of Chevalier des Grieux and Manon Lescaut

4.1 The role of the data model

As we stressed in Chapters 1 and 2, the development of a database application, or the design of an information system, starts with the drawing up of a conceptual model of the system to be implemented. This model must be the transcription, into terms that can be used by the system, of that part of the real world that the application is going to manage. In mathematical terms, a data model consists of a formalism which describes the data and a set of operations for manipulating it.

The hierarchical, network and relational models, which we discussed in the first part of this book, are often too limited to represent the real-world directly. There is therefore a semantic gap between the real-world and existing systems, which are, for the most part, relational.

In order to bridge this gap, design methodologies, based on intermediate models, have been developed which are more powerful than the relational model. These models are generally called *semantic models*. As they are intermediate models and supports for design methodologies, most semantic models have not been implemented and have remained propositions 'on paper'.

There is an interesting analogy between the needs that led to the definition of *semantic models* and those that led to the generation of high-level programming languages. The aims of languages descended from Algol have been to provide the programmer with a richer and more useful level of abstraction and to get rid of, as far as possible, implementation problems. Similarly, the aim of semantic models is to provide more powerful concepts for modelling the real-world than those the relational, network or hierarchical models provided. In effect, the richer the model and the greater its power of expression, the easier it is to model an application faithfully without errors.

The first models proposed in a research context go back to the 1970s with the entity-relationship model, Smith and Smith's models and the SDM model. The 1980s saw a real flowering of work in the area as well as its formalization.

Our aim is not to give an exhaustive picture of the various semantic models proposed, but rather to synthesize their features and the requirements they satisfy, in order to guide the reader through this vast domain where differences are often a question of nuance. In Chapter 3 we showed that the new database management systems must provide richer modelling primitives than the relational systems. Therefore it is from amongst the diversity of primitives provided by semantic models that the new systems must choose those they implement.

In the next section, we describe the main concepts of semantic models. In Section 4.3 we define the main characteristics of the data manipulation languages associated with these models. Section 4.4 gives the characteristics of several important models by way of illustration. In Section 4.5 we establish the links between the semantic models and the area of artificial intelligence. Section 4.6 is concerned with the links with object-oriented languages. As a conclusion, in Section 4.7 we give some criteria for evaluating semantic models and in Section 4.8 we mention some modelling problems for which there is no satisfactory solution at present.

4.2 General principles

The terminology used in the semantic models domain is very varied and the same concept often goes by different names depending on the different schools of thought. So as not to be overwhelmed by several parallel terminologies, we have chosen just one with which to present the general ideas of semantic models. In Section 4.4, we will see a certain number of synonyms which are in current use for these concepts.

A semantic model is made up of a certain number of modelling primitives, that is, *abstractions*. For the most part, these models propose to represent the real-world as a vast collection of *entities* (sometimes called *objects* or *instances*) and of *links* of various kinds between those entities. Most of the models also allow *constraints* to be defined describing the static, dynamic or even temporal aspects of the entities and the application.

4.2.1 Classes and entities

In most models, *entities* that share common characteristics are grouped together in *classes*. The class' name is used to denote the elements in that class that are present in the database at any given time. In general, an entity's existence is dependent upon it belonging to a class. An entity cannot exist unless it belongs to at least one class.

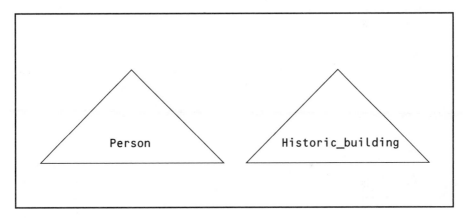

Figure 4.1 Classes

An entity can have an *identity* which is constant over time and independent of any eventual modifications. This idea of identity is fundamental to semantic models. It allows us to express the fact that a person's identity does not depend, for example, on his or her name or address, and that two people with the same name who live at the same address remain two separate people. The lack of this idea of identity is one of the main faults of the relational model because it prevents it from distinguishing between two tuples that have the same contents but represent two different real-world entities. We saw in the previous chapter that CAD applications are amongst the new database applications. The entities handled by these applications are often artefacts, which means there is a direct and strong link between those entities and real-world objects. The idea of identity is therefore essential if we are to be able to deal with this type of application.

4.2.2 Aggregation

Aggregation is the process of grouping various entities into a new 'higher-level' entity. Thus, an address is formed by aggregating a town, a road and a number, as shown in Figure 4.2.

From a formal point of view, an entity that is an aggregation of other entities is the Cartesian product of those entities. The identity of such an entity is determined by its components.

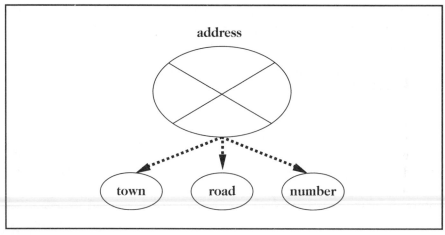

Figure 4.2 Aggregation.

4.2.3 Association

Unlike aggregation, which builds a new entity from lower-level entities, *association* does not build an entity but links several entities together. The difference between the two concepts is somewhat subtle, but it can be important, depending on the use you make of the semantic model.

The description of an association may contain cardinality constraints. The example in Figure 4.3 shows an association between a person and a historic building. The constraint (N : 1) expresses the fact that a historic building may be managed by several people but that each person only manages one historic building. We use an association because we want to express a link between people and historic buildings without having to define a new entity. We could represent the same situation by defining an aggregation Management with person and historic building as its components. This would allow us to associate attributes to that aggregation, as we shall see in the next paragraph, which we cannot do to an association. One of the characteristics of semantic models is that they provide a large range of constructs which are partially overlapping.

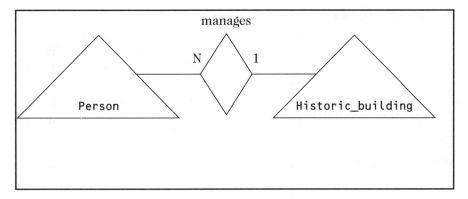

Figure 4.3 Associations

4.2.4 **Attributes**

Attributes are one of the main means used to link entities in semantic models. Formally, we can define an attribute as a bi-directional relationship between two classes of entities. An attribute can be mono-valued or multi-valued. A *mono-valued* entity (represented by a single-headed arrow) associates an entity in the class it starts from with an entity in the class it points to, whereas a *multi-valued* attribute (represented by a double-headed arrow) associates an entity in the class it starts from with several entities in the class it points to.

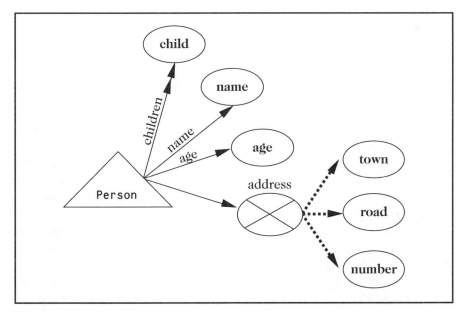

Figure 4.4 Attributes

Intuitively, we use an attribute to represent certain characteristics of a class of entities. Thus, in the example in Figure 4.4, the name, age and address of a person are linked to that person by attributes. A person's children are linked to that person by a multi-valued attribute. This modelling by attributes expresses the fact that a person *is* something more than the simple aggregation of name, age and address. A person is an entity with characteristics which are expressed via the attributes.

4.2.5 Grouping

The grouping is a primitive that is used to build an entity from a (finite) set of entities with a given structure. The identity of this entity is determined by all its elements. The difference between a grouping and a class is that a grouping is an entity, whereas a class is not an entity but a 'meta'-level construct.

The example in Figure 4.5 shows a grouping of entities in the **Person** class that is associated with a **Historic_building** by the personnel attribute. Notice that a degree of redundancy can be detected between the grouping constructor and the multi-valued attributes. The situation described above could be represented using a multi-valued personnel attribute rather than a grouping. The difference is that if we use a grouping we can talk explicitly about the set of people who work in a historic building, whereas if we used a multi-valued attribute we could only talk about the association of each of the people with the historic building, case by case.

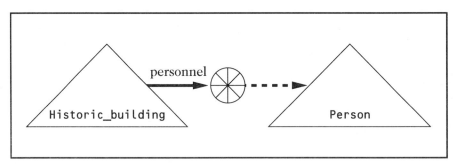

Figure 4.5 Groupings

4.2.6 Different approaches

We can distinguish between two major trends in semantic models, depending on how they tackle the problem of representing links between entities. In the above presentation, we have described the main constructs used in existing models. In reality, depending on the models, the emphasis is either on representing links using aggregations and groupings or on using attributes to do the same thing. In the first case, data representation (called the schema as in the relational model) is seen as a set of structures built using constructors like the tuple (aggregation, association), the set (grouping), and so on. In the second case, new structures are not built but classes of entities are linked using attributes. Figure 4.6 illustrates these two approaches by showing the same situation modelled using constructors and using attributes. In both cases, the entities are people, who have a name and children, and historic buildings, which have a name and are managed by one or more people. Notice that if an association is considered as an entity (the second approach) you can attach additional data to it using attributes. Thus, you could define an `average_age` attribute for a person's children, or a `salary` attribute to indicate the pay of a manager of a given historic building.

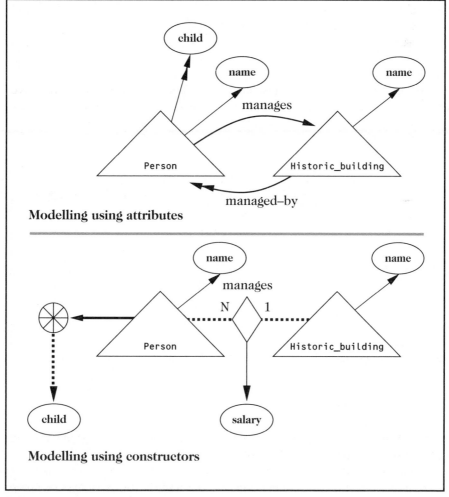

Figure 4.6 The two main trends

4.2.7 Specialization and generalization

Specialization consists of refining a class into a subclass. This allows us to represent everyday situations such as the `Employee` class which is a subclass of the `Person` class, or the `Mansion` class which is a subclass of the `Historic_building` class. An entity in the `Employee` class is also an entity in the `Person` class. Therefore the subclass is included in the superclass. Specialization of a class can be either *explicit* or *derived*. Specialization of the `Person` class in the `Employee` class is explicit in the sense that whether an entity belongs to one of these two classes is explicitly determined by the users when they create the entity. They create either a person or an employee. On the other hand, a derived subclass is defined using a predicate that specifies a subclass of the original class. Thus the `Young_person` class can be defined as the set of entities in the `Person` class whose age is less than 30.

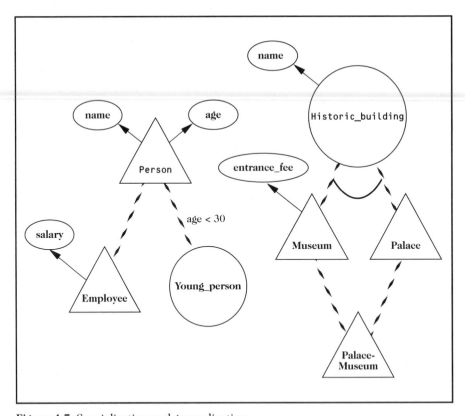

Figure 4.7 Specialization and generalization

We may want to specialize several classes at the same time in order to represent, for example, palaces that serve as museums, or researchers who are at the same time students and employees. In each of these cases, we have to define a class as a specialization of *several* other classes. An entity in the Palace_Museum class will also be an entity in both the Palace class and the Museum class.

Generalization consists of defining a class as the union of several other classes. The union class will thus generalize these various classes. In the example shown in Figure 4.7, the Historic_building class is the generalization of the Palace class and the Museum class. When we choose to represent the Historic_building class as a generalization of two other classes, it means that the database does not contain any entities that belong to that class. All the class does is to group together museums and palaces. If we also wish to represent historic buildings that are neither palaces nor museums, we must define the Historic_building class as an ordinary class and then effect two specializations of that class.

Some models allow you to specify whether the classes that are part of a generalization are mutually exclusive. The generalization in the above model is not exclusive because there can be museums which are also palaces.

The specialization/generalization graph forms a hierarchy which is traditionally known as the ISA hierarchy or the *inheritance hierarchy*. Not all the models distinguish between specialization and generalization and some only talk of the inheritance hierarchy. However, it seems important for us to distinguish clearly between these two concepts which have important repercussions for the database. Similarly, some older models only allow specialized subclasses to be defined using a predicate, like the Young_person class.

We have said that the entities in a subclass (such as Employee) are also entities in the superclass. Consequently, all the attributes defined for the superclass apply to the entities in the subclass. In the example shown in Figure 4.7, an employee has name, age and salary attributes. Therefore we say that the attributes of the superclass are *inherited* by the subclasses, whence the terms inheritance and inheritance hierarchy come. If a class has several superclasses, conflicts of definition can arise between several inherited attributes. In most models, these conflicts are resolved by renaming some inherited attributes.

4.2.8 Derivation of components

The mechanism for the derivation of components is fundamental to semantic models because it allows the concept of computed information to be modelled. A derived schema component describes both the structure of the data items that represent the information and the way that information was derived (computed) from other schema components. In most models, two types of derived components can be defined, derived classes and derived attributes.

We have already seen two examples of derived classes in the preceding section. The `Young_person` class, obtained by specialization using a predicate, is a derived class of the `Person` class. Similarly, the generalization of the `Museum` and `Palace` classes is a derived class. Classes created by specialization using a predicate and generalization are the main types of derived classes. However, some models allow classes to be derived from arbitrarily complex set expressions. In that case, there is no *a priori* ISA link between the derived class and the class(es) from which it is derived.

A derived attribute is defined using an expression that links it to other schema components. The language used to specify a derived attribute can be any programming language, but in many of the models it is a restricted query language (*see* Section 4.3).

One essential point is that derived components in a schema are manipulated in exactly the same way as the other components. Derived components have a direct link with the concept of a view in relational systems. However, in semantic models, the type of data manipulated is much more general. As in the relational model, derived components cause problems when updates are implemented. If a component forms part of the computation that is modified, that modification is by definition propagated to the derived value. Thus if we add a person who is younger than 30 to the `Person` class, that entity is automatically visible in the `Young_person` class. On the other hand, the delete operation makes no sense for the `Young_person` class. A young person is a `Person` entity whose age is less than a given threshold. The only way a young person can stop being one is to see his or her age increase. Explicitly deleting a young person from the `Young_person` class makes no sense because it implies nothing about his or her age. As a general rule, semantic models drastically reduce the updates that can be implemented on derived components to those that can be propagated to the data in a very evident way. As no general solution has been found to the problem of view updates in the context of the relational model, which is relatively simple, we can hardly expect a general solution in the context of semantic models, which are much more complex.

4.2.9 Integrity constraints

Even though semantic models provide the user with numerous tools for structuring the data, they are not always sufficient to express the great diversity of links between objects in the real-world. Integrity constraints are commonly used to enrich the expressive power of these models. This is also true for the relational model, which very quickly found itself enriched with numerous integrity constraints.

Semantic models express most of the relational model's integrity constraints in a structural way, that is, directly by their constructs. In particular, this is the case for key constraints. In the relational model you can specify that a subgroup of attributes in a given relation is the unique key to the relation's tuples. For example, the national insurance number will be a key because there will never be two distinct tuples in the Person relation with the same national insurance number. A key constraint will be translated as a mono-valued attribute or will not be necessary because the object has its own identity. Similarly, the multi-valued dependencies of the relational model can be expressed using multi-valued attributes. Semantic models are therefore at a much higher level of abstraction than the relational model.

Among the most common constraints in semantic models are those that allow you to express the fact that an attribute is partial or total. A person's maiden_name attribute will be defined as partial (because it is optional) whereas their name attribute will be total (because it is mandatory).

Cardinality constraints are another very important class of constraints. This class was popularized by the entity-relation model (ER). In this model associations between entities are characterized as being either 1 : 1, 1 : N, N : 1 or M : N.

4.2.10 The functional approach

Functional data models can be considered to be a particular category of semantic models. The functional approach has been, and still is, very vigorous and it has the distinction of having been the basis for numerous implementations, which is why we are giving it its own section in this chapter.

Functional programming languages first made their appearance with Lisp and were consecrated in Backus' manifesto and a whole host of proposals (Miranda, SASL, ML and so on). They are now a fully fledged distinct research area. In databases, the functional model dates from the start of the 1970s and was rediscovered in the 1980s. It was inspired independently by the application of the semantic model's ideas and by the extension of functional programming languages to data manipulation languages.

The functional data model was introduced jointly by Buneman and Frankel and by Shipman. It is also reminiscent of Abrial's *Data Semantics* model. This model is very attractive to part of the research community. Here we will present the principles behind the definition of a functional model by giving an example of such a model. Even though this is not an exact replica of an existing model, it is strongly based on the Daplex model.

At the start, a set of basic domains are available: Integer, String, Boolean, Real and Entity. Note that these sets are presumed to be exclusive. The Entity domain includes all objects that are only known by their structures and not by their values (a person as opposed to an integer).

It is then possible to declare a set of functions. The functions have a definition domain and a target domain. They are either simple (as in the case of a true function in the mathematical sense) or multi-valued (as in the case of a relation). A function is declared as follows:

$$f(D_1, D_2,..., D_n) \rightarrow D \text{ or}$$
$$f(D_1, D_2,..., D_n) \rightarrow\rightarrow D$$

This declares a function whose name is f which maps from the Cartesian product of D_i to D (in the case of a $\rightarrow$ type arrow) or to all of the parts of D (in the case of a $\rightarrow\rightarrow$ type arrow where the function is multi-valued). The domains are either the basic domains or domains defined by the user in the following manner:

$$d() \rightarrow\rightarrow D$$

This declaration defines a domain called d which is a subset of D. This type of definition allows us to define an inheritance hierarchy between the domains. The functions are of course inherited throughout that hierarchy. Let us consider the following schema:

```
Person() →→ Entity
Employee() →→ Person
name(Person) →→ String
age(Person) →→ Integer
salary(Employee) →→ Integer
```

The **Person** and **Employee** functions are constant functions which return a set of entities. All employees are people. The **name** function is therefore defined for people and for employees. The **salary** function, on the other hand, is only defined for employees.

We can then declare a certain number of integrity constraints for this schema, for example inverse functions or the cardinality of target sets.

All the functional model propositions have contained appropriate query languages. Curiously though, the associated query and data manipulation languages have not necessarily been functional themselves. Adaplex, which we describe in Chapter 8, is a case in point. Finally, notice that certain functional query languages have been used with models that are not functional at all. This is the case with the O_2 system's query language described in Chapter 10.

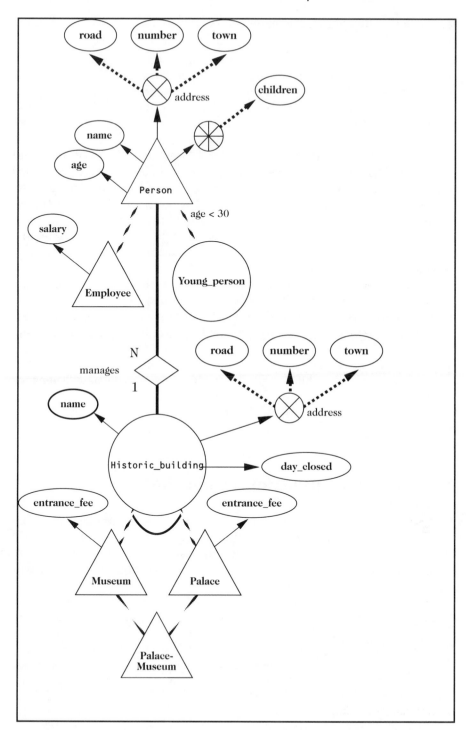

Figure 4.8 A complete example

4.2.11 A complete example

Figure 4.8 gives a complete example showing all the modelling primitives that we have described in the preceding sections. The example is made up of five main classes (Person, Employee, Museum, Palace and Palace_Museum) and two derived classes, one by specialization (Young_person) and the other by generalization (Historic_building).

A person has four attributes, two of which are atomic and two structured, one by an aggregation (address) and one by a grouping (children). The fact that we have defined addresses as aggregations rather than creating an Address class shows that we are interested in addresses as structures attached to people but not as entities in their own right. The children attribute is a grouping because we are interested in all of a person's children and not each individual child. On the other hand the day_closed is a multi-valued attribute, rather than a grouping, because in this case we are interested in each individual day rather than the set of days.

The Person class' attributes are inherited by the Employee subclass which also has its own salary attribute. The Young_person derived class does not have any attributes of its own. The Museum and Palace classes each have an entrance_fee attribute and a shared Palace_museum subclass. Depending on the model, that subclass should either rename the entrance_fee attribute in order to resolve the inheritance conflict or specify the class the attribute comes from when it is manipulated. The name and day_closed attributes attached to the Historic_building class are inherited by all its subclasses. Finally there is an N : 1 association between people and historic buildings.

4.3 Data manipulation languages

A data model should define how data is structured and the operations for manipulating that data. In the world of databases and semantic models, those operations and the ways in which they are combined are designated by the term *data manipulation language*. In the preceding section we have explained how the data is structured. Now we are going to study the characteristics of the data manipulation languages (DMLs) associated with semantic models.

These languages are similar to the relational data manipulation languages and in particular to SQL. However, they have to be able to manipulate more complex data structures than their relational counterparts and to manage the hierarchy of classes and associations. More precisely, the data manipulation languages associated with semantic models have to be able to perform the following functions:

- Create entities in a given class or delete them from it.

- Consult or update an attribute or a component of an aggregation.
- Add an element to a grouping or delete one from it.
- Set up or break off an association between two entities.
- Iterate through all the elements in a grouping and all the entities in a class.
- Migrate an entity over the length of the hierarchy of classes.

Not all the semantic models allow all these manipulations and in particular the migration of an entity over the length of the hierarchy of classes is rarely allowed. The semantics of this operation can be difficult to define when, for example, a person becomes an employee and a salary attribute has to be added.

Several styles of languages have been proposed for defining these operations. In the main, they are imperative languages, logical languages descended from the relational calculus or even functional languages. We will describe each category in detail.

4.3.1 Imperative languages

An imperative data manipulation language is essentially made up of a list of commands corresponding to each of the required manipulations. Generally these commands are constructed around an expression that allows iterators with a sufficiently general scope to be defined. Let us presume that we want to find out the names of all the people older than 20: in the language associated with R. Hull and R. King's GSM model we would write:

```
for each p in Person
    such that age(p) > 20
    print name(p)
```

If we wanted to know the names of all the people between 20 and 30 years of age, we could write the same expression but replace the Person class by the Young_person class, because the latter is derived from the former but only retains those people under 30. The manipulation of derived components is therefore totally transparent during data manipulation. The following example prints the list of addresses that are common to at least two people:

```
for each p in Person
    such that for some q in Person
    p ≠ q and address(p) = address(q)
    print address(p)
```

Classes can be created using commands similar to the following examples:

```
create subclass Employee of Person
create subclass Young_person of Person
   where age < 30
```

Updates are done using a specific command (**update** for example) which takes the components to be modified as parameters:

```
for each p in Employee
   such that age(p) < 40
   update salary(p) to 1.5 * salary(p)
```

These imperative data manipulation languages are made up of a set of commands centred around fairly general iterators. In order to program a complete application these commands must be encapsulated in a general programming language.

4.3.2 The logical approach

The logical approach (also called the deductive approach) to databases is, along with the object-oriented approach which we will describe in detail in Chapter 9, one of the classic approaches to building systems that are richer in features than the relational systems.

The idea of using logic as a data manipulation language is directly descended from the relational model and its calculus. Work on deductive databases has mainly been concerned with extending this approach to more complex manipulations than relational manipulations. The Datalog language is at the centre of these considerations. Datalog can be seen as a version of Prolog appropriate for databases. We can summarize the essential characteristics of Datalog as follows:

- The function names are not used to construct terms. The only terms used are constants and variables.

- A Datalog program can be given semantics based on the model's theory, as opposed to Prolog whose semantics is, *grosso modo*, a 'true fact' proving algorithm and which is, therefore, totally operational.

- The underlying data is essentially relational and the names of predicates are identified with the names of relations. The essential difference from

Prolog is that in Datalog the attributes become positional because a predicate's arguments are not named.

- When using Datalog to describe relational data manipulation we can distinguish two types of relations: extensional relations and intensional relations. An extensional relation is stored in the database whereas an intensional relation corresponds to a predicate derived by a Datalog program. This distinction is similar to the one made in Chapter 2 between relations and views. However, we can demonstrate that Datalog allows us to derive relations that cannot be defined as views, and in particular to calculate the transitive closure of a relation.

A Datalog program is made up of a set of Horn clauses formed entirely from atomic formulæ, which in turn are built up from predicates that represent relations and basic predicates which correspond to the classic arithmetic comparators. The following example shows a Datalog program which builds a colleague predicate which returns those people who manage a historic building together or who are colleagues of such a person:

```
immediate_colleague(X,Y):- manage(X,H), manages(Y,H), X <> Y
colleague(X,Y):- immediate_colleague(X,Y)
colleague(X,Y):- colleague(X,Z), immediate_colleague(Y,Z), X <> Y
```

This extremely simple example shows that the power of Datalog lies in the fact that you can define recursive predicates. The efficient evaluation of the rules of recursion is a subject that has blackened of lot of paper since the early 1990s. A more detailed study of Datalog is outside the scope of this chapter but the interested reader can refer to Chapter 7.

The Datalog language is limited to the manipulation of relational data. Extensions of the language capable of manipulating more complex data have been proposed. In particular, the COL language is an extension of Datalog which can manipulate data structured as sets and tuples, that is, according to the constructors **aggregation** and **grouping**. The main difference between COL and Datalog is in the construction of the terms. COL terms are defined as follows:

- Constants and variables.

- External functions (*data functions*) defined and *evaluated* outside the language.

- A tuple values constructor $[a_1: x_1, ..., a_n: x_1]$.

- A set values constructor $\{x_1, ..., x_n\}$.

The predefined predicates are equality and set membership. A COL program (like a Datalog program) is made up of a set of clauses. The following program finds those people who live near a given historic building (in the same road) and have a child called 'Eric'. We assume that the database is made up of two predicates Person (with a name, an address, structured as a tuple, and a set of children) and Historic_building (with a name and an address structured in the same way).

```
Near(X, H):- Person(X, [ town: T, road: R, number: N1], E)
             Historic_building(H, [ town: T, road: R, number: N2])
             [name: "Eric", age: A] ∈ E.
```

To sum up, the logical approach to data manipulation languages is centred around Datalog and its extensions. The main interest of this language is that it makes it possible to use recursion when defining predicates. which gives us a much greater power of expression than that of relational languages. The logical approach to data manipulation is particularly interesting because it is declarative. The obvious disadvantage of this declarative nature is that it can be difficult to guarantee the determinism of such programs and to find efficient evaluation methods. In this approach updates present a difficult problem for which satisfactory solutions have not always been found.

4.3.3 The functional approach

In the context of databases, functional languages are usually defined as languages in which the only concept used is that of the function. There are therefore no variables (in programming language terms, not in mathematical ones). Nor is there an assignment operation and, therefore, there is no state. The functions have no side-effects and each time you apply the same function to the same arguments you get the same result; the language is said to be *applicative*. In order to define a functional language, you must specify:

- The domains that represent the data and the basic functions that can be applied to them.

- How to define new functions.
  It is possible to define new functions using existing functions; generally this is done by using equations to link the function being defined to known functions. These functions can be recursive.

- Functionals or function constructors.
  Functionals are operators that work on functions to create new ones. Function composition is an example of a functional that you find in practically all languages but there are others such as the conditional (**if-then-else**), the conditional iterator (**do-while**) or a filter constructor (**filter**).

We will illustrate this approach using the FQL language. This language is not the data manipulation language of one particular system. It is a query language defined to provide a functional interface for existing systems, and in particular CODASYL systems.

The functions' domains are defined in the following manner: you start with the atomic types (**integer**, **boolean**, and so on) and then you build more complex values by applying the *flow* and *tuple* constructors to these atomic values. In FQL's own terminology a flow is a list of values, and the **flow** constructor corresponds exactly to the grouping described in Section 4.2. The *tuples* are positional, that is, the components of a tuple are not named, as in the relational model, but referenced by position.

The basic functions are (1) the functions associated with the different domains and defined in the basic schema, (2) the predefined arithmetic and logical functions, (3) particular functions such as constant functions and identity, and (4) the functions associated with the **flow** and tuple constructors. Flows are manipulated like Lisp lists, using the head, tail, cons and length functions. There are functions for accessing tuple components. For example, the i function extracts the ith component of a tuple. As FQL is a query language, no update primitive has been provided and it is therefore purely applicative.

```
types Historic_building, Person

function                type
!Historic_building      → *Historic_building
!Person                 → *Person
Tourist                 → Person
!Tourist                → *Tourist
Hb_name                 Historic_building → string
Hb_town                 Historic_building → string
Hb_road                 Historic_building → string
Hb_day_closed           Historic_building → string
Hb_entrance_fee         Historic_building → num
T_name                  Tourist → string
S_town                  Staying → string
S_road                  Staying → string
```

Figure 4.9 The Tourism database in FQL

The function constructors are composition (written o); extension (written *), used to map from a function of A in B to a function of **flow**(A) in **flow**(B) with the usual semantics; restriction (written |), which takes a function of A as the input to a **bool** (a selection condition) and returns a function of **flow**(A) in **flow**(A) and which operates as a selection function corresponding to the condition given. The last function constructor is the tuple constructor which takes n functions f_i of A_i in B_i and returns a function of $[...A_i...]$ in $[...B_i...]$. This function associates the tuple $[f_1(x_1), f_2(x_2), ..., f_n(x_n)]$ with the tuple $[x_1, x_2, ..., x_n]$.

Notice that all the functions in FQL are unitary and that the language does not use variables. The definitions in Figure 4.9 are the expression of the Tourism database's schema in FQL. The schema is made up of two main types, in FQL terminology, Historic_building and Person. The extensions of these types (corresponding to classes in the terminology of Section 4.2) are written !Historic_building and !Person. These functions are functions without arguments which return respectively a **flow** of historic buildings and a **flow** of people. The Tourist function is used to define a subtype of Person, because a tourist is a person. Then come the functions that play the role of attributes in this functional vision of the database. The example below computes the average entrance fee and the variation in entrance fees for the historic buildings in Paris.

```
average = [/+, len] o div
square = [id, id] o times
variance = [id, average] o distrib o *(- o square) o average
Charges = !Historic_building | ([Hb_town, "Paris"] o =) o
*(Hb_entrance_fee)
Average = Charges o *average
Variance = Charges o *variance
```

We have already described some of the function constructors used in the above example. The other important constructors are the summation of all the elements in a **flow** (/+), the len function which returns the number of elements in a **flow**, the id function which is the identity function and the times function which performs multiplication.

To sum up, the advantages that can be derived from using a functional data manipulation language are as follows:

- The language is concise.

- There is a natural fusion between a functional data model and a functional style of programming. It is obviously a good idea to have a data model where the basic data items are functions and a programming language style where all programs are functions. You only have to handle a single concept in a uniform way.

- It is connected to an advanced programming technology. Functional programming technology is particularly rich. Two models of execution have been proposed: *lazy evaluation* or *data driven evaluation*. There is an analogy between the different evaluation modes of functional languages and the evaluation techniques of Datalog programs, database logicians having tried, in their formalism, to copy the well-established results of functional programming.

On the other hand, functional programming poses certain problems. This programming style was created by theoreticians and is used mainly in artificial intelligence, rapid prototyping and compiler circles. It is not well adapted to management applications. The power of some of the tools seems excessive for applications which are, after all, relatively simple in terms of the computations executed. As with the logical approach, updates are not easy to define because these languages are purely applicative. More generally, it is not easy to make a language where the notion of a state does not exist cohabit with a database which describes, by definition, a state. Finally, as the example shows, the syntax of functional languages is often off-putting for inexperienced users.

4.4 Some important models

In this section we will describe the main semantic models. As we have already described their general principles in Section 4.2, we will limit ourselves here to mentioning briefly their characteristics.

Figure 4.10 describes nine of the most interesting models. The first three (ER, FDM and SDM) are generally considered to be the most important and have had great influence in the modelling domain. The next two (SAM* and IFO) are models which provide a rich variety of means for structuring data (including statistical data in the case of SAM*). Then we have two models (RM/T and GEM) which are extensions of the relational model. Finally the last two models (Format and LDM) have been defined for theoretical purposes in order to study a certain number of modelling and/or data manipulation tools.

In the table shown in Figure 4.10, the Comparison criteria column allows the models to be compared according to three criteria: their aims, the primitives they provide for modelling the data and the general design principles they follow. The aim of some models is to provide a general context for modelling while others are dedicated to the investigation of theoretical solutions. The modelling primitives are either explicit or an extension of the relational model's primitives. The general design principles are based either on the idea of attributes, or on that of aggregation (relational extensions), or on more general constructors, as in the case of the models used for research purposes.

The second column, Schema components, gives a picture of each model according to the schema construction tools it makes available. The first two sub-columns show the aggregation and grouping constructors, the next three describe the possible types of attributes and the last two the inheritance hierarchy. The initials EXP or IMP indicate whether the function is

| | Comparison criteria | | | Schema components | | | | | | |
| | | | | Constructors | | Attributes | | | | |
	Research aims	Modelling primitives	General design principles	Aggregation	Grouping	Printable	Objects	Multi-valued	Inheritance	Derivation
ER	General	Explicit	Aggregation	EXP	IMP	EXP	IMP	IMP		
FDM	General	Explicit	Attributes	IMP	IMP	EXP	EXP	EXP	EXP	EXP
SDM	General	Explicit	Constructors Attributes	IMP	EXP	EXP	EXP	EXP	EXP	EXP
SAM*	General	Explicit	Constructors	EXP	EXP	EXP	EXP	EXP	EXP	EXP
IFO	General	Explicit	Constructors	EXP	EXP	EXP	EXP	EXP	EXP	
RM/T	General	Extended Relational	Aggregation	EXP	IMP	IMP	IMP	IMP	EXP	
GEM	General	Extended Relational	Aggregation	EXP	IMP	IMP	IMP	IMP	EXP	
Format	Theoretical	Explicit	Constructors	EXP	EXP					
LDM	Theoretical	Explicit	Constructors	EXP	EXP	IMP	IMP	IMP	IMP	

Figure 4.10 Classification of the main semantic models

explicit or whether it is obtained via other functions. A blank means that the function is not available in the model. In the rest of this section we will describe the main aspects of the most representative models in the table.

4.4.1 The entity-relationship model

The entity-relationship model (ER) was proposed in the mid-1970s and is still very important. Along with Abrial's Z model, which follows a different approach, it can be seen as one of the first semantic models. The basic components of the ER model are the entities and the relations between sets of entities. The entities, like the relations, can be characterized by attributes whose values are 'printable'. The relations can have associated cardinality constraints which specify whether they are 1 : 1, M : 1 or M : N. In Figure 4.11 we give an example of a schema in the ER model formalism.

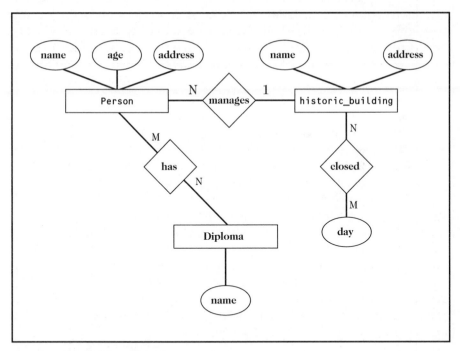

Figure 4.11 An ER model schema

In the entity-relationship model, an attribute is always mono-valued. Relations are used to represent multi-valued attributes, as in the case of the diplomas belonging to a person.

Originally, the entity-relationship model was conceived as a high-level design tool for designing schemas which were subsequently translated and integrated into a relational or network model. It also allows you to define insertion and deletion constraints, which you can use to express existential integrity constraints. Thus, it is possible to express the fact that a town only exists if a Historic_building or a Person entity has a relation with it. If the person or the historic building is deleted then the town is also deleted.

The entity-relationship model, as originally defined, does not allow you to define an inheritance hierarchy but numerous propositions for extensions have been made in order to take this concept into account.

4.4.2 SDM

The SDM model differs from most of the semantic models in that it proposes a great range of modelling primitives via a single abstraction, the *class*. Therefore the SDM model places the emphasis on the grouping constructor and allows the designers to have multiple views of their data using derived schema components. In SDM, the subclass concept is divided into four categories in which we find the categories described in Section 4.2.7. The first category contains the subclass defined by specialization using a predicate. The second covers the subclasses obtained by applying set operators to the existing classes. Subclasses in the third category are used as domains for a given attribute and the last category contains the subclasses whose entities are explicitly inserted by the user.

An example of the first category is the Young_person subclass of the Person class. The second category is represented by the Historic_building class obtained by the union of the Museum and Palace classes. An example of the fourth category is the Employee class.

You can also define a concept of meta-class as in the SAM* and TAXIS models. Thus, you could define a Class_of_historic_building class whose entities would be the Palace and Museum classes. That class' attributes would be the class attributes for the Palace and Museum classes and would therefore be attributes shared by all the entities in those classes. For example, we could define the attributes number_of_entities and average_price, which could be derived from all the entities in the classes at a given moment. As you can see from the table in Figure 4.10, SDM does not explicitly provide an aggregation constructor.

4.4.3 IFO

IFO is a good example of a model developed for studying the structural aspects of semantic models. IFO provides the concept of attributes, the aggregation and grouping constructors and two types of ISA links. In particular, this model has been used to study updates in the context of semantic models and the interactions between constructors and ISA links.

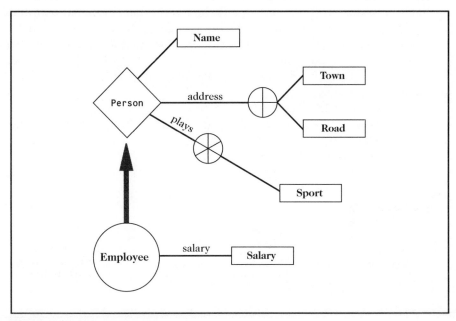

Figure 4.12 Three fragments in IFO

The basic structure in an IFO schema is the *fragment*. A fragment contains the definition of a class' internal structure along with the attributes that characterize it. Figure 4.12 shows a schema composed of the fragments Person and Employee.

The fragment concept is close to the *frame* concept used in artificial intelligence models. IFO also allows attributes to be associated with groupings. For example, you can associate with a person's children an attribute that gives the average age of those children.

4.4.4 RM/T

The RM/T model is an extension of the relational model proposed by E. F. Codd himself. In this model, a class is represented by a relation called an *E-relation* which contains the objects' permanent identifiers (*surrogate* in RM/T terminology). In fact this approach is an implementation, in the form of relations, of the concept of the entities' internal identifiers. These identifiers cannot be referenced explicitly by the user. The concepts of mono- and multi-valued attributes are represented by relations between identifiers and 'printable' values.

Similarly, aggregations can have identities (*entity aggregation*) or not (*non-entity aggregation*). The second category can neither have multi-valued attributes nor be used in an ISA link.

RM/T proposes two types of ISA link: *unconstrained specialization* and *generalization*. In the first case, we can distinguish the idea of an explicit subclass, that is, that the superclass contains all the entities in the subclasses. In the second case, the entities in the generalizing class must belong to one of the subclasses but generalization is not necessarily the union of the subclasses.

This model is mainly interesting because of its direct descent from the relational model. The use of *surrogates* (which make the identifiers of the entities modelled explicit) is an *ad hoc* way of getting round the lack of object identity in the relational model.

4.4.5 Daplex

Daplex is a model defined by D. W. Shipman at CCA[1]. Abrial's Z language is a precursor of the approach followed by Daplex. As the model is essentially functional, the only concepts in the model are entities and functions.

```
declare Person() ⇒ entity
declare Employee() ⇒ Person
declare name(Person) ⇒ string
declare age(Person) ⇒ integer
declare road(Person) ⇒ string
declare number(Person) ⇒ integer
declare town(Person) ⇒ string
declare salary(Employee) ⇒ integer
declare boss(Employee) ⇒ Employee

declare Town() ⇒ entity
declare name(Town) ⇒ string
declare historic_buildings(Town) ⇒⇒ string
declare Historic_building() ⇒ entity
declare name(Historic_building) ⇒ string
declare town(Historic_building) ⇒ Town
declare day_closed(Historic_building) ⇒⇒ string
declare manages(Employee) ⇒ Historic_building
define is_managed(Historic_building) ⇒⇒ inverse of
   manages(Employee)
```

Figure 4.13 The Tourism database in Daplex

1 Computer Corporation of America

A Daplex function is declared in the schema using the **declare** clause. This clause inserts a new basic function in the schema, that is, a new link between entities. In terms of the principles described in Section 4.2, the functions inserted using the **declare** clause correspond to attributes, that is, directional links. Like attributes, Daplex functions can be mono- or multi-valued. In Figure 4.13, the name function is mono-valued but the day_closed function is multi-valued.

Daplex allows you to create functions from the basic functions defined in the schema. Figure 4.13 contains the is_managed function which is defined as the inverse of the manages function. The inverse clause allows you to express simply inverse links to the links declared in the schema (and therefore stored). Daplex functions can also be created using more general operators (aggregates, set operations, iterators and so on) as in the following examples:

```
define TownHbs() ⇒⇒ town(Historic_building) over
 Historic_building()
define AverageSalary(Historic_building)
   average(salary over is_managed(Historic_building)
define Hierarchy(Employee) transitive of boss(Employee)
define ParisianEmployees() intersection of
   Employee(), inverse of town(Person) = "Paris"
```

These examples demonstrate both the power and the conciseness of the model. In Daplex updates are done in the following way:

```
for a new Historic_building
   begin
      let name = "Eiffel tower"
      let day_closed = "Monday", "Tuesday", "Sunday"
   end

for the Employee such that name = "Henri Dupond"
   begin
      let manages = the Historic_building such that name =
      "Eiffel tower"
   end

for the Historic_building such that name = "Eiffel tower"
   begin
      exclude "Sunday" in day_closed
      include "Saturday" in day_closed
   end
```

The **new** clause creates a new historic building and specifies the values of each of the declared functions using the **let** clause. The second example modifies the **manages** link of the employee with the name 'Henri Dupond'. The **the** clause means that the system will only execute the update on the single entity with that name. If there are two entities with the same name when the update is performed an error will be signalled. The same update could be performed without the **the** clause, in which case all the entities with the same name would be updated. The last example shows how values can be added to and removed from a multi-valued function using the **include** and **exclude** operators.

As the Daplex model allows both the representation of derived data and updating, the problem of updating via derived functions arises. Daplex offers an original solution to this problem. We said earlier that there is no general solution to the problem of automatic propagation of updates to the derived classes. In Daplex, the user must specify how an update is propagated by using the **perform** clause in the following manner:

```
perform
    exclude TownHbs() = a_town
using
    for Historic_building such that town = a_town
    exclude Historic_building()
```

This expression specifies that the update which consists of removing a town's name from the multi-valued **TownHbs** function must be interpreted as the deletion of all the historic buildings found in that town,

In conclusion, the Daplex model is of interest because it is an example of a functional model that integrates a large part of the semantic model's concepts into a set that is coherent and easy to use. In particular, the Daplex data model is functional, yet the data manipulation language is imperative and based on a few simple and powerful constructs. In Chapter 8, we will see how well Daplex can be integrated with a general programming language.

4.5 Links with Artificial Intelligence

Semantic models and the models used to represent knowledge have different aims but a certain number of concepts and tools in common. That is why we think a brief description of the similarities is of interest in a book dedicated to the evolution of database management systems, given that these models have evolved due to the need to increase the computing power of the data manipulation languages on the one hand and to the semantic richness of the database models on the other.

Research into knowledge representation has introduced the concepts of *semantic nets* and *frames*. Semantic nets organize knowledge about the real-world into graphs. These graphs allow complex and recursive data items to be defined and organized in categories according to their properties. The most important links are the *instance of* and *part of ISA* (inheritance) links (similar to aggregation). In contrast to semantic models, semantic nets do not distinguish between data and structure, that is, they provide no means for separating the definition of the data item's structure from the data item itself. In practice, this means there must be a node in the net for each object represented.

The approaches based on *frames* allow greater structuring of object classes as well as links between classes. The *frames* theory is a result of M. Minsky's work on perception in vision systems. Minsky was influenced by psychological theories. The general idea is that in order to understand a new concept, human beings use elementary structures that they have remembered from situations they have faced previously. They choose the most appropriate structure and modify it if necessary so that it is better adapted to the new situation. A *frame* is characterized by a list of properties and a tuple whose attributes (called *slots*) play the same role as the attributes in the semantic model. The *frames* are organized into an inheritance hierarchy and the attributes are inherited. Models inspired by the *frames* theory allow exceptions to be made to either the attributes or their values. For example, we can express the fact that people can see but that blind people are people who cannot see. These models have also been extended so that operations can be performed on the attributes. We will briefly illustrate the mechanisms of an approach based on frames using the KRL language, which was its precursor. KRL is both a programming language and a knowledge representation language. The *frames* are put into categories according to their level of abstraction. The most general are placed in the `Basic` and `Abstract` categories. The `Basic` category is used to partition the knowledge into simple inheritance trees. The `Abstract` category only includes general data and cannot be specialized. The `Specialization` category includes *frames* which are a refinement (finer grain) of the *frames* in the `Basic` category or of other frames in the `Specialization` category. Here is an example of `Basic` and `Specialization` frames:

```
[ Historic_building UNIT Basic
<SELF>
< name ( a String)>
< entrance_fee ( an Integer)>
< day_closed (( a Day) Monday ; DEFAULT)>
< address (( a Town) Paris ; DEFAULT)> ]
```

```
[ Palace UNIT Specialization
<SELF ( a Historic_building)>
<category { (XOR normal luxury)
            (using (the entrance_fee from Historic_building
              ThisOne)
                  selectfrom (which isLessThan 30) normal
                  otherwise luxury) } > ]
```

The first *frame* describes the historic buildings (**UNIT** is the KRL term for frame). It is a basic *frame*. The predefined **SELF** attribute is used to define the inheritance link; in this case there is none, but in the case of the **Palace** *frame* an inheritance link with the historic buildings has been defined. The attributes' types are preceded by the **a** or **an** keywords. They may be either predefined (**Integer**) or a reference to another *frame*. Values can be associated by default, as in the case of the historic building's address. The **Palace** *frame* represents a case of simple inheritance. The category attribute is computed according to the value of an inherited attribute (**entrance_fee** in this case). The **ThisOne** keyword designates the current value of the frame. The **using...selectfrom...otherwise** construct is the equivalent of a *case* instruction in Pascal. Up till now, we have defined the equivalents of classes. An entity is an **Individual** category frame. The originality of this approach is that an entity can be defined from different 'points of view', called *perspectives*, which are attached to the **SELF** attribute. Here is an example:

```
[versailles UNIT individual
<SELF> { ( a Historic_building with
           name = "Palace of Versailles"
           entrance_fee = 40)
         ( a Palace with
           owner = "French State")
         ( a Park with
           area = "100")}]
```

The versailles *frame* has three perspectives: **Historic_building**, **Palace** and **Park**. The **Park** perspective allows this *frame* to be seen as a leisure park. This mechanism allows you to include attributes in the entity which are not present in the frames from which it inherits when they are specified. This allows you to specify multiple inheritance functions. Note also that these perspectives may vary from one entity to another.

Finally, *frames* are designed to be used in main memory. In relation to semantic models, they place far less emphasis on the structuring of data (used for security and efficiency purposes) and far more on the dynamic nature and flexibility of the constructions. Nevertheless, the similarities between the concepts used should be noted.

4.6 Links with the object-oriented approach

As we will show later in this book, and particularly in Chapter 9, the object-oriented approach is extremely popular among database management system designers. One of the reasons is that it offers a satisfying solution to the numerous problems posed by the creation of database management systems more powerful than relational systems. As we shall see, object-oriented systems provide greater flexibility than relational systems as well the capability to manage and handle data more complex than relations.

One difference between object-oriented models and semantic models is that the former stress the behaviour of data by encapsulating in the concept of an object both the data and the operations that can be performed on that data. Most object-oriented systems provide an inheritance mechanism that allows you to refine classes into more specific subclasses, as in the schema shown in Figure 4.8. The object identity concept of object-oriented systems covers the semantic models' entity concept.

Superficially, we could say that object-oriented systems, which have their origins in the areas of both object-oriented programming languages, such as Smalltalk, and databases with complex objects, implement a certain number of the key functions of semantic models efficiently. However, generally they do not provide declarative languages, integrity constraint management, definition of views or data manipulation like those found in semantic models.

4.7 Criteria for using a model

As the reader has no doubt realized, the semantic models which have been proposed are varied and of interest to the areas of both databases and artificial intelligence but the same concepts are often repeated or re-invented. In the context of databases, the common aim of these propositions is to make the design *and* use of databases easier. There is a consensus about the fact that in order to achieve this aim you need a model that provides links between objects that correspond as closely as possible to the user's view of the real-world, and that those links need to have clear semantics which formally define the possible states of the database and the transitions from one state to another.

The various existing models differ on the following points:

- *Target applications.*
  Some models are general and have been created for research purposes, while others are designed to be used in a specific application area.

- *Degree of freedom to define links.*
  Some models, such as SDM and SAM*, provide totally specified links with insertion/deletion and cardinality constraints. Other models leave it up to the user to define the links' semantics in a specific way. The ER model is one of these.

- *Degree of complexity of the links.*
  Some models offer a very simple type of link. Thus the binary models only manage binary links. Even though it is possible to represent more complex relations using those links, most current models, such as the SDM model provide constructors for sophisticated links directly.

- *Distinction between links and entities.*
  In models like the ER model, the links are a basic modelling element and have different semantics from the entities. By contrast, functional models often have a uniform approach and model both links and entities as functions.

- *Privileged abstractions.*
  We have already seen that certain models stress certain abstractions rather than others. According to the case in hand, the model may be built using aggregations or tuples or both. Once again, there is no universal truth and users will choose according to their own needs.

- *Handling of data dynamics.*
  Few models provide a way of handling data dynamics. We will see in Chapter 9 that object-oriented models provide good solutions to this problem via the concept of the object.

The points described above should be used when you want to evaluate the suitability of a semantic model to your own needs. The table in Figure 4.10 can be enriched to take these factors into account and can be used to select a model according to a particular need. Three other criteria are often used to measure the ease with which a semantic model can be implemented for a particular application:

- *Ease with which the model's concepts can be understood.*
  If users cannot understand, or find it difficult to understand the tools the model they are using provides, it is obvious that any advantages it has are completely lost. There is often a delicate balance between the model's richness and its clarity. Here, as elsewhere, 'an abundance of riches can be harmful'.

- *Ease with which data queries can be formulated.*
  One of the problems with standard database management systems is that they do not allow data to be manipulated easily in the context of very complex applications. It is imperative that a semantic model that

provides tools for constructing sophisticated schemas also provides a powerful and easy to use query language.

- *Ease with which the semantics of the constructions in the schema can be formulated and maintained.*
  Whether the model limits itself to the specification of insertion and deletion constraints or provides tools for defining general constraints, the semantics must be easy to define and maintain.

A classic technique for comparing the various models consists of weighting the characteristics you want to take into account and then measuring the 'weights' of the respective models according to these characteristics. The score obtained by model M shows that, in the context of the particular application, that model is judged by the designer to be the most suitable. Obviously, the evaluation criteria we have given do not claim to be exhaustive and the weights assigned may vary according to the preferences of the person doing the evaluation. Subjectivity is inevitable and justified because the most important thing is that the user of a semantic model understands it well and likes using it.

4.8 Conclusion

As a conclusion, we will point out the deficiencies of semantic models and describe briefly their probable evolution. We have already mentioned, in Section 4.6 that the object-oriented approach allows numerous features of semantic models to be implemented and also offers modelling of object behaviour. The two areas where semantic models are the most limited are the dynamic and temporal domains, that is, in managing events and explicitly taking account of time. All the semantic models take into account the static aspects of data but very few offer propositions for the dynamic and temporal aspects. Among the methodologies for representing temporal aspects, we have picked out the following. The TODM model (Temporally Oriented Data Model) adds temporal data to the relational model. This model generalizes relational operations so that they manage temporal data. Another proposition, put forward by Snodgrass and Ahn, also starts from the relational model. The authors distinguish between 'transactional' time, that is, the time when the data was actually recorded, and validity time, which represents the data's useful life. Starting from these concepts, they define the ideas of historic relations and *static roll-back relations*. Schiel's THM model (Temporal Hierarchical Model) manages the temporal aspects as one of the basic abstractions. More particularly, this model studies the impact of time on the semantics of generalization and specification. In most of these propositions, there is a generalization of the constraints which allows the users to include temporal data as well as classic data in the specifications of the constraints.

Finally, we must stress that the semantic models area is above all a research area. The market is increasingly obsessed with relational database management systems and will not turn to systems based on semantic models until reasonably high-performance implementations of them exist. The systems we describe in the following chapters, in particular the extended relational systems and the object-oriented systems, provide implementation solutions for a large number of the features of semantic models. They may also provide a response to market needs.

Bibliographical notes

The semantic models area has a very rich literature. We have relied heavily in this chapter on two articles which anyone who wants to have a clear view of the area must read. The first, [HK87], is very synthetic and is as much in the form of a lecture as in that of a review of a certain number of models in the light of a typical model called GSM. The second, [PM88], describes numerous models in detail.

The reader will find more extended accounts of semantic nets and models based on frames in [Min75], [BW79] and [MNC*89].

The models we have mentioned in this chapter are described in the following articles: Data Semantics ([Abr74]), the entity-relation model ([CD74], [Che76]), the Smith and Smith model ([SFL80]), the Kent model ([Ken78]), FDM ([KP76], [Shi81]), SDM ([HM83]), SAM* ([Su83]), IFO ([AH87]), RM/T ([Cod79]), GEM ([TZ84], [Zan83]), Format ([HY84]), LDM ([KV84], [Kup85]), TAXIS ([Bor85]), ADAPLEX ([SFL80]), SEMBASE ([Kin84]), INSYDE ([KM 85]).

In the context of the logical approach to data manipulation, we refer to COL ([AG88]), LDL ([BNR*87], [NT89]) and RDL1([KdMS89]).

The functional approach originates with Backus's manifesto ([Bac78]). In the context of databases, this approach first appears in the 'Data Semantics' article ([Abr74]), and in the articles describing FQL ([BF79], [BFN82]) and Daplex ([Shi81]).

The temporal aspects of semantic models are described in relation to the TODM model ([Ari86]) and the THM model ([Sch83]) and in ([SA86]).

Exercises

1. Draw a diagram illustrating a Painting entity which is an aggregation of the Name, Artist and Date entities.

2. Draw a diagram illustrating an association which expresses the fact that several Painting entities can be housed in one Historic_building entity.

3. The situations described above could be expressed using attributes. How would the diagram differ?

4. We might want to classify our paintings into subclasses of, for example, old masters and the Italian school. We could do this by specialization, derived in the first case (old masters date from before 1600) and explicit in the second case. Draw a diagram to illustrate this.

5. It is said that subclasses defined by specialization or superclasses defined by generalization form an inheritance hierarchy. What does this mean in practical terms?

6. Why would updates of the old master class, defined above, present a problem?

7. What are the essential functions of data manipulation languages?

8. How do logical data manipulation languages differ from imperative data manipulation languages and what are their advantages?

9. Functional approaches have great appeal to many researchers. Give reasons for this and also say why they may not appeal to general users.

10. Daplex is really a hybrid between a functional approach and an imperative approach. Why could this statement be considered to be true?

11. Both semantic nets and frames are ways of representing knowledge which have many advantages. However, because semantic nets do not distinguish between data and data structures, frames have received more attention from the database community. What are the advantages frames offer?

12. What do object-oriented systems offer that is lacking in semantic models and what is missing from them that semantic models provide?

5

Type systems

*You can only design the simple well
after you have studied the complex in depth.*
Gaston Bachelard
Le nouvel esprit scientifique

5.1 The concept of type

In the last chapter, we saw that the purpose of a data model is to represent the data pertinent to an application. The concept of type is very closely related to the concept of class, as used in data models, but it is used in another context and for another purpose.

The role of a type in a programming language is to distinguish between values handled dynamically during program execution. In many cases, a type can be seen simply as a set of values.

A type system is used to manage a collection of types and the links between them, which may be complex. There are several very good arguments for using types in programs:

- They help you to understand and organize your data better. Seen from this point of view, a typing system has a modelling role much like a data model.

- They help you to detect programming errors as early as possible.

- They help the compiler to decide how the data should be represented physically.

5.1.1 Untyped programming languages

Not all languages have type systems, and there are famous examples of programming languages where the concept of type does not even appear. Lisp, being a realization of the lambda-calculus, is one of the most famous examples of this approach. Every value in Lisp is a list and you use the language to define and execute functions which operate on those lists. Smalltalk is another example of an untyped programming language, even though the concept of a class in Smalltalk can be compared to that of a type.

One of the main advantages put forward by the designers and users of these untyped languages is their flexibility. This approach can be seen as a reaction against the languages around at the end of the 1960s, which had too rigid and too restricted type systems. The Pascal type system, for example, is very limited and does not allow you to write a general sorting function that can be applied to arrays containing different data types. As the sorting operation does not depend on the nature of the data sorted, you should be able to write such a function, which would be called a *polymorphic* or *generic* function because it could be applied to data items with different types (and therefore forms).

Considerable progress has been made since these earliest type systems (Fortran, Pascal) in defining types and type systems and in understanding them from a theoretical point of view. In particular, modern type systems allow you to define polymorphic functions, types with other types as parameters, abstract data types, ordered relations between types and so on.

Given the progress made in type systems during the past 20 years, the arguments in favour of designing and using untyped languages have become outmoded because the typed approach offers great advantages.

Furthermore, as the size and complexity of software packages and systems are continually increasing, the detection of inconsistencies and programming errors has become a question of prime importance. The whole technology of the rapidly expanding discipline of software engineering is based on languages with type systems that are both powerful and supple yet rigorous.

5.1.2 Type checking

We said that it is important to detect programming errors, that is, type errors, and to detect them as early as possible. Let us list the different types of errors:

1. An operation is applied to arguments whose types are not the same as the ones it was designed for.

2. A variable is assigned a value whose type is not the one in the variable declaration.

3. An array is processed using an index that is outside the bounds of the array.

4. An illegal arithmetic operation occurs (division by zero, de-referencing the nil pointer, overflow, and so on).

It may seem strange to consider a division by zero as a type error, because type errors are traditionally confined to the first two categories, if not solely to the first one. It all depends, really, how you view types. If you decide that the `Real` type can be divided into two types, `Real_not_null` and `Real_null`, you can define the division operation as an operation with a first argument, whose type is `Real_null`, and a second argument, whose type is `Real_not_null`. Seen in this way, division by zero is a type error. You can find similar examples for arrays.

Type checking consists of detecting type errors. It might seem natural to think that these errors should be detected when the programs are executed. However, this has several important disadvantages:

- If types are checked on execution, the data must retain information about its type during execution.

- Checking slows down execution.

- The program is difficult to validate, because there is always a possibility that it may halt because of an undetected type error.

In order to avoid these problems, type checking must take place, as far as possible, when the programs are compiled. The list of the different sorts of errors shows clearly that it is impossible to guarantee that a program will execute without errors once it has been compiled. Type checking is, therefore, a carefully balanced mixture of checking during compilation (static checking) and checking during execution (dynamic checking). The language should also provide programmers with tools that they can use to specify a program's behaviour when an error is detected during execution.

The following program is an example which defines two variables and a function in an imaginary language resembling C, and uses those declarations. The **any** keyword is used to declare a variable without specifying its type.

```
int x;
any y;

int f (int p) { ... }

{
f(3); f(x); f(y);
}
```

During compilation, the first call to the function is validated, because the argument (the literal 3) is of the type expected by the function. The same happens for the second, for we assume that the compiler ensures that a variable declared with the **int** type corresponds to a value of the **int** type. However, the third call cannot be validated during compilation and the compiler must generate code to check the type during execution.

5.1.3 Type inference

Type inference is a natural extension of the concept of type checking. In a traditional compiler, the checking algorithm uses the type information provided by the programmer. Type inference means that the compiler extracts the type information from the program itself, thus freeing the programmer from the (sometimes laborious) task of specifying all the type information for each variable and each operation. A language that uses type inference provides a simpler and more user-friendly interface than a traditional language. On the other hand, from a theoretical and algorithmic point of view, it is much more difficult to understand than type checking, which obeys fairly simple laws. We will have the opportunity to come back to this problem, in greater detail, in Section 5.3.2 when we discuss the language ML, which is one of the languages that provide this kind of mechanism. The following example shows how a compiler can infer the types used in an ML program:

```
fun append(nil, l) = l | append(hd:: tl, l) = hd:: append(tl,l);
```

This is the definition of a function (**append**) which concatenates two lists. The **::** operator concatenates an element (**hd**) to a list (**tl**). The **nil** value represents the empty list. Notice that no type information appears in this definition. Nevertheless, the ML compiler can type this expression and return its type, in the form of the expression:

```
val append = fun: ('a list * 'a list ) -> 'a list
```

This expression means that the **append** function takes as input two lists of elements of the same type and returns a list made up of elements *of the same type* as the input lists. The **'a** symbol denotes a type of some kind (in the above example, the type of the elements in the input and output lists). If you wish, you can try to trace the ML compiler's procedure and deduce from the expression defining the append function that the elements in the input and output lists must be of the same type.

This example also shows that type inference is strongly linked with polymorphism (*see* Section 5.3), because if you free a program from its type information you open the door to its functions being used in different contexts.

5.1.4 Abstractions

It is impossible to define the notions of type and type system without talking about the underlying facilities of the languages that use this system. For example, we saw that a language must provide programmers with a mechanism that allows them to manage dynamically type problems that cannot be resolved during compilation.

In programming language terminology, the term *abstractions* is used to refer to a language's basic facilities, because they translate the physical mechanisms (processor, memory, and so on), which are used to execute the language, into abstract terms. Variables are the most common example of abstractions.

5.1.4.1 Functional abstraction

Another example of abstraction is functional abstraction. This facility allows you to define functions and to call them from different places in the program. A primitive language like Basic does not have this facility.

Even though functions have been known and used for a long time now, not all languages define them in the same way. In particular, you find the following differences:

- *Functions with or without side-effects.*
  Some languages allow functions to access a global state and to update that state, so that if you apply the same function to the same arguments

twice in succession you may get different results. Other languages, which are closer to the lambda-calculus, define functions in a way that is more like the mathematical concept. The FQL database language, described in the preceding chapter, is an example of that approach.

- *The semantics of parameters.*
Different languages have different semantics for passing parameters. The standard semantics, that is, that of the lambda-calculus, is that parameters are passed by value. Languages like Pascal and C++ allow parameters to be passed by reference. The function can then update the corresponding value, thus creating side-effects in the calling context.

- *Definition of local functions.*
Pascal allows you to define functions inside functions, thus providing a mechanism with an unconventional scope.

5.1.4.2 Control abstractions

Control abstractions are mechanisms that you can use to control program execution. Traditionally, in this category, you find **if..then...else**, and the iterators **do...while**, **repeat..until** and **for**.

Apart from these traditional mechanisms, there is a very interesting and original facility in the Clu language that allows you, within limits, to define your own control abstractions. You can use this facility to program iterators. An iterator takes the form of a function but has the ability to give results iteratively and be used in combination with the **for** iterator, as the following example shows:

```
strings_to_chars = iter (s: string) yield (char)
   index: int = 1;
   limit: int = string$size(s)
   while index <= limit do
         yield (string$fetch(s, index));
         index:= index + 1;
   end;
end string_to_chars
...
for x: char in string_to_chars("hello!")
   ...
end
```

This Clu program defines an iterator which transforms a string into a character stream which can then be processed. The **string$fetch** term designates the **fetch** operation defined in the **string** module. The **yield** instruction produces an element in the result stream. In system terms, the iterator can be seen as a server that produces a stream of characters which are consumed in a **for** loop. The Clu iterator allows you to express this stream in an abstract way so that you do not have to know the details of the transformation.

5.1.4.3 Exceptions

Another basic facility of modern programming languages is exceptions which allows programs to take exception events, like division by zero or array overflow, into account. The following example, using Ada, shows how you can write a division function that handles the problem of division by zero:

```
function divide (x, y: float) return float is
begin
   return x / y;
exception
   when DATA_ERROR =>
           if y = 0 then
                   return 1;
           else
                   return sign(x) * MAXINT;
           end if
end
```

In this example, the function uses standard division to return the result. When the value of parameter y is 0, this primitive operation fails and returns the predefined exception DATA_ERROR. This exception is handled by an *exception handler* which specifies the program's behaviour if there is an exception. In the example it returns an alternative value as the result. This facility is very important when you are building very large software packages which must be able to handle unexpected events and which cannot be allowed to crash suddenly, as, for example, a C program would.

You can also use this facility as a programming discipline that allows you to separate particular cases from the general case and handle them differently. The main part of the code only takes the general case into account, whereas the particular cases are grouped together in the exception handler.

5.1.4.4 Other abstractions

We have described some of the basic facilities which found in modern programming languages; these facilities structure the corresponding type systems. Obviously, there is no comprehensive list of these facilities and each language provides specific abstraction mechanisms depending on the types of applications for which it was designed.

In the context in which we are interested, the programming of database applications, we will concentrate on defining the abstractions that can be used to manipulate large volumes of data easily. A set or list construction may be one of these abstractions, but we will see in Chapter 6 that they are not the only possibilities.

In Section 5.2 we consider one particular abstraction whose invention has certainly caused the greatest upheaval in the programming languages area. This is data abstraction.

5.1.5 The expressive power of a type system

When we are comparing different type systems, we generally consider the following characteristics:

- The system's set of basic types.

- The set of type constructors.

- The degree of polymorphism allowed by the system.

- The syntactic constructions used to construct types (the algebra of types).

Among a type system's basic types, you usually find **integers**, **floats**, character **strings**, **booleans**, and so on. The type systems of more sophisticated languages also include enumerated types, bit strings or images. These basic types vary according to the programming language's application domain.

Among the most common type constructors, you find the tuple constructor popularized by languages like Pascal and C:

```
record
   name: string,
   age: int
end
```

You also find constructors that allow you to create unions of types or tuples with variants.

```
union
   animal: desc_Animal,
   vegetable: desc_Vegetable,
   mineral: desc_Mineral
end
```

```
record
name: string,
age: int,
case sex Sex of
   Woman: m_name: string
end
end
```

Very often, languages have a constructor that allows you to build collections of values of the same type. The main constructions are as follows:

- *Array.*
  An array is a collection indexed by an integer value which represents an entry in the array. In most languages the boundaries of the array are specified in the type definition and checked dynamically.

- *List.*
  Lists are the sole data structure in Lisp. In most cases the elements in the list are accessed sequentially using the **car** (extract the first element) and **cdr** (extract the sublist that does not contain the first element) operations.

- *Set.*
  The languages whose type systems allow sets to be constructed are rare. In Pascal there is a **set** constructor but it is so restrictive that it is almost unusable. In the following chapters, we will see that a set constructor is one of the essential components of a database programming language's type system and, in the fourth part, we will see that implementing this constructor is a difficult problem.

- *Sequence.*
  Certain languages (like Galileo, described in Chapter 8, or O_2, described in Chapter 10) allow you to construct sequences. Sequences unite the features of lists and arrays. You can index them like arrays and handle them like lists.

In most languages you also find a function constructor, a pointer (or reference) constructor or even an abstract data type constructor.

A polymorphic typing system allows you to construct types with other types as parameters (thus allowing you to define your own type constructors) and functions that can take values of different types as inputs. In Section 5.3 we describe the different kinds of polymorphism in detail.

The algebra of types is the set of syntactic constructions that can be used to construct types. One of the main features of modern type systems is the principle of orthogonality. All the types that can be constructed have the same rights and all the constructions can be applied to all the types.

The Pascal type system does not have this property because a Pascal set cannot contain atomic values and a function can only return an atomic value.

5.1.6 The theory of types

We are not going to go into the details of the mathematical constructs used to describe the semantics of programming languages and type systems. However, it may be useful to consider the general principles behind these formal models in order to understand the different constructions offered by certain languages.

Constructing a good type system is not an easy task and language designers always have to make compromises between the power and the security of their type system. It must be strict enough to ensure that the programs developed are reliable, yet flexible enough to allow fragments of the programs to be used in other similar contexts. The theory of types is the formalism used in order to construct good type systems. By isolating a few fundamental concepts it makes it possible to construct all the others.

However, the theory of types is not just useful for designing programming languages it is also a tool that you can use when thinking about types. From a practical point of view, the theory of types is used to study problems such as:

- the decidability of type checking;
- whether it is possible to check types during compilation;
- if this is not possible, the kinds of errors that may arise during execution;
- the creation of type checker generators, using a declarative specification of the type system.

The theory of types has close links with logic, in that its aim is to describe the properties of a world made up of all the values a language can handle.

From a syntactic point of view, a theory of types can be seen as a set of rules used to deduce true statements about the types from other true statements. For example, one of those rules can describe the typing of a function in the following way:

$$\frac{\Gamma \vdash f : A \to B \qquad \Gamma \vdash a : A}{\Gamma \vdash f(a) : B}$$

This rule expresses the fact that if you *know* that f is a function of A in B and that a is a value of A, then *you can deduce* that $f(a)$ is a value of B.

From a semantic point of view, the theory of types consists of defining a mathematical structure that gives a meaning to the above rules, which means that it associates a truth value with each assertion in such a way that all the true assertions, and only true assertions, can be derived from the rules. Generally, defining such a construction is complicated. In particular, you have to find a domain of values that can represent atomic values (such as integers), functions and Cartesian products at one and the same time. Such a domain can be seen as a solution to the equation:

$$V \approx \text{Int} + (V \to V) + (V \times V)$$

Different solutions to these equations have been proposed, in particular by Dana Scott [Sco76]. The roots of most of these constructions lie in the theory of categories.

One of the simplest domains was first proposed by Scott. The set of values V is defined as a complete ordered set. A type is a subset of V with certain properties that make it an *ideal* of V. The set of all the ideals of V form a *lattice* whose summit is the set V itself (the **any** type), and whose smallest element is the singleton containing the smallest element of V (the **void** type).

The phrase 'v is of type t' is interpreted as meaning that the value v belongs to the ideal representing t. In this model, it is evident that a value can have several types because the ideals are not necessarily exclusive. Certain type systems only use a restricted set of the ideals in V to construct their types.

A language is called *monomorphic* when the type system dictates that the ideals associated with two different types are exclusive. It is called *polymorphic* when two types can share values. As types are represented by sets, the concept of a subset is used to represent the concept of a subtype, found in some languages, or the concept of inheritance, found in object-oriented languages.

The semantics of ideals is not the only possible semantics for the theory of types. In relation to other semantics, it has the advantage of being intuitive (types are interpreted as sets of values) and explaining, to a certain extent, polymorphism and inheritance. Scott has proposed other more complex semantics, based on *retracts*, in which the types themselves are values.

5.2 Data abstraction

5.2.1 Motivations and examples

The concept of data abstraction was generated by a simple observation: the quality of a software package depends above all on the methodology used to develop it. Numerous proposals for methods, more or less formal, were made in the 1970s. Mostly, these methods aimed at defining a software package incrementally, by decomposing problems into isolated subproblems which could then be solved individually. When using such a method, you must carefully isolate the links, of various kinds, between the various system components.

The ease with which a methodology can be implemented in a particular language depends upon whether the language provides constructors similar to those used in the methodology. Furthermore, a methodology, however useful and efficient, runs the risk of not being used much if it is too far removed from the application programmers' world and unless the language's constructions force them to respect a certain discipline.

This is why the 1970s saw the emergence of the first languages proposing new data types, called abstract data types, which allow for a more formal style of programming. These propositions culminated, at the start of the 1980s, in the appearance of the Ada language, which was the fruit of considerable human and financial investment.

Let us consider, as an example, an imaginary application which has been broken down into various subproblems, and let us suppose that one of those subproblems is managing a stack of words. The methodology leads the designer to specify this subproblem in the following terms:

```
problem Stack_of_words
   operations   create a new stack
                add a word to the stack
                remove the last word from the stack
                test to see if the stack is empty
   constraints You can only take a word off the stack if it is
                not empty.
```

This (informal) specification gives no information about how the stack is defined physically or how the operations are carried out. This specification only describes the problem's external aspects, that is, what the application's other components need to know in order to use the stack.

If you wanted to solve this problem using the C language, you might write the following code:

```
/* SPECIFICATION */

typedef char[256] word;
typedef struct stack {
   int size;
   word * elements; } * stack;

stack stack_create();
void stack_insert(stack, word);
```

```
void stack_drop(stack);
char stack_empty(stack);
```

In this definition a `stack` is defined as an array of words and the `stack` type designates a pointer to a structure that describes that array. The corresponding implementation is as follows:

```
/* IMPLEMENTATION */

stack stack_create() {
   stack st = malloc(sizeof(struct stack));
   st->size = 0;
   st->elements = (word *) malloc(1024 * sizeof(word));
return st;
}

void stack_insert(stack st, word w) {
   strcpy(st->elements[++st->size], w);
}

void stack_drop(stack st) {
   --st->size;
}

char stack_empty(stack st) {
   return (st->size == 0);
}
```

This code could be seen as a reasonable solution to the problem posed. In order to use a list of words, another of the application components could contain:

```
char w1[] = "hello";
char w2[] = "world";
stack s;

s = stack_create();
stack_insert(s, w1);
stack_insert(s, w2);
stack_drop(s);
if (stack_empty(s)) {...}
```

Leaving aside the fact that the C language has no appropriate mechanisms for constructing such software components, the programmer must know the details of the implementation of a stack and the language allows illicit operations on stacks, such as directly modifying the size field.

If you now want to solve the same problem in a language adapted to this style of programming, like Ada, you would write the following code:

```
/* SPECIFICATION */

package STACKS is
   type stack is private;
   type word is private;
   function create () return stack;
   function insert (s: stack, w: word) return stack;
   function drop (s: stack) return stack;
   function empty (s: stack) return boolean;
private
   type word is string
   type stack is
       record
            size: integer;
            data: array(1...1024) of word;
       end record
end
```

This specification consists of a module (package) which contains the set of types and operations that contribute to the definition of a stack. The stack and word types are private. This means that only their names will be known to the module's users and these users will not be able to make use of the fact that, for example, the stack type is a structure with two fields. The implementation is as follows:

```
/* IMPLEMENTATION */
package body STACKS is
   function create () return stack is
   begin
        s: stack;
        s.size:= 0;
        return s;
   end;

   function insert (s: stack, w: word) return stack is
   begin
        s.size:= s.size + 1;
        s.data(s.size):= w;
        return s;
   end;
```

```
function drop (s: stack) return stack is
begin
        s.size:= s.size - 1;
        return s;
end;

function empty (s: stack) return boolean is
begin
        return (s.size = 0);
end;
end STACKS;
```

This Ada definition is used in another component in the following way:

```
uses STACKS
s: stack:= create();
s:= insert (s, "hello");
s:= insert (s, "world");
s:= drop(s);
s:= drop(s);
s. size:= 0;      Type error
```

The Ada compiler checks that a **stack** is used exclusively as specified in the **package** declaration and does not allow any attempt to access the internal elements of the **stack** type.

This example has shown that programming using abstract types is first and foremost the product of a methodology whose aim is the development of better quality software. This methodology can be used with any programming language; it is even possible to program in C using abstract types. However, the approach only becomes completely meaningful when the programming language provides specific facilities that support the methodology and guarantee that it is really applied.

To summarize, the advantages of programming with abstract types are as follows:

- Data abstraction is a software development technique for designing and implementing quality software.

- Data abstraction groups together in the same unit an application's data and the operations that can be carried out on that data.

- Data abstraction allows you to separate a type's specification from its implementation and to make only the pertinent information visible.

- Data abstraction allows you to specify several different implementations for the same specification. The choice of one implementation rather than another can only be motivated by performance considerations.

5.2.2 Formalization

The first languages that implemented abstract data types, such as Clu and Ada, were not based on a formal mathematical theory.

During the 1980s, several propositions were made for the formalization of data abstraction. Two main approaches can be distinguished: the algebraic approach and the logical approach.

5.2.2.1 The algebraic approach

The mathematical concept of algebra automatically comes to mind when you think about finding a theoretical support for the concept of data abstraction. An algebra is a mathematical entity made up of a set of values and a set of operations for manipulating those values. This definition is very close to the informal definition of an abstract type given in Section 5.2.1. In order to define an algebra, you start by stating its *signature*, which is a set of type and operation definitions. An algebra's signature is similar to an interface's specification in a programming language. The following example shows the information contained in a signature:

```
integer, boolean: type
plus (integer, integer) -> integer
≤ (integer, integer) -> boolean
zero () -> integer
one () -> integer

true () -> boolean
false () -> boolean
and (boolean, boolean) -> boolean
or (boolean, boolean) -> boolean
```

This signature defines two types (integer and boolean) and the operations that manipulate values of those types. A signature is not an algebra. It is just a set of specifications and there may be several algebræ that correspond to a given signature. To define an algebra completely you have to associate a set of values with each type in the signature (integer and boolean in the above example) and a function with each operation defined in it. The following example shows two different algebræ for the same signature, that is, two different semantics for the same declaration.

First possibility:

```
integer ==> N¹
boolean ==> {0, 1}
```

---

1   The set of natural integers

```
plus(x, y) ==> the addition function applied to integers
≤(x, y) ==> the relation ≤ applied to integers
zero() ==> 0
one() ==> 1

true() ==> 1
false() ==> 0
and(x, y) ==> if x and y are 1 then 1 else 0
or(x, y) ==> if x and y are 0 then 0 else 1
```

Second possibility:

```
integer ==> {0, 1}
boolean ==> {0, 1}

plus(x, y) ==> if x and y are 0 then 0 else 1
≤(x, y) ==> if x is 0 and y is 1 the 1 else 0
zero() ==> 0
one() ==> 1

true() ==> 1
false() ==> 0
and(x, y) ==> if x and y are 1 then 1 else 0
or(x, y) ==> if x and y are 0 then 0 else 1
```

This example shows that an algebra's signature is sufficient for representing an abstract data type's interface, but gives no information about the semantics of the operations it describes. The second algebra gives an interpretation of the **integer** type that does not correspond in the least with reality. In order to specify an abstract type's operations more precisely, a signature can be enriched with axioms. These axioms are properties an algebra must satisfy if it is to be a valid representation of the abstract type. We could rewrite the signature in the following way:

```
integer, boolean: type
plus (integer, integer) -> integer
≤ (integer, integer) -> boolean
zero () -> integer
one () -> integer

true () -> boolean
false () -> boolean
and (boolean, boolean) -> boolean
or (boolean, boolean) -> boolean
```

```
≤ (x, plus(x, y)) = true()
≤ (y, plus(x, y)) = true()
plus (x, y) = plus (y, x)
...
and (true(), true()) = true()
and (true(), false()) = false()
and (false(), false()) = false()
and (x, y) = and (y, x)
...
```

The above axioms eliminate the second algebra and only retain the first. In the second algebra, the function associated with ≤ is such that the axiom ≤ (x, plus(x, y)) = true() would be false in the majority of cases.

This algebraic approach has aspects that transcend the context of the theory of types itself. These techniques are usually used as a support for formal program specification. In this context, a program is seen as a set of abstract types which communicate via interfaces represented by signatures whose semantics are given by axioms. Formal specification is the logical conclusion of the abstract types approach, seen as a design methodology. On the other hand, if we restrict ourselves to the problem of checking (or inferring) a program's typing, we do not have to take the axioms, which describe the semantics of the operations, into account. The operations' interfaces are sufficient. This correlation between the formal specification of a program and the theoretical basis of a type system brings us back to the comment made in Section 5.1: a program's typing can be seen as a partial specification of that program, and depending on the type system involved, that specification is more or less precise.

The main limitation of the algebraic approach is that an abstract type's operations, along with the type itself, are not ordinary values and cannot, for example, be used as parameters for other operations. The interpretation of an abstract type is not of the same nature as the interpretation of an ordinary type.

5.2.3 The logical approach

The logical approach was described briefly in Section 5.1.6. In this approach, an abstract type is a type like the others, and data abstraction is simply one way among others of constructing types. The immediate advantage of this way of seeing things is that resulting type systems do not have to use several 'categories' of types, some of which have prerogatives that the others lack.

However, when we introduce data abstraction as a primitive for constructing types it means that we have to specify on the one hand the semantic rules that govern those types and their interactions with the other types, and on the other how those types and those rules are interpreted in terms of ideals. This task, undertaken by Cardelli and Wegner, led to the definition of existentially quantified types. An existentially quantified type has the form $\exists \tau \cdot \mathtt{exp}(\tau)$ where $\mathtt{exp}(\tau)$ is a type expression using the free variable τ. The semantics of such an expression is expressed as an infinite union of ideals. A value v is of the type $\exists \tau \cdot \mathtt{exp}(\tau)$ if and only if there is (at least) one type τ such that v is of the type $\mathtt{exp}(\tau)$. The ideal associated with the type $\exists \tau \cdot \mathtt{exp}(\tau)$ is therefore the union of the ideals associated with the types $\mathtt{exp}(\tau)$ for all τ. Using this definition, we can associate numerous types with the pair `<12, 45>`, for example:

```
<int, int>        ∃τ · τ        ∃τ · <τ, τ>
```

The first type is an ordinary type which describes the `<12, 45>` object in a concrete way. In the second case, we have $\tau = $ `<int,int>`, and in the third $\tau = $ **int**.

Cardelli and Wegner defined a language, called Fun, using these existentially quantified types. In order to be able to statically type this language, they introduced a specific construction for generating instances of abstract types. For example, if `incr` is the name of a function which adds 1 to an integer, and you want to represent the pair `<12,incr>` using the type:

```
∃ ref · <val: ref, op: ref → int>,
```

then you can use the following construction:

```
x = pack[ref = int in ∃ ref · <val: ref, op: ref → int>]
         <12, incr>
```

The **pack** keyword indicates that the object that follows the construction is an instance of an existential type and specifies the type in question. The value x is considered to be an instance of the type $\exists$ ref · `<val: ref, op: ref → int>`, and can be written `x.op(x.val)` in order to evaluate the expression `incr(12)`; thus you get the value 13. The `ref` type used in the **pack** construction is called the reference type of value x. In the above example, the instance denoted by x is constructed with **int** as its reference type. Thus, you can construct different instances of the same existential type with different reference types. The expression `x.op(x.val)` is valid only because it uses two components of the same instance x. As a general rule, the expression `x.op(y.val)` is badly typed because the instances x and y may have different reference types.

In order to prevent instances with different reference types being mixed illegally, Fun introduces the **open** construction:

```
open x as id in id.op(id.val)
```

This construction is used to give a local name (**id**) to an instance of an existential type (**x**) and defines the scope *opened* for that instance. The following expression is considered to be illegal by the Fun compiler, because it combines two instances of an existential type:

```
open x as id1 in
    open x as id2 in
          id2.op(id1.val)
```

This expression is illegal because the **id1.val**'s type is the reference type of **id1**, whereas the **id2.op** function expects a value with **id2**'s reference type. Furthermore, **id1** and **id2** are considered to be different values because they are generated by two different **open** clauses. The Fun compiler cannot determine *statically* that the two names, **id1** and **id2**, come from the same instance **x**.

The following two derivation rules give the semantics for Fun's **pack** and **open** clauses:

$$\frac{\Gamma \vdash e : s\{t/a\}}{\Gamma \vdash \textbf{pack}[\, a = t \text{ in } s\,]e : \exists\, a \cdot s}$$

$$\frac{\Gamma \vdash e : \exists\, b \cdot s \quad \Gamma, x: s\{a/b\} \vdash e' : t}{\Gamma \vdash \textbf{open } e \text{ as } x[a] \text{ in } e' : t}$$

The first rule expresses the fact that e is of the type $s\{t/a\}$[2], therefore the expression **pack**[$a = t$ in s]e is of the type $\exists\, a \cdot s$. The second rule expresses the fact that if e is of the type $\exists\, b \cdot s$ then the type of **open** e as $x[a]$ in e' is the type of e' obtained by supposing x to be of the type $s\{a/b\}$. The fact that a is a free variable in the expression $s\{a/b\}$ corresponds to the semantics of reference types in Fun: the reference type in an **open** clause is considered to be a new atomic type, that is, a type about which nothing is known.

The semantics of the **open** clause and the reference types can be a serious limitation in certain cases. Let us suppose, for example, that we want to define an abstract type representing points in a plane in Fun. We could give the following definition:

---

2   $s\{t/a\}$ is the type produced by substituting t to the variable of type a in s.

```
type Point = ∃ rep.     <value: ref
                         x_val: ref → real
                         y_val: ref → real
                         plus: <ref, ref> → ref>

value create(x, y): Point =
      pack[ rep = <real, real> in <
            value: ref
            x_val: ref → real
            y_val: ref → real
            plus: <ref, ref> → ref>]
      <value = cons(x, y);
       x_val = fun(p) car(p);
       y_val = fun(p) cdr(p);
       plus = fun(p1, p2) cons(car(p1)+car(p2),
cdr(p1)+cdr(p2));
       >
```

This Fun definition of the Point abstract type is very natural and corresponds to the general form of definitions we saw in Section 5.1. However, the particular semantics of the Fun language makes this definition unusable. What happens is that the 'create' function applies the **pack** operator and creates instances of the Point existential type. Now, all the instances created by this function have the same representation, that is, the same reference type (ref = <real, real>). However, as we said earlier, the Fun compiler cannot use this information, and all the instances of Point are considered to have different representations. Therefore, the following expression is considered to be illegal:

```
open create(2,5) as p1 in
   open create(0,1) as p2 in
         p1.plus(p1, p2)
```

In reality, it is impossible to use the addition of two points operation with the above definition because that operation is based on the hypothesis that the two arguments have the same representation. A correct definition of the Point abstract type in Fun could be written thus:

```
type Point = $ rep .     <create: <real, real> → ref
                          x_val: ref  → real
                          y_val: ref  → real
                          plus: <ref, ref> → ref>
```

```
value point: Point =
    pack[ref = <real, real> in <
        create: <real, real> → ref
        x_val: ref  → real
        y_val: ref  → real
                    plus: <ref, ref> → ref>]
    <create = fun(x, y) cons(x, y);
     x_val = fun(p) car(p);
     y_val = fun(p) cdr(p);
     plus = fun(p1, p2) cons(car(p1)+car(p2),
cdr(p1)+cdr(p2));
        >
```

This abstract type is used in the following way:

```
open point as p in
    p.x_val(p.plus(p.create(1.3),p.create(4,5)))
```

This time, the definition and the use of the Point type do not correspond to the intuitions derived from the examples in Section 5.2.1. Here, the Point type has *one* and *only one instance* (the point value) which is used to group together different operations, one of which is a creation operation.

The existential types formalism is therefore caught in the crossfire: on the one hand, the semantics of reference types make it extremely difficult to combine two abstract types, even two instances of the same abstract type. On the other hand, in order to obtain the required semantics for an abstract type, you have to write definitions in a counter-intuitive manner.

At this point, several alternative definitions, aimed at resolving the problems, were proposed: the definition of recursive types (self-referencing) and an original approach based on the Amber language.

5.2.2.3 Recursive definitions

The problem we had in defining the Point type in the previous example can be resolved if recursive type definitions are allowed. The declaration of the plus operation in the example takes two ref type arguments and returns a ref type value. This definition implies that the arguments and the result have the same representation. In the following example, the Point type is used inside its own definition to indicate that the second argument is a point, but does not necessarily have the same representation as the first argument:

```
type Point = ∃ rep.<value: ref
                    x_val: ref → real
                    y_val: ref → real
                    plus: <ref, Point> → Point>

value create(x, y): Point =
   pack[ref = <real, real> in <
                    value: ref
                    x_val: ref → real
                    y_val: ref → real
                    plus: <ref, Point> → Point>]
   <value = cons(x, y);
   x_val = fun(p) car(p);
   y_val = fun(p) cdr(p);
   plus = fun(p1, p2)
     create(car(p1)+p2.x_val(p2.value),
cdr(p1)+p2.y_val(p2.value));
   >
```

Now we have this definition, we can use the `Point` type in the way we wanted to above, that is, we can write:

```
open create(2, 5) as p1 in
   open create(0,1) as p2 in
       p1.plus(p1, p2)
```

The expression's type result is a `Point` type value. The drawback of this definition is that we are getting further away from the intuitive semantics of the Fun language based on an infinite union of ideals.

5.2.2.4 Abstract types with status: Amber

One of the important aspects of the abstract type formalized by the Fun language is that they correspond to a purely functional approach. An instance groups together the functions that can be applied to the arguments. In the Amber language, Cardelli uses a formulation that differs slightly from that of Fun in that it introduces both recursively defined types, like those above, and the concept of status, denoted by the **self** keyword. This symbol designates the current instance to which the functions are applied and therefore allows that instance to be referred to inside those same functions.

Externally, this approach manifests itself by a style of definition and usage which is similar to that of most object-oriented languages, and in particular Smalltalk. To define the `Point` type, we would write:

```
type Point = ∃ ref.<value: ref
                     x_val: real
                     y_val: real
                     plus: Point → Point>

value create(x, y): Point =
  pack[rep = <real, real> in <
                     value: ref
                     x_val: real
                     y_val: real
                     plus: Point → Point>]
    <value = cons(x, y);
     x_val = car(self.value);
     y_val = cdr(self.value);
     plus = create(self.x_val + p.x_val, self.y_val + p.y_val);
    >
```

The x_val and y_val functions have an implicit argument which is of
the Point type and can be referred to using self. The plus function has two
arguments, the first of which is also implicit. You use this type in the same
way as in object-oriented programming:

```
r = create(23,4).plus(create(1,9)).x_val
```

5.2.2.5 Conclusion

We have reviewed the various propositions that have been made for formali-
zing the concept of abstract types in programming languages. Firstly, we
described the algebraic approach, which, because it represents an abstract
type as an algebra, seems the most natural. The main defect of this
approach is the distinction it makes between abstract types and other
types. We then described an alternative approach which models abstract
types as existentially quantified types whose semantics are an infinite union
of ideals. This approach has the merit of modelling ordinary types and
abstract types on the same level, but its main limitation is that it is difficult
to get several different abstract types or even several instances of the same
abstract type to interact. The semantics given to an abstract type's reference
types mean that the representations of two instances of an abstract type are
always presumed to be different.

We then looked at two propositions derived from Fun which allow this
interaction to be handled in a better way. These two propositions allow you
to define recursive types, that is, types whose name appears in the
definition. They provide the facilities and the flexibility which is lacking in
Fun. However, in Fun there is an immediate correspondence to the model of
typing by ideals, which becomes much more problematic in the cases of
these propositions.

In conclusion, the formalization of type systems, and of abstract data types in particular, is a very active research area. The Fun language formalism is an important benchmark in this research but it will almost certainly be improved upon, in order to take better into account, for example, the interactions between different instances of the same type.

5.3 Polymorphism

5.3.1 Different forms of polymorphism

Traditional languages like Pascal are based on the principle that the language's values have unique types which can be determined when the program is compiled. Such languages are called *monomorphic*. We saw in Section 5.1 that static type checking is an important requirement because it provides better security and better performance, but that, in a traditional language, it may impose great limitations on the programmer.

Polymorphic languages are languages in which a value, and in particular a function, may belong to several types at the same time.

Traditionally, we distinguish between several types of polymorphism: *parametric polymorphism* and *inclusive polymorphism*, which are grouped together under the term *universal polymorphism*, on the one hand, and *ad hoc polymorphism* on the other. A type system provides parametric polymorphism when functions can be applied to a whole category of types that have a similar structure. A function that calculates the length of a list, whatever the types of the elements in that list, is an example of parametric polymorphism because that function applies to a whole category of types (lists). When a function can be applied to a collection of types linked together by an order relation it is called inclusive polymorphism. This is the kind of polymorphism implemented in object-oriented languages. Functions that are said to have universal polymorphism (parametric or inclusive) all share the characteristics that they can be applied to a number of types (the length function can be applied to any type of list), normally infinite, and that they behave in exactly the same way when applied to arguments of different types.

On the other hand, *ad hoc* polymorphism only involves a finite (and restricted) set of types with no *a priori* links between them. The classic example of a function with *ad hoc* polymorphism is the **+** function which can be applied to the types: **integer**, **real**, **complex**, **matrix**, and so on. The addition function has different semantics in each case and the polymorphism involved is therefore only a *notational convention* which allows them all to be subsumed under the operation's name. The language's compiler sorts out the ambiguity by looking at the arguments applied to the function. This kind of polymorphism can be found in all languages[3], but it is more fully developed in Ada and C++ where the programmer can define new

---

3   The addition operation is polymorphic when the language uses **integers** and **reals**.

functions that subsume different semantics. Figure 5.1 summarizes the different types of polymorphism.

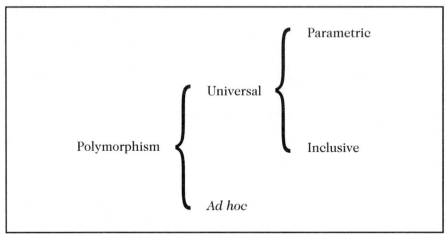

Figure 5.1 The different kinds of polymorphism

From a practical point of view, the difference between universal polymorphism and *ad hoc* polymorphism is that a function has universal polymorphism if it executes the same code on a set of types with similar structure and has *ad hoc* polymorphism if it executes different code for each type of argument.

We should also mention the kind of polymorphism used in Ada, where you can define generic procedures or functions and use them in different contexts. This kind of polymorphism is like parametric polymorphism but it is purely syntactic in Ada. In reality, the generic procedures or functions must be instantiated with known parameters during compilation. They can, therefore, be seen as abbreviations representing sets of monomorphic procedures or functions. The advantage of this approach is that the compiler can generate optimized code for each instantiation.

5.3.2 Polymorphic functions

Programming languages that allow parametric polymorphism in function definitions are rare. Among them is ML, which was designed around this concept and was certainly the first to use it. Let us look again at the definition of the **append** function given in Section 5.1.3:

```
fun append(nil, l) = l | append(hd:: tl, l) = hd:: append(tl,l);
```

This function is polymorphic because it can be applied to any type of list. The particular feature of ML is that the compiler uses the function definition to determine the set of all the types to which it can be applied. In the above example, the compiler returns the following result:

```
val append = fn : ('a list * 'a list) -> 'a list
```

which means that the function can be applied to two lists of elements of the same type and produces a list of elements of the same type as the parameters. The 'a symbol in this type expression is a variable representing any type. This variable is implicitly instantiated by a particular type, depending on the context in which the function is used. The programmer is not asked for any explicit information.

In a more traditional language, which does not use type inference, in order to define a polymorphic function you have to explicitly specify and instantiate a type parameter, as in the Napier language (described in Chapter 8) where you can define the generic identity function in the following way:

```
let id = proc[t] (x: t → t) x;
```

The t symbol denotes the type parameter, and x denotes the function's parameter which is of the t → t type. The body of the function is simply x, which makes this function the identity function whose type is proc[t] (t → t). The essential difference from ML is that the language makes the programmer specify that the function is a polymorphic function and give the types of the arguments and the result in the definition of the id function. In order to use the id function in Napier, you have to instantiate the type variable, as in the following example:

```
let three = id[int](3);
```

Therefore, you have to instantiate the function twice in order to use it: the first time with a type parameter and the second time with a value of that type. A type system such as that in Napier (or ML) clearly separates the instantiation of a polymorphic function with a type parameter from 'ordinary' instantiation, that is, the passing of arguments. This separation arises from the fact that types are not values in the language.

There have been propositions for type systems and languages in which the types are values like any others. In such a language there is no difference between a type parameter and an ordinary parameter. However, the designers of these languages are forced to introduce constraints on the construction of types, in order to be able to type programs statically.

5.3.3 Parametered types

When type definitions with similar structures, even though they are different, appear in a program, you may want to parameter those definitions in order to be able to factorize them. If, for example, you have:

```
type Pair_of_integers = int × int
type Pair_of_reals = real × real
```

you can define a parametered type Pair[t] in the following way:

```
type Pair[t] = t × t
type Pair_of_integers = Pair[int]
type Pair_of_reals = Pair[real]
```

A type definition such as Pair_of_integers does not create a new type. It simply associates a name with a type expression. A definition of a parametered type, on the other hand, introduces a *new operator* that operates on the types. The Pair parametered type is an operation that associates the type t × t with the type t. Consequently, a parametered type is not a type but an operation that operates on types. In particular, you should not confuse the following definitions:

```
type A[t] = proc(t → t)
type B = proc[t](t → t)
```

Actually, A is an operation that associates any type t with the type of the functions of t in t, whereas B is the type of the functions that transform the values of a type t into a value of the same type. B is the type of the identity function. Parametered types may be provided by a type system for generating constructors for types such as sets, lists, and so on.

5.3.4 Formalization

5.3.4.1 Polymorphic functions

The types of polymorphic functions can be modelled by existentially quantified types in the same way as Cardelli and Wegner modelled abstract types as existentially quantified types. The identity function's type can therefore be written:

$$\forall t \cdot t \to t$$

The semantics of the universal quantifier is an infinite intersection of ideals. The ideal that represents the type ∀ t · t → t is the intersection of the ideals of the types t → t for any type t.

In order to understand this definition intuitively, we must go into a little detail about the semantics of functions in the model using ideals. If A and B are two types, that is, two sets of values, type A → B is the set of all the functions of V in V that transform any value in A into a value in B. The intersection of types A → B and C → D is therefore the set of all the functions that transform any value in A into a value in B and any value in C into a value in D. By generalization we obtain that the type ∀ t · t → t is the set of all the functions of V in V that transform any value of any type t into a value of the same type.

Fun introduces two clauses for defining and handling polymorphic functions. We can define the identity function in the following way:

```
id = all[t] fun(x: t) x;
```

and instantiate this function in an expression:

```
four = id[int](4)
```

The typing rules that govern these two clauses in Fun are as follows:

$$\frac{\Gamma \vdash e : t}{\Gamma \vdash \textbf{all}[a]e : \forall a \cdot t}$$

$$\frac{\Gamma \vdash e : \forall a \cdot t}{\Gamma \vdash e[s] : t\{s/a\}}$$

The first rule states that the Fun language's **all** clause creates a polymorphic value (function), whereas the second expresses the instantiation of a polymorphic value (function) by a type. Notice the similarity between these two rules and the typing rules for functions, given below. This takes us back to the comment made in Section 5.3.2.

$$\frac{\Gamma \vdash e : t}{\Gamma \vdash \textbf{fun}(x : s)e : s \to t}$$

$$\frac{\Gamma \vdash e : s \to t \quad \Gamma \vdash e' : s}{\Gamma \vdash e(e') : t}$$

5.3.4.2 Parametered types

In Section 5.3.3, we said that parametered types are not types but operations that operate on types. Consequently, we cannot assign semantics to these types without going outside the scope of the model, because the model only describes types.

Syntactically, we can use the following rule in order to take the definition of parametered types into account:

$$\frac{\Gamma \vdash e : t\{s/b\}}{\Gamma \vdash e : a\{s\}} \quad \text{if } a[b] = t \text{ is a type definition}$$

5.4 Subtyping

Many programming languages introduce an order relation for the terms representing the types. These order relations can be used to organize automatic type conversion in the compilers, to resolve operator overloading or even to formalize the inheritance concept. In this section, we are interested in this last type of order relation, called subtyping.

5.4.1 Implicit and explicit subtyping

There are different ways of defining subtyping in a programming language. You can define a subtype relation implicitly, explicitly or by a combination of the two. In the case of an implicit subtype, the types are defined independently of one another and the subtype relation is inferred using the rules of subtyping. In the case of an explicit subtype, the subtype relation is declared when the types are defined. No inference (other than consulting the types catalogue) is then necessary in order to determine whether one type is a subtype of another.

A combination of the two approaches consists of having implicit subtyping for certain categories of types and explicit subtyping for others. Languages like Galileo (described in Chapter 8) or O_2 (described in Chapter 10), in particular, take this combined approach because abstract types have explicit subtyping and all other types have implicit subtyping.

A combination like the one above can be justified from the modelling point of view. In reality, an abstract type models a type of entity in the real-world. Establishing a subtype link between two abstract types is the same thing as modelling a specialization link between those types of entities. It is therefore logical to leave the responsibility for establishing the link to the database designer. On the other hand, the concrete types represent general data structures, without a direct link with the application entities. Implicit subtype definition then provides the programmer with greater flexibility.

5.4.2 Examples of subtyping

5.4.2.1 Scalar types and functions

Let us first look at a very simple special case of subtyping using integers. Let us call the subtype of the **int** type corresponding to the set of integers from n to m, inclusive, n..m. We can then define the subtype relation $\preceq$ on those subtypes in the following way:

$$n..m \preceq p..q \text{ if and only if } p \leq n \text{ and } q \geq m$$

Thus we can define the type $2..5 \rightarrow 4..9$. This type of function transforms an integer between 2 and 5 into another integer between 4 and 9. Given the semantics of the function types in the model by ideals, described in Section 5.3.4.1, a $2..5 \rightarrow 4..9$ type function is also a $3..4 \rightarrow 2..11$ type function. In general, we can give the following subtyping rule for these functions:

$$s \rightarrow t \preceq s' \rightarrow t' \text{ if and only if } s' \preceq s \text{ and } t \preceq t'$$

Notice that the domain of the subtype is larger than the domain of the supertype, whereas its target is smaller. This is called the contravariance rule and is a characteristic of function subtyping in the model by ideals. The intuitive justification for this semantics is that a function of a subtype can be used coherently in a context where a function of the supertype can be used.

5.4.2.2 Tuple types

A tuple **type** is constructed in the following way: [age: **int**, name: **string**]. The semantics of a tuple **type** $[a_1:t_1, ..., a_n:t_n]$ is the set of tuples defined *at least* on $a_1, ..., a_n$, and such that the value associated with a_i is of type t_i. A tuple **type** does not therefore represent *one* tuple structure, but an infinity of tuple structures with common fields. One consequence of this definition is that we can deduce the following subtyping rule for tuples:

$$[a_1: t_1, ...,a_n: t_n, ..., a_m: t_m] \preceq [a_1; u_1, ..., a_n: u_n]$$
if and only if $t_i \preceq u_i$ for all i between 1 and n.

We can therefore define types like `Vehicle` and `Car`:

```
type Car = [name: string, speed: int, fuel: string]
type Vehicle = [name: string, speed: int]
```

We then have the `Car` $\preceq$ `Vehicle` subtype relation meaning that the `Car` type is a subtype of the `Vehicle` type, and therefore that `Car`s are also `Vehicle`s. We assumed, in this example, that the subtyping of the `Car` and `Vehicle` types was implicit. In a language with explicit subtyping, you would have to write:

```
type Vehicle = [name: string, speed: int]
type Car subtype Vehicle
     = [name: string, speed: int, fuel: string]
```

5.4.3 Parametric polymorphism

Subtyping is a particular form of polymorphism because a function that can be applied to a type's values can, by definition, also be applied to the values of all its subtypes. Let us consider the following function:

```
value g fun(x: [age: int]) x.age
```

This function's type is `[age: int]` $\rightarrow$ `int`. It can therefore not only be applied to a tuple `[age: 31]`, but also to a tuple `[name: "jean", age: 34]`.

In this paragraph, we are going to show cases where it can be useful to combine subtyping, that is, inclusive polymorphism, with parametric polymorphism. In this context, let us consider the following function:

```
value f = fun(x: [age: int]) x.age:= 29; x;
```

This function's type is: `[age: int]` $\rightarrow$ `[age: int]`. It changes the age field of x and returns the modified value. According to the definition of subtyping for tuple types, it can be applied to arguments that have *at least* one **integer** type **age** field, but that can have any other fields. Now if we look at the type definition of function **f**, it is impossible, during compilation, to formulate any hypothesis other than that the type of the value returned by **f** is **[age: int]**. Consequently, when the function is applied to an argument whose type is **[name: string, age: int]**, part of the type information about the value returned by **g** is lost because it is presumed *only* to be of the **[age: int]** type when it really returns a value of the **[name: string, age: int]** type.

This example shows how there has to be interaction between inclusive polymorphism and parametric polymorphism. In the definition of function **f** above, we need to be able to express the facts that it takes an **[age: int]** type value, or any of its subtypes, as an argument and that it returns a value of the same type as its input argument. Neither the subtype nor parametric polymorphism, when considered separately, can solve this problem. Only the combination of the two mechanisms will allow us to express the required semantics for this type of function. In Fun we can write:

```
value h = all[a ⪯ [age: int]] fun(x; a) x.age:= 29; x;
```

The **h** function is a polymorphic function, like those constructed in Section 5.3.4.1, with the sole difference that the set of types that can be used to instantiate this function is not the set of all possible types, but only the set of subtypes of a given type. This combined use of polymorphism and subtyping is a form of *constrained polymorphism*. You can imagine other ways of limiting the set of types that can be used to instantiate a function, such as, for example, specifying that the type has a particular operation with some particular property. We will not go into further details of the various possibilities in this section.

5.4.4 Subtyping rules

We said previously that in the model by ideals subtyping was interpreted in terms of inclusion of ideals. The interpretation of the concept of subtyping is therefore easy from a semantic point of view. But we still have to see how the subtype relation is translated at the syntactic level, that is, in terms of typing rules.

First of all, there is a set of rules which express the simple properties of the subtype relation (reflexiveness, transitiveness, and so on) as well as the subtyping rules for the various types and constructors in the language:

$$\Gamma \vdash t \preceq \mathbf{any}$$

$$\Gamma \vdash t \preceq t$$

$$\frac{\Gamma \vdash s \preceq t \quad \Gamma \vdash t \preceq u}{\Gamma \vdash s \preceq u}$$

$$\frac{\Gamma \vdash s' \preceq s \quad \Gamma \vdash t \preceq t'}{\Gamma \vdash s \rightarrow t \preceq s' \rightarrow t'}$$

$$\frac{\Gamma \vdash s_1 \preceq t_1 \ ... \ \Gamma \vdash s_n \preceq t_n}{\Gamma \vdash [a_1 : s_1, \ ..., \ a_n : s_n, \ ..., \ a_m : s_m] \preceq [a_1 : t_1, \ ..., \ a_n : t_n]}$$

The last rule expresses the fact that a value belonging to the subtype can be used where a value belonging to the type is expected:

$$\frac{\Gamma \vdash e : t \quad \Gamma \vdash t \preceq u}{\Gamma \vdash e : u}$$

5.5 Conclusion

A type system is a formalism which is used to structure the values manipulated by a programming language. Types are used both to structure the data, in other words to model an application, and to protect it against illicit manipulations.

The evolution of languages and type systems has led to the definition of languages which are strongly and statically typed but whose type systems are more flexible and more powerful than those of second-generation languages such as Pascal.

In particular, these new languages have two characteristics, data abstraction and polymorphism, which have allowed us to make progress in both modelling and flexibility of use.

Numerous propositions have been made for ways of defining abstract types, from Ada *packages* to Clu *clusters*, not forgetting classes in C++. Efforts have been made to formalize abstract types, leading mainly to two approaches: the algebraic approach which sees an abstract type as the specification of an algebra, and the logical approach which attempts to see an abstract type as an ordinary type. Formalization of type systems, and type theory in general, is still a developing area. The Fun language, which we have used to illustrate this chapter, is an important benchmark in that development.

Parametric polymorphism and subtyping are the other essential charac-teristics of modern type systems. Among the main problems in the design of a type system are the interactions between subtyping and parametric polymorphism and between polymorphism and data abstraction. There is still much work to be done on formalization.

Bibliographical notes

The concept of type in a programming language is almost as old as programming itself. In the 1970s, the principles of structured programming were defined ([DHD72]) and with them, the general principles of type systems. The Pascal language and its type system are the classic representatives of this approach. Towards the end of the 1970s the need for more flexible and more powerful type systems was felt and their general principles established. The [Weg77] conference marked an important turning point in setting out the basis for programming using abstract data types. You can find a summary of the main points made at [Weg77] in [GG77]. These points found concrete expression in languages such as Clu ([LZ74], [LS79]) and Ada ([Ich79], [Dep83]). An overview of the main principles of type systems can be found in [Cle86] which is a good introduction to the problems of defining and using modern type systems.

Programming using abstract data types was introduced in the 1970s as a logical extension of structured programming. The Clu language ([LZ74]) was the first to implement these principles. The OBJ and OBJ2 languages ([GT79], [FGJM85]) used the abstract type approach as a support for formal program specification. The logical approach to abstract data types was proposed by Mitchel and Plotkin in [MP84] and then reformulated in a more general context in [CW85] and [Mit86].

Milner's article ([Mil78]) was crucial to the understanding and the implementation of type systems that use polymorphism. It gives the bases for a type inference algorithm in the context of polymorphic functions. This algorithm was explained in detail and implemented in [Car87a]. The ML language ([Har86], [MH88]) was directly based on this work. There are also other, more complex, approaches to polymorphism, in which types are considered as ordinary values. This approach has led to the development of languages such as Russel ([Hoo84]) and Poly ([Mat83]).

The concept of subtyping is quite old, because you can find it in a restricted form in Pascal. The [KPM84] conference (and in particular [Mit84] and [Car84a]) contributed to establishing the principles. In [Car84a], [Car84b], [CW85] and [Car88], the authors define and use a form of subtyping that can model certain aspects of inheritance in object-oriented languages. The semantics of subtyping for tuple types, in particular, was introduced in [Car84a]. The [DT88] article is a compilation of the main approaches to the problem of abstract data types and subtyping, whose aim is to formalize the object-oriented approach.

Exercises

1. What are the functions of a type system?

2. What are the disadvantages of checking types during execution?

3. What is the difference between the functional abstraction of procedural languages, such as Pascal or C, and those based on the lambda-calculus?

4. Give a definition of the algebra of types.

5. Two example programs showing the implementation of a stack are given in Section 5.2.1. What does the Ada program, using data abstraction, prevent you from doing that is perfectly possible in the C program?

6. What problems in the use of the Fun language can be solved using recursive definitions or Amber?

7. Why is a function that can return the length of any type of list said to have parametric polymorphism?

8. In what way does the code for a function with *ad hoc* polymorphism differ from the code for a function with universal polymorphism?

9. It terms of types, explain the difference between these two types:

   type A[t] = **proc**(t → t)
   type B = **proc**[t](t → t)

10. What is the relationship between subtyping and parametric polymorphism?

6

Integrating models and type systems

*I feel that I am making progress because, once again, I am beginning to
understand absolutely nothing about anything at all.*
Charles Ferdinand Ramuz
Diary

In the last two chapters we have described two areas which, until the past
few years, had remained distinct. On the one hand data models had been
set up to represent certain aspects of the real-world, often in very fine
detail, and to be used as tools in the design of database applications. On the
other hand more highly evolved languages had been developed, languages
that use much more sophisticated type systems.

Designing a database application and writing a program in Ada are
similar activities, and the resulting product is often the same: an executable
program. In reality, the difference lies in the procedure adopted to arrive at
the result, as well as the tools provided by the programming environment.

A database application is a data-oriented application. A special effort is
made to model the data itself and the links between data items. Data
manipulations are often managed separately from the data descriptions. The
concepts of type and type checking are very rarely included. The idea of
consistency that the development environment implements is more like a

notion of semantic consistency linked to the data and the links between data items. The checking of that consistency is essentially dynamic.

The programming of a traditional application proceeds according to the classic 'triangle': design, programming, validation. Generally, programming is not centred on the data but on the functions the system must implement. The idea of type is central and is used as a basis for validating the application. Statically typed languages are used because they allow certain properties of consistency, which the programs will have when executed, to be guaranteed during compilation.

The aim of database programming languages (DBPL) is to unite these two previously separate currents, or more precisely to find the highest common denominator. A DBPL is a complete general language. Therefore, it is based on a type system and must allow programs to be validated and their consistency guaranteed, by secure and if possible static typing. A DBPL is used to write data-oriented programs. Therefore, it also allows complex data and the links between data items to be modelled easily.

There is no difference between the type system and the data model in a DBPL. The great difficulty in designing such languages is to find constructions that produce a type system that can be used to model data and at the same time to provide a data model that can be used to type programs.

In this chapter, we will give some clues to help you understand how the differing traditional constructions of semantic models and type systems can be combined. Nevertheless, we do not propose a complete solution for integration, which remains the subject of research.

6.1 Abstract types and modelling

The concept of data abstraction is at the heart of integration of data models and type systems. The ability to talk about abstract data is a characteristic of semantic models. For instance, a person is not represented as a concrete data structure but as an abstract entity with certain characteristics. At the same time, the introduction of abstract data types into programming languages has been one of the significant developments in those languages.

However, semantic models and programming languages such as Clu or Ada do not have the same definition of an abstract type.

6.1.1 Abstract types and semantic models

In a semantic model, an abstract type corresponds to an essentially structural definition. A person is an abstract entity characterized by a name, an age and an address. The difference between an instance of the Person type and a three-field tuple is that an instance of an abstract type would not be *printable* as such, and could only be known via its attributes.

The abstract type in a semantic model corresponds to the intuition that a real-world entity *is* always more than what we know about it. An abstract type's attributes only model that knowledge.

In most models (*see* Chapter 4), an abstract type's properties are only attributes. The type's behaviour is not described in the type itself. The modelling of behaviour is one of the advantages that object-oriented models have over many of the semantic models.

6.1.2 Abstract types and languages

In a programming language, the abstract data type is first and foremost an abstraction of the language, by which we mean a device that can be used to construct a software structure that can be combined with other structures. In these approaches, the modelling aspect, properly speaking, receives scant consideration. The following example illustrates this difference:

```
package STACKS is
    type stack is private;
    type word is private;
    function create () return stack;
    function insert (s: stack, w: word) return stack;
    function drop (s: stack) return stack;
    function empty (s: stack) return boolean;
private
    type word is string
    type stack is
        record
            size: integer;
            data: array(1...1024) of word;
        end record
end
```

This Ada *package* defines a *stack* abstract type which can be used to manage stacks of words. In their definition, the designers are not interested in modelling what a stack is but rather in modelling what you can do with a stack. Therefore, they have declared the *stack* type itself as a private type and given the list of the operations you can execute on a stack.

The view of an abstract type in a programming language is clearly a parallel view to that in semantic models. The first is mainly concerned with the representation of instances of the type, that is, with the type's attributes, whereas the second is mainly concerned with the behaviour of instances of the type and with the various functions that can be applied to them. Figure 6.1 summarizes these approaches.

Data abstraction	
Language	– Separation between specification and implementation – Extensibility and reusability of components – Security – Formal specification and validation
Modelling	– Specification of domains – Data independence – Modelling of attributes

Figure 6.1 Different views of data abstraction

6.1.3 Towards a more global approach

A DBLP should provide a concept of an abstract type that brings together these approaches. The definition of an abstract type in a DBLP must be sufficiently structural to allow the semantic models' attribute concept to be modelled. It must also be close enough to the traditional abstract type to preserve the considerable advantages of data abstraction in programming languages.

The definition of abstract types proposed by object-oriented languages may be a step towards just such a global view of data abstraction. Let us look at an example using the Eiffel object-oriented language in order to appreciate this point:

```
class Point export
    x, y, translate, scale

feature
    x, y: real
    scale (f: real) is
        do
            x:= x * f;
            y:= y * f;
        end
    translate (a, b: real) is
        do
            x:= x + a;
            y:= y + b;
        end
end Point
```

This example defines an Eiffel class which is nothing other than an abstract type translated into the object-oriented approach's terminology. This abstract type defines a point as being made up of properties (*features*) x, y, scale and translate. The x and y properties are attributes which describe an instance of the Point abstract type, just as a semantic model would. The scale and translate properties describe the operations you can perform on points.

Therefore, object-oriented languages in general, and the Eiffel language in particular, provide a mechanism for defining abstract types which is at the boundary between abstract types as they are seen by semantic models and the 'traditional' abstract types of programming languages.

6.2 Different concepts of inheritance

The concept of inheritance is used intensively in most data models as well as in object-oriented systems. Unfortunately the concept of 'inheritance' does not always mean the same thing in all the models and languages that use it.

The concept of subtyping, on the other hand, is precisely defined in the context of programming languages as one of the possible forms of polymorphism. Subtyping is the 'natural' equivalent of inheritance in a DBPL, but certain forms of inheritance are not covered by subtyping. Inheritance is a heavily overloaded concept in many models, and in order to integrate it into a programming language we must distinguish its different facets.

In this section we are going to describe in detail the different uses made of the concept of inheritance in semantic models while at the same time showing, in each case, what they correspond to in programming languages. Figure 6.2 summarizes the different uses.

Inheritance	
Language	– Subtyping – Parametered types – Modules – Classification
Modelling	– Incremental specification – Parametric polymorphism – Implementation – Modularity – Specialization and generalization

Figure 6.2 Different views of inheritance

6.2.1 Incremental specification

The original form of inheritance is the one that is used to model real-world objects incrementally. For example, the `Employee` class can be defined by refining the `Person` class. This idea of inheritance is clearly the equivalent of subtyping in programming languages. It expresses the fact the all employees are people, independently of any specific extension. The characteristics of people are 'inherited' by employees and an employee can be used wherever a person is expected, which can be translated as inclusive polymorphism in programming language terminology.

This use of inheritance is intensional because it describes the links between types of entities. In this context, inheritance is an abstract data type construction primitive. Figure 6.3 illustrates this equivalence.

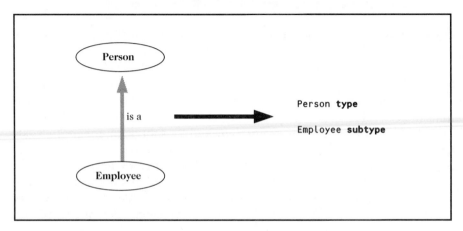

Figure 6.3 Incremental specification

6.2.2 Parametric polymorphism

The concept of inheritance is often used to simulate a form of parametric polymorphism. In both semantic models and object-oriented languages there are definitions of generic collections (like the `Set` class) which define the standard behaviour of those collections. The inheritance mechanism is used to define sets of people and express the fact that a set of people is a set. Inheritance is therefore used to represent parametered types. This solution relies, in most cases, on the fact that the languages associated with these semantic models are typed dynamically, if they are typed at all. In a programming language, this form of inheritance would be represented by defining parametered types and polymorphic functions. The construction of a subclass would be replaced by the instantiation of a parametered type, as shown in Figure 6.4.

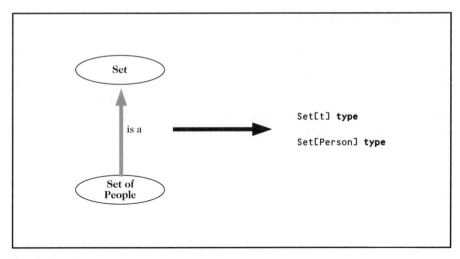

Figure 6.4 Parametered types

6.2.3 Implementation

Inheritance is also used as a support for implementation. An example of this use can be found in the Smalltalk object-oriented language. In that language, a **Set** class describes the behaviour of sets and a subclass **Dictionary** describes that of dictionaries. There is no semantic link between sets and dictionaries. The only link between the two definitions is an implementation link. A dictionary is constructed from the set construction by considering a dictionary as a set of key/value associations. In a database programming language, this type of inheritance would be expressed as a simple usage dependency between the **Set type** and the **Dictionary type**, as shown in Figure 6.5.

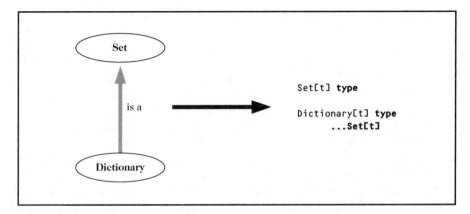

Figure 6.5 Implementation

6.2.4 Modularity

The example of inheritance shown in Figure 6.5 can be generalized. In some object-oriented languages, such as Eiffel, `class` also fulfils the role of a `module`. Inheritance is then used to express the dependency links between various modules. The `Dictionary` **module** uses the `Set` **module** as an implementation support. A `Table` **module** can be refined into an `Indexed_table` module by adding characteristics or access methods. In this case, inheritance is not a question of subtyping but of modularity, and a database programming language would represent this type of inheritance by using a system of modules and links between classes, as shown in Figure 6.6.

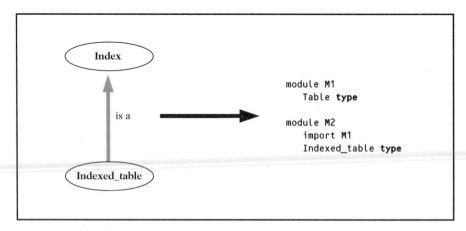

Figure 6.6 Modularity

6.2.5 Generalization and specialization

The definition of generalization and specialization hierarchies is an important aspect of semantic models which is often implemented using inheritance mechanisms. In contrast to other forms of inheritance, this is an extensional form of inheritance in that it defines links between sets of specific entities and not between types of entities. Generalization consists of defining a set of entities as the union of various sets. The set of `human being` is the generalization of `men` and `women`, that is, the union (in this case exclusive) of the set of men and the set of women. An important feature of this definition of human beings is that a human being is necessarily either a man or a woman. Specialization consists of characterizing a subset of a set of entities according to a given property. The set of `red cars` is the subset of cars which are red. In a database programming language, a classification mechanism would have to be specifically provided to represent this type of hierarchy, as suggested in the next section. Figures 6.7 and 6.8 summarize this discussion.

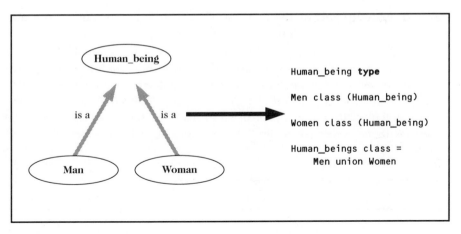

Figure 6.7 Generalization

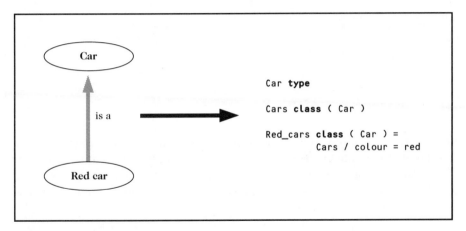

Figure 6.8 Specialization

6.3 Classes and relations

Classes and relations are two essential data model constructions for which traditional programming languages provide no equivalent.

6.3.1 The concept of class

Class is an extensional concept. A class groups together various entities that have common properties. As a first approximation, you might think about representing the concept of class in a programming language using a collection (a set, for example) of values of a given type. This representation does not faithfully mirror the concept of class and, in particular, does not take the following aspects into account:

- The semantics of creating or deleting entities in a class are specific. In most models, adding an element to a class or deleting an element from it is different from adding an element to a set or collection or deleting an element from it. The concept of an entity's *existence* is linked with its belonging to a class (or several classes) but not with its belonging to any set.

Classes	
Modelling	– Extension, existence – Specialization, generalization
Language	???

Figure 6.9 Classes

- Classes can be linked by a hierarchy of generalization and specialization. These hierarchies differ from simple set inclusion because of their semantics: for example, a class can be decomposed into subclasses which form a partition. This property of partition, and its verification, is attached to the hierarchy of classes.

These points are sufficient to demonstrate that the concept of a class is richer than the concept of a set or a collection in a programming language. A database programming language must therefore provide a specific mechanism to represent that concept which will allow classes to be defined and manipulated independently of the various types of collections it provides.

6.3.2 The concept of a relation

A relation represents non-directional links between entities. From a modelling point of view, it is very important to be able to represent and manage such links simply. However, programming languages do not provide a comparable construction. In a programming language you find the concept of a structure or of an attribute which can be used to represent *directional* links from one entity to another.

Relations	
Modelling	– Non-directional M-N links – Concept of the key – Specific accesses
Language	???

Figure 6.10 Relations

A person has an age and an address, and these two attributes establish a link between a person and his or her age, or between a person and his or her address. The first-generation database systems were based upon this style of link, and it is precisely because they were incapable of expressing more general links that they were supplanted by relational systems.

Nor can the concept of a relation be simply 'simulated' by using sets and tuples. As with the concept of class, indirect representation leaves out certain important aspects:

- A relation may have a key which expresses the equality of two associations.

- Specific access methods may be defined for relations, particularly filtering operations and update operations. Accesses and updates for collections (and particularly for sets) are not necessarily adapted to handling relations.

6.3.3 The difference between classes and relations

In relational systems, classes are represented by relations because the relation is the only abstraction the systems provide. However, most of the design methodologies that use those systems take two kinds of relations into account: those that represent classes and those that represent non-directional links between entities belonging to different classes. An entity's existential property, which is linked to its belonging to a class, is represented in those systems by inclusion dependencies or by external keys which express the fact that any entity that appears in a relation representing a link also appears in another relation representing a class.

This observation leads us to conclude that classes and relations really are independent mechanisms and that a database programming language must provide them both.

6.4 Views and derived data

6.4.1 The concept of the view

The concept of the view is essential in a database management system because it allows individual users to have selective accesses to certain parts of the conceptual schema, according to their needs. The concept of the view is also an element in the system's logical independence because, as long as the existing views are preserved, it allows the schema to be updated without the users being aware of the change. A view mechanism also forms part of the system's security because it can be used to specify which parts of the schema (and therefore of the database) a user can access.

In a relational system, a view is defined as a set of virtual relations which are mapped onto the relations in the database using the query language. The queries made about those virtual relations are then simply translated into queries about the database by simple composition. A DBPL's data model is much more complex than the relational model and data manipulation is performed by languages which are more complex than relational query languages. The concept of a view in these new systems cannot therefore be directly inspired by the relational concept of a view.

6.4.2 Derived data

In Chapter 4, we saw that many semantic models allow us to define components (often attributes) which are not physically stored in the database but which are derived from other components. Using this we can express, for example, that an employee's manager is the manager of the department in which that employee works, that the entrance fee of a historic building is the regulated entrance fee set by the town in which that historic building is located, and so on. In all these examples, the derived components are used to show different views of the same information without introducing redundancy in the data stored.

This is very rarely possible in traditional programming languages. It is only found in some languages derived from Lisp and used in artificial intelligence. The definition of derived components is not however inconsistent with the static typing of programs. If the designers of modern languages such as Clu and Ada have not provided this facility it is because of the principle of minimality. This principle stipulates that a language should not provide several mechanisms with similar functions. From a programming point of view, a derived attribute is not very different from a function type attribute. Why then should you be allowed to model function type attributes and derived attributes at the same time?

Once again, a DBPL should differ from an ordinary language by clearly separating the two mechanisms and allowing you to construct both functions and derived components. From a modelling point of view, there is no conceptual difference between two components one of which is stored and the other derived. The decision to derive a component or to store it is often arrived at late in the design process, mainly when the designer wishes to reduce data redundancy and thence update anomalies.

In Section 6.2.5, we saw that the concepts of specialization and generalization are represented in a DBLP in terms of classes derived from other classes, either by predicate (specialization) or by union (generalization). These are particularly important cases of derived information, allowing us to express, for example, the fact that a sportsperson is a person who participates in at least three sports, or that a human being is either a man or a woman. In an application, when we need to manipulate the set of sportspeople or the set of human beings, we do not want to have to do it in a different way depending on whether one of the components is derived or not.

6.4.3 Abstract types and logical independence

In the previous chapter, we saw that an abstract type is the interface data that describes the structure and behaviour of instances of that type, and that the interface can have several physical representations. In Fun, in particular, two instances of the Person abstract type can have different representations. Let us consider the following example, which uses abstract type definitions, taken from [LR90]:

```
type Town is abstract
    name: string
    regulated_entrance_fee: float
end

type Historic_building is abstract
    name: string
    town: Town
    entrance_fee: float
end

let Create_historic_building = fun(n: string, t: Town, e: float)
        Historic_building   (name = n,
                             town = t,
                             entrance_fee = e)

let Create_regulated_historic_building = fun(n: string, t: Town)
        Historic_building   (name = n,
                             town = t,
                             derived entrance_fee:
                               town.regulated_entrance_fee)
```

In this example, we have defined two types (Town and Historic_building) and want to express the fact that there will be two types of historic buildings in the database, some whose entrance fees depend on the historic building itself and others (regulated) whose entrance fees are determined by the town in which the historic building is located. However, this difference does not justify the definition of two types of historic buildings, because only the way the entrance fee is determined varies. Therefore, we have one type (Historic_building), and two functions which create either ordinary or regulated historic buildings. In the case of ordinary historic buildings, the function creates an instance of Historic_building, specifies that the three fields (name, town and entrance_fee) are stored and specifies their values during creation. In the case of regulated historic buildings, instances are created with an entrance_fee field derived from the Town.

This example shows how, by using the concept of a derived component and that of an abstract type at the same time, you can represent complex situations, while at the same time preserving a simple interface for data manipulation. This possibility of abstraction is an important step towards the logical independence application designers dream about. If a third category of historic buildings is discovered or if the way of calculating entrance fees changes, it will be possible to reflect these changes without changing the definition of the Historic_building type.

We have seen, therefore, how derived components (classes, attributes, and so on) can be used in a DBPL to preserve the flexibility and logical independence provided by the views mechanism in a relational system.

6.4.4 Modules and database schemas

A relational schema, even if it has views, is a very centralized view of the real-world. The conceptual schema always represents the totality of the information represented and the views allow you to derive various secondary representations. If you exploit the idea of a module used in modern languages, you can envisage a less centralized schema definition. A database schema could be defined as a set of modules linked by various kinds of links. A module is then mainly a name space, that is, a set of definitions of types, classes, values, and so on, each definition being associated with a name that characterizes it within the module.

For example, let us consider an application that handles the administration of historic buildings. It must know the concepts of people, employees, towns, historic buildings, and so on. These various concepts can be grouped together in the following way[1]:

---

1   We are using an imaginary syntax here.

```
module Personnel
   export Person, Employee
   type Person
      ...
   type Employee subtype of Person
      ...
   ...
end

module Property
   export Town, Historic_building, ...
   type Town
      ...
   type Historic_building
      ...
   ...
end

module Application
   import Personnel, Property
   export Consult, Create, Modify
   ...
end
```

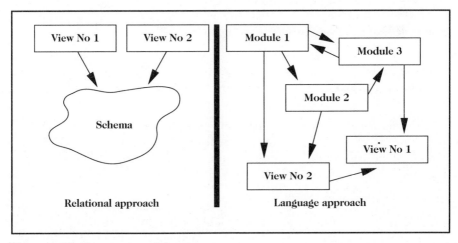

Figure 6.11 The concept of the view

An approach such as this offers numerous advantages both in terms of the application design and in terms of understanding the schema produced and therefore being able to reuse and maintain it:

- *The definition of the schema is less complex.*
  A schema defined in a modular way will be less difficult to understand and to analyse than an unstructured global schema. In the above example, the Personnel and Property modules can be seen as independent sub-applications which form part of the complete application.

- *Controlling the evolution of the schema.*
  Because a more structured schema is simpler, the designer can exercise better control over the evolution of the schema. The links between the different parts of the schema are explicitly defined and the repercussions of an update are easier to control.

- *Defining and integrating views.*
  In this context, a view is simply a module that interacts with other modules. There is no need to define an *ad hoc* mechanism. Such an approach would, as you can imagine, help greatly with the problem of integrating views, which, in relational systems, consists of deriving a global conceptual schema from different user views.

It is interesting to note that the arguments that you can put forward to justify the structuring of a database schema are exactly the same ones that led to the adoption of structured programming and modular languages in the 1970s and 1980s. We can, therefore, assert that there should be, in addition to the integration of languages and databases, a synthesis between the techniques of database application modelling and those of software engineering. The definition of a development environment for a DBLP involves not only design techniques but also programming, debugging and validation techniques. Seen from this angle, the structured definition of a schema in terms of modules seems obvious.

6.4.5 Updates

In the relational context, the problem of updates on views is a difficult problem for which no satisfactory solution has ever been found. As a relational view is defined as a query language expression, the translation of updates on views to the database is as difficult (in most cases) as the translation of queries is easy.

Even though there is no satisfying theoretical solution, most systems provide partial solutions to the problem, either by restricting the set of views on which updates are possible or by making the system administrator responsible for the view's transactions.

The problem arises, but in a different way, in DBPLs. We have looked at various mechanisms that provide the flexibility and logical independence needed by applications. Each of these mechanisms behaves in a different way when confronted with updates.

When a component (for example an attribute) is derived from other components, the problem of updating that component arises. We said that the decision to store or to derive components can be made late in the design process. Under these conditions, it must be made possible to update derived components. The following example, taken from [LR90], modifies the one given in Section 6.4.3 in order to handle the update of an entrance_fee:

```
type Town is abstract
   name: string
   regulated_entrance_fee: float
end

type Historic_building is abstract
   name: string
   town: Town
   entrance_fee: float
end

let create_historic_building = fun(n: string, t: Town, e: float)
   Historic_building    (name = n,
                         town = t,
                         entrance_fee = e)

let create_regulated_historic_building = fun(n: string, t: Town)
   Historic_building    (name = n,
                         town = t,
                         derived entrance_fee:
                            town.regulated_entrance_fee
                                entrance_fee:= e:
                                town.regulated_entrance_fee:= e)
```

The difference from the example in Section 6.4.3 is that in the creation of a regulated historic building, the clause that defines the entrance_fee attribute specifies not only how the attribute is derived, but also how it should be updated. If this information was not included, an attempt to update the entrance fee would probably cause an exception error.

This approach to the problem of updates is very different to that used in relational systems. It is not realistic, given the complexity of the data being handled, to try to find general algorithms in order to derive updates automatically. But the use of abstract data types provides programmers with a context in which they can simply specify the updates.

We also saw that if we structure the schema in modules we can define several views of the same data and make them cooperate. The same thing applies as above, the problem of the update of data shared by several views is the responsibility of the designer.

In conclusion, the problem of updates on views should not be approached in the same way in a DBPL as in a relational system. Such languages are so complex that any attempt to define a general algorithm to handle them automatically would be totally illusory. On the other hand, it is important that the language's main constructions allow the designer to define them simply. We saw, in the above example, that data abstraction is one of those constructions.

6.4.6 Views and interface generators

Finally, the concept of a view in a DBPL can be considered from the point of view of user interfaces, that is, display and output. From this angle, a view of an entity is defined as a graphic *presentation* of an entity.

A presentation is defined as the set of data items visible on the screen at any given moment. A presentation is interactive in the sense that it also describes which of the data items displayed can be edited. A presentation is therefore a displayable mask which represents an application entity on the screen, and from this point of view we can consider that a presentation is a view of that entity.

The usefulness in a DBPL of a mechanism that can generate multiple presentations of the same entity is obvious and we can see easily that this facility extensively covers the relational concept of a view. However, such a mechanism is restricted to the dialog between the user and the application and cannot be used to program that application.

6.5 Constraints and transactions

6.5.1 The definition of constraints

The purpose of integrity constraints is to preserve the integrity of the data stored in the database, that is, to protect the data against incorrect manipulations. In relational systems, a distinction is traditionally made between structural constraints and domain constraints. Structural constraints express equalities between values in the database. Functional dependencies and, in particular, key dependencies are famous examples of structural constraints. Domain constraints express the fact that certain attributes of a relation can only take their values from certain domains. For example, a person's age must be an integer between 0 and 150. Inclusion dependencies can also be seen as domain constraints.

More generally, in relational systems the constraints are predicates that restrict the set of possible states of the database in order to describe the set of consistent states. It seems that integrity constraints are used in those systems in order to make up for the relative weakness of relational constructions and to make it possible to express the semantics of an application more precisely.

The classic problems linked to handling integrity constraints are how to express those constraints and above all how to check them. It is essential to be able to check these constraints efficiently. Efficiency considerations are the reasons why most commercial systems only allow keys to be defined on relations with indices. The link between the definition of the constraints and the query language is also an important aspect of the problem in the relational context.

The structural constraints and domain constraints mentioned above are *static constraints*, which means they define conditions that must be true at any given moment. It can also be useful to describe, not the database's permissible states, but the permissible transitions between two states. This means you have to define *dynamic constraints* that describe the conditions under which an update is possible. Notice that very few relational systems provide the user with this facility.

6.5.2 Integrity constraints and typing

A type system and a constraint definition system have similar purposes. A type system specifies a set of permissible states just as a system of constraints does. In Chapter 5, we saw that a type system can express domain and structural constraints.

In reality, the difference between the two concepts lies at the checking level. In Chapter 5, we said that a type system must allow the consistency of a program and of the database to be checked statically. Checking an integrity constraint is done dynamically.

If a language has dynamic type checking, then there is no reason to distinguish between typing and integrity constraints. If, on the other hand, a language has static type checking, then the two mechanisms need to be separated.

Notice also, that data abstraction, via the encapsulation mechanism, is already a data protection mechanism. A person's age can only be modified by a `Person` type operation and not directly, as in a relational system. We can assert that a great many of the problems of data protection are solved simply by using abstract types. However, it is clear that we must be able to describe more global constraints declaratively and that they must be checked by the system.

Dynamic constraints have natural equivalents in programming languages: preconditions and postconditions. These two mechanisms, which are used in languages such as Eiffel, allow you to set conditions that must be checked before and after the execution of an operation. This analogy between dynamic constraints and the pre/postconditions shows how the techniques of database modelling and software engineering for programming languages have converged.

6.5.3 Constraint violation

In a relational system, the integrity constraints are checked when updates are implemented in the database. Specific techniques have been developed to reduce the costs of checking. When an update causes an integrity constraint violation it is refused.

In a database programming language, constraints checking can be based on an exceptions facility. Several modern languages, such as Clu, Ada and Eiffel, have a facility that can be used to manage asynchronous events in a program and therefore, in particular, violation of an integrity constraint, whether it be static or dynamic.

An exceptions facility allows you to define exception handlers and associate them with exception identifiers. When an exception is raised, either by the programmer (synchronous exception) or via an external event (asynchronous exception), control is passed to the handler for the exception that has been raised. The languages differ in the semantics they ascribe to exception handlers. In Clu, for example, an interrupted function returns immediately and it is up to the calling function to handle the 'premature' return. The exception is, therefore, an alternative way to quit a function. In Ada, a function can handle exceptions that occur during its execution and continue after handling the exception. The Eiffel language has similar semantics.

6.5.4 Transactions

The purpose of a transaction is to make complex operations atomic. The atomic nature of transactions is an essential principle of database management systems. It means that if, for some reason, a transaction is not completely executed then the database is restored to the state it was in before the transaction started.

In a relational system, all interactions with the system are handled via transactions, but systems in which transactions can execute sub-transactions are very rare. In most cases the transaction execution model is a flat model.

In a database programming language, it is important to be able to construct complex operations that have this atomic property. Yet a flat execution model is unsatisfactory and you must be able to combine atomic operations and ordinary operations at will.

Defining transactions in a database programming language when there are integrity constraints is particularly interesting. The constraints described for a database can be randomly complex. You could, for example, say that the husband of the wife of any given person is that person. If you want the database to be consistent at any given time vis-à-vis that integrity constraint, it would not be possible to declare two people and declare them to be husband and wife. You would have to establish the links one after the other and there would necessarily be a time when the constraint was violated. If you can put these basic operations into one transaction the problem is resolved because the establishment of the links between the two people would then be seen as one operation.

Finally, in traditional systems, the transaction is used as the logical unit for controlling concurrency between several users. When a user accesses data via a transaction, that data is locked, and then unlocked when the transaction terminates. The situation in a database programming language is therefore complex and, as we shall see in the fourth part, the specification of a system facility for such a language is a difficult research problem.

6.6 Conclusion

A database programming language must profit from the advances both in the data modelling domain and in the programming languages domain. The concepts used in these domains have common features but often differ in the use made of them.

The concept of abstract data types is at the centre of this integration. An abstract data type can be used both to model the application's entities and to construct reliable reusable programs. We saw that the object-oriented view of the abstract data type is particularly suited to this integration.

Classes and relations are two important but different concepts, even though they are complementary. The concept of subtyping is also very important. In particular, it allows an application's types to be defined incrementally. The concept of inheritance used in object-oriented languages can be formalized using the concept of subtyping.

The concept of the module is essential and must be clearly separated from that of the abstract type. The links between modules must not be represented as inheritance links.

In a DBPL, the concept of the view cannot be approached from the same point of view as in relational systems. However, the concept of derived data is important and must be taken into account.

Even though typing in general, and data abstraction in particular, allows data to be handled in a much more controlled way than in relational systems, the designer must be able to specify integrity constraints at a global level in a declarative way. An exception facility may be adapted for checking these constraints.

Finally, the concept of the transaction is still essential in the context of databases. The complexity of the processing carried out by a DBPL requires a more sophisticated transaction model than that used by relational systems, and one that will handle nested transactions.

Bibliographical notes

The concept of a database programming language has been around for quite some time. A language like Pascal-R ([Sch77a]), for example, was already an attempt to integrate a data model (the relational model) with a programming language (Pascal).

However, DBPLs have become much more important since relational systems revealed their limitations when confronted with new applications. An international conference on this subject was instituted in 1988 and [RH89] contains numerous articles on type systems adapted to database programming.

Exercises

1. A database programming language is said to unite the properties of database applications and those of high-level programming languages. What are these properties?

2. Semantic models and programming languages define abstract types in different ways. How do object-oriented languages resolve the differences between these two types of definition?

3. A Mansion class is defined by refining the Historic_building class. What does this tell us about it in terms of inheritance and how would it be implemented in a programming language?

4. If a Menus class is defined as a set in an object-oriented language, what does it inherit from the Set class and how would this inheritance be expressed in a programming language?

5. How does specialization differ from the refinement of a class?

6. What is the difference between deleting an entity from a class and deleting it from a set?

7. How is the concept of class represented in design methodologies for relational systems?

8. Use the example in Section 6.4.3 to show how a historic building without an entrance fee could be created, assuming that a town where such a historic building is located will not have a regulated entrance fee.

9. If you now look at the example in Section 6.4.5, would you modify your decision in Exercise 8 in order to take account of updates? What would happen if the town wanted to start charging? Is there a problem with

these examples in terms of updates? What happens if a town decides to regulate/deregulate its historic buildings?

10. How do abstract types provide integrity constraints?

Part III

From concepts to systems

The first relational database systems date from the early 1980s. The subsequent years saw considerable development of these systems in industrial circles at the same time as research circles were becoming conscious of their limitations. In the second half of the 1980s very varied propositions were made about how to go beyond relational systems and resolve, in particular, the problems linked with malfunction and the poverty of the relation concept.

We can classify these propositions into three broad categories. The first category covers those systems directly descended from relational systems. The aim of these systems is to add to the relational model the facilities it lacks while remaining centred on the relation concept. The second category of systems concentrates more on programming languages. These systems have either extended existing languages in order to integrate them with database management systems, relational systems for example, or defined languages whose data is managed in secondary memory and persists after the programs terminate. Finally, the third category contains the object-oriented systems. These systems are conceptually similar to persistent programming languages but they are based on the object-oriented programming paradigm, which is sufficiently different to merit its own category.

In this part, we will attempt to describe some representative systems from each of the categories. The aim of these presentations is not to give a precise syntactic or semantic description of each system but rather to show their distinctive features and to draw out the links between these systems and the fundamental aspects we described in Part II.

The figure on page 157 illustrates the evolution of database systems. In this figure, we show the origins of each evolution and the concepts that contributed to each one, situating them either in the world of programming languages or in the world of databases. The roots in the programming world are: programming languages (PL), abstract data types (ADT), object-oriented programming languages (OOPL) and Datalog. The location of Datalog in this world is disputable. This logic programming language was the result of work in the database community aimed at better integrating the relational model with the principles of logic programming. It could be considered as the confluence of two worlds.

On the database side, we have taken the relational model and the semantic models as roots. This last category could have been subdivided because, as we saw in Chapter 4, it also contains elements that have their origins in artificial intelligence as well as functional programming. Even if this classification is a little arbitrary, it allows us to show the main lines of evolution.

Chapter 7 describes the main extended relational systems. Chapter 8 describes persistent programming languages, while Chapter 9 presents the principles of object-oriented programming and example systems. The O_2 system, developed under the auspices of Altaïr, is described in detail in Chapter 10.

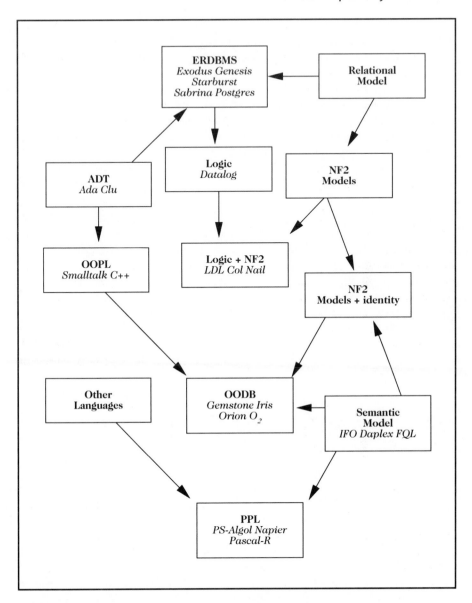

Figure III.1 General view of the evolution of DBMSs

7

Extended relational models and systems

There is no set measurement if you wish to develop.
There is no model if you are looking for the unknown.

Paul Eluard
Poetic evidence

7.1 The different approaches

The management applications that were current when the relational systems first appeared only used simple data structures built from atomic types like integers, reals and character strings. The relational approach satisfied these requirements for which the relation structure (sets of tuples with atomic type attributes) was adequate. However, as we showed in Chapter 3, new applications, such as computer-aided design and office automation, required data models with a richer expressive power. Thus the limitations of the first normal form relations, that is, those whose attributes take their values from the atomic types, soon seemed too restrictive. These new fields of application needed hierarchical structures. Therefore the concept of a *complex object* or *structured object* was created. In the context of this chapter, rather than use the expression *structured object*, we will use the

159

expression *structured value*. The term 'structured object' is the original term, but with the emergence of object-oriented databases it may lead to confusion. Therefore, we will reserve the term 'object' for the data items handled by object-oriented DBMSs.

The structured value approach originated in the late 1970s. In [Mak77] the author proposes abandoning the first normal form of the relational model. From then on, numerous studies extend the relational model in order to make it able to manipulate relations whose attributes are themselves relations. This corresponds to a hierarchical view of an attribute's domain. These models are often known by the term NF2[1]. The first part of this chapter deals with models of this type and describes their type systems and the operations you can execute on them.

When the relational system first appeared, a number of researchers pointed out the close relationship between the model and first order logic. This interaction opened the way for the use of the logic programming paradigm for databases and for the birth of deductive database systems. In so far as they provide users with new facilities for describing processing, these systems can be seen as extensions of relational systems. Later, we will show how the concepts of logic programming and structured values can be combined.

Structured values and logic programming are not the only extensions of the relational model. Actually, they are inadequate for handling the new database applications efficiently. Application programmers need to manipulate data which is even richer than that provided by systems with structured values. Above all, they must be able to describe the operations they can use to manipulate the corresponding data. In Chapter 1, we stressed the problem of the malfunctions between a programming language like C or Cobol and a database system. In order to avoid those problems, it is important that the user data is manipulated directly at database level and not solely by the application written in a general programming language. Generally, the solutions that content themselves with this latter course suffer from significantly degraded performance. In reality, crossing the interface between the application layer and database software is a costly operation. Having made these observations, one obvious solution consists of extending the facilities of the relational model by basing it on an extensible type system. The system is said to be *extensible* when application programmers can define new types and new operations themselves. We say that the system is *externally* extensible when these new types are defined outside the database, that is, at application programmer level. The basis for implementing this approach is the use of abstract data types in programming languages. Extensibility may apply to storage and data access methods, as well as to the type system.

---

1 NF2 is an abbreviation of 'Non-First Normal Form'.

Finally, amongst the developments of the relational model and systems, we should mention those that take account of the concept of object identity. In a model with structured values, it is not easy to model the following facts: Peter loves Alice and John loves Alice. In order to resolve this problem, one simple solution is to say that the people Peter, Alice and John are distinct entities with their own identities, independent of their values. Object identity is one of the essential characteristics of semantic models (*see* Chapter 4) and object-oriented models.

The purpose of this chapter is to describe these four developments: models with structured values, deductive models, models with object identity and models with abstract types. All four are important because, taken separately or in combination, they are at the roots of the new database systems: the extended relational systems, the deductive systems and the object-oriented systems.

For reasons of presentation, we will consider them as developments of the relational system. In reality, the interactions between the various models are more complex and the causal links are not simple. For example, the models with object identity developed in parallel to the relational model and have their roots in the semantic networks used in artificial intelligence. Similarly, the extensible systems and certain principles of object-oriented systems are closely linked to the concept of an abstract type in programming languages.

7.2 The model with structured values

7.2.1 Preliminary concepts

In this section, we give a general definition of the concept of a structured value, based on the work described in [AB87a]. In Chapter 2, we said that the relational model's data was made up of sets of flat tuples. Therefore, there are two privileged constructors: the tuple constructor and the set constructor. These constructors are used in a limited way. You cannot repeat the use of one in relation to the other. We can establish a parallel with programming languages like Pascal, where certain type constructors do not have the same rights as others. For example, a Pascal function can only return values belonging to a limited number of types. It therefore appeared natural to give greater flexibility to the use of these constructors and to define structured values as follows.

Let us presume there is a set of attributes $\{a_1, a_2, ...\}$ and of constants $D = \{d_1, d_2, ...\}$ which make up the atomic values. We will use the generic notation $[a_1: ..., ..., a_k: ...]$, where k is a positive integer, to denote a tuple built with k distinct attributes. The empty tuple and the empty set are written as [] and $\emptyset$ (or {}) respectively.

The set of *structured values* (*Val*) on D is defined by the following rules:

- Any element of D is a value of *Val* (called *atomic*).

- If v_1, ..., v_n are values and a_1, ..., a_n are distinct attributes, then $[a_1: v_1,$ ..., $a_n: v_n]$ is a tuple type structured value.

- If v_1, ..., v_n are distinct values, then $\{v_1, ..., v_n\}$ is a set type structured value.

The { and } symbols are part of the structured value definition language. They also represent the set symbol. Depending on the types of values of the attributes in a tuple, relations may be either in first normal form (atomic values), hierarchical relations (tuple values) or nested relations (set type values). You can also model sets of atomic or other values.

According to this definition, the following are examples of structured values:

```
1. [ name: "Eiffel Tower",
     address:    [town: "Paris",
                  road: "Champ de Mars"],
     days_closed: {"Christmas", "Easter", "Assumption"},
     entrance_fee: 25F]

2. {[ name: "Eiffel Tower",
      address:    [town: "Paris",
                   road: "Champ de Mars"],
      days_closed: {"Christmas", "Easter", "Assumption"},
      entrance_fee: 25F]

   [ name: "Palace of Versailles",
     address:    [town: "Versailles",
                  road: "Place d'Armes"],
     days_closed: {"Christmas", "Assumption"},
     entrance_fee: 30F]

   [ name: "Pantheon",
     address:    [town: "Paris",
                  road: "Place du Pantheon"],
     days_closed: {"Christmas", "Easter", "Assumption"},
     entrance_fee: 18F]}

3. {[ name: "Eiffel Tower",
      address:    [town: "Paris",
                   road: "Champ de Mars"] ],

   [ name: "Palace of Versailles",
     address:    [town: "Versailles",
                  road: "Place d'Armes"],
```

```
[name: "Richard"
   address:    [town: "Le Chesnay",
               road: "Pottier"],
   age: 31,
   profession: "researcher"]}
```

The first value is a tuple describing a historic building in Paris. You can see that one attribute (**address**) has a tuple value and another (**days_closed**) has a set value. The second value is a set of tuples with non-atomic fields. The third value is a heterogeneous set. It contains tuples representing historic buildings and a tuple representing a person.

A structured value can be represented in the form of a finite tree whose nodes are labelled differently according to their nature: the atomic nodes (□) correspond to the elements in D; the tuple nodes (⊗) have k subnodes and the arcs are labelled with the names of the attributes; the set nodes (⊙) have a number of subnodes equal to the cardinality of the set and the arcs attaching those subnodes are not labelled. So as to ensure that duplicated values are eliminated when representing a set, we assume that all the subnodes of a set node are the roots of distinct trees. Figure 7.1 shows the tree related to the first example given above for the Eiffel tower.

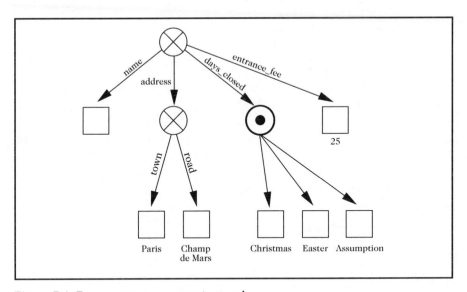

Figure 7.1 Tree structure representing a value

7.2.2 Types for structured values

In database technology, heterogeneous sets are not usually allowed. We prefer to group homogeneous sets of values together so that we can apply set operators to them efficiently. The concept of a database schema is used, among other things, to exclude these types of values. Before introducing the concept of the schema, we will first define a world of *types*.

$$t::= \emptyset \mid D \mid [a_1 : t, ..., a_k : t] \mid \{t\}$$

D represents the atomic types **string**, **float**, **bool**, **real...** Examples of types that satisfy this definition are:

```
1. [name: string,
      address:    [town: string,
                   road: string],
      description: string,
      days_closed: {string}
      entrance_fee: float]

2. {[name: string,
      address:    [town: string,
                   road: string],
      description: string,
      days_closed: {string}
      entrance_fee: float]}
```

The first structured value in the example in the previous section corresponds to the first type and the second set type value corresponds to the second type. But the third set type value, which is made up of heterogeneous values, cannot be associated with a type using the above definition. The set of atomic types usually used in databases contains the integer, real and character string types and there are also multimedia types like image and text. In the next section, we will give an example of a schema and we will describe the various data manipulation languages using that example.

The *interpretation* $[\![t]\!]$ of a type t is defined as follows:

- $[\![\emptyset]\!] = \emptyset$

- $[\![D]\!] = D$

- $[\![[a_1 : t_1, ..., a_k : t_k]]\!] = \{[a_1 : v_1, ..., a_k : v_k] \mid v_i \in [\![t_i]\!], i = 1, ..., k\}$

- $[\![\{t\}]\!] = \{ \{v_1, ..., v_m\} \mid v_i \in [\![t]\!], i = 1, ...,m$

In practice, *D* is not seen as the set of all atomic values. There is a list of atomic types: integer, real, Boolean, character string. These atomic types are interpreted in the usual way.

A type expression can be represented by a tree, in the same way as a structured value. An atomic type corresponds to a square node ($\square$), a tuple type of the form $[a_1 : t_1, ..., a_k : t_k]$ corresponds to a round node ($\odot$) with n subnodes, where the ith subnode is the tree related to t_i, and a set type of the form $\{t\}$ corresponds to a round node ($\odot$) with a single subnode whose tree is t.

7.2.3 Database schema and instance

Let us presume there is a finite set of relation names $\mathbf{R} = \{R_1, R_2, ...\}$. An *assignment* for $\mathbf{R}$ is an application ρ which makes a set of finite structured values in **Val** correspond to each element R in $\mathbf{R}$. Under these conditions, a *schema* S of a given database is a pair $S=(\mathbf{R},\mathbf{T})$ where $\mathbf{T}$ is an application of $\mathbf{R}$ in **Type**.

```
T(Historic_building)=[name: string,
                      address: [town: string,
                                 road: string],
                      themes: {string},
                      days_closed: {string},
                      entrance_fee: float]

T(Restaurant)=[name: string,
               address: [town: string,
                          road: string],
               days_closed: {string},
               menus: {[intitule: string},
                        price: integer]}]
```

Figure 7.2 Historic_buildings and Restaurants

An *instance* I of schema S is an assignment ρ for $\mathbf{R}$ such that:

$$\rho (R) \subseteq [\![\mathbf{T}(R)]\!], \text{ for each } R \text{ in } \mathbf{R}$$

This condition expresses the fact that each element of an assignment for a relation name R is a set of values of the type associated with R. Figure 7.2 shows a schema:

$$S = (\{\text{Historic\_building, Restaurant}\}, \mathbf{T})$$

where **R** is made up of the relation names Historic_building and Restaurant and **T** gives the types of the relations Historic_building and Restaurant. The structured value made up of the Eiffel Tower, Palace of Versailles and Pantheon historic buildings could be an assignment for the Historic_building relation.

If I is an instance of a schema $S = (\mathbf{R},\mathbf{T})$, then this information can be represented in the form of an interpretation using first-order logic:

$$facts(I) = \{R(v) \mid v \in \rho(R), r \in \mathbf{R}\}$$

where R is the predicate name and $R(v)$ is a basic fact.

7.2.4 Manipulating structured values

In this section, we will present a calculus for structured values. We have based this on the calculus described in [AB87a]. The language is made up of an alphabet of constants D, a set of variables, written x, y, z, a set of predicates R, S...,which designate sets of values associated with a type, a set of logical connectors $\vee$, $\wedge$, $\neg$ and the quantifiers $\forall$ and $\exists$.

The *terms* are either constants of D, or variables, or expressions '$v.a$' where v is a variable and a is an attribute.

The *atomic formulæ* are defined as follows:

1. $u = v$, where u and v are terms of the same type t.

2. $u \in v$ where u is of type t and v is of type $\{t\}$.

3. $R(u)$ where u is a term of type t and R is a predicate of type $\{t\}$.

4. $\{x|\phi\}$ where x is the only free variable in the well-formed formula ϕ.

The *well-formed formulæ* are defined as follows:

1. any atomic formula is a well-formed formula,

2. $\phi \vee \phi'$, $\phi \wedge \phi'$, where ϕ and ϕ' are well-formed formulæ,

3. $\neg\phi$ where ϕ is a well-formed formula,

4. $\forall x(\phi)$ and $\exists x(\phi)$ where ϕ is a well-formed formula.

A *query* is an expression in the form $\{x|\phi\}$ where x is the only free variable in ϕ. Predicates in the form Historic_building(y) are interpreted as 'y is a value of the Historic_building relation' or if we use the above definition $y \in \rho(\text{Historic\_building})$. We will give some examples of queries based on the above schema:

Set of Parisian historic buildings:

$\{x \mid \exists y \, (\text{Historic\_building}(x) \wedge (y =x.\text{address}) \wedge (y.\text{town} = \text{``Paris''}))\}$

The set of the restaurants in the same road as the Musée d'Orsay in Paris, with a menu for less than 100F:

$\{x \mid \{x \mid \exists y \exists v \, (\text{Historic\_building}(y) \wedge (v = y.\text{address}) \wedge (v.\text{town} = \text{``Paris''}) \wedge$
$\quad (y.\text{name} = \text{``Musée d'Orsay''}) \wedge$
$\quad \exists w \, (\text{Restaurant}(x) \wedge (w = x.\text{address}) \wedge (w.\text{road} = v.\text{road}) \wedge$
$\quad (w.\text{town} = \text{``Paris''})))\}$

The evaluation rules for a formula in a given interpretation are those of first-order logic and are analogous to those used for the relational model. The interpretation used is that relating to *facts*(I) which represents the basic facts about the database. In spite of the analogy with the relational model, the calculi for structured values are more powerful than the relational calculus because they can handle more complex structures. They are also more powerful even when they only manipulate first normal form relations. Thus, it is possible to express the transitive closure of a relation with the calculus for structured values. Interested readers who want more details should refer to [AB87a].

7.2.5 Conclusion about structured values

The model with structured values is a generalization of the relational model. It has liberated itself from the constraint of only having atomic domains for attributes: the use of a type system built from set and tuple constructors means that the value of an attribute can be complex. The data manipulation language is still based on the same principles of first-order logic. In the relational model, one of the fundamental results involved the equivalence of the relational calculus and the relational algebra. Even though we have not described an algebra for structured values here, the results are similar. The fact that the algebra and the calculus for structured values have equivalent expressive powers was first demonstrated by Kuper. Abiteboul and Beeri also proposed an algebra and a calculus with the same expressive power. In the model with structured values, a single value cannot be shared between several values. Only by introducing a new concept that allows a value to be identified as a universal can this objective be achieved: we would then be talking about a model with *object identity*.

7.3 Deductive models and logic programming

7.3.1 General principles

Logic programming for databases stems from the idea that you can infer certain facts from the facts physically stored in the database. You can then, on the one hand, save memory and, on the other hand, provide answers to queries by using inference mechanisms like those used in Prolog. Deductive databases resulted from this approach. Two paths can be followed: when a new data item is input, new facts are generated by deduction and stored, or the facts are generated when queries are evaluated. The difference mainly affects performance but the procedures are conceptually similar.

Having arrived at this point, it seemed natural to question the database using a logic programming language. The nature of the data in a relational model is well suited to this idea because data items are sets of tuples and a Prolog predicate can be interpreted as a set of tuples. The great differences from the Prolog approach are that in this case performance is crucial, that the data items handled are of the set type and that the quantities of data are very large. Another interesting feature of the logical approach to data manipulation is the extension of the data manipulation language's power in a natural way so that it has the power of a complete programming language.

There are several approaches that handle the integration of structured values into logic programming. Here, we have chosen the approach proposed by LDL (*Logic Data Language*) because it seems to us to be the closest to the model of structured values we introduced earlier. In what follows, we will demonstrate more precisely how logic programming deals with the problem of defining and manipulating structured values.

Most logic programming languages were designed as extensions of Datalog. Datalog is a rule-based language which uses Horn clauses and does not use functions. Generally, the reasons given for using a logical approach such as this for database applications are as follows:

1. The logical approach provides a uniform high-level formalism for defining data, views and integrity constraints. Furthermore, this formalism is based on solid and well-known theoretical foundations.

2. Logic languages are based on the rules of deduction. Therefore they can be used to deduce additional facts from initial facts.

3. Logic languages for databases are general in that no distinction is made between general programming and processing the data in the database. Everything is uniform (as opposed to the imperative approaches such as C + SQL described in Chapter 2).

In contrast to Prolog which has a 'one tuple at a time' type computing model, LDL, like the relational query languages, has a 'one set at a time' type computing model. In fact, coupling Prolog to a relational database, even though it is more natural than the C + SQL coupling, may suffer from the same malfunctions and therefore performance problems. In order to resolve these problems, LDL has adopted a compiled approach and carries out a complete analysis of the rules in such a way as to produce queries in a relational type of target language. This allows it to apply all the relational optimization techniques to the processing of large quantities of persistent data and to achieve acceptable performance.

7.3.1.1 The features of LDL

LDL is an extension of Datalog which contains symbols of uninterpreted functions, sets, predefined functions and primitives for manipulating sets. In the formal definition of first-order logic, a term is a complex structure composed of function symbols, variable symbols and constant symbols. Here, the function symbols are not interpreted, which means that the semantics of those functions depends entirely on the program in which the symbols appear. They should not be confused with the computable function symbols which are automatically evaluated when the program is executed. The addition of uninterpreted functions is one of the essential features of LDL.

An LDL program is a rule-based language, that is, a set of rules in the traditional form:

$$A \leftarrow L_1, ..., L_n$$

A is the *head* of the rule and its *body* is the conjunction of the literals $L_i, (i = 1, n)$. There are syntactic conventions for writing expressions in the language. Function symbols are written in lower case, as are the constant and predicate symbols. Variable symbols are written in upper case. For example, the expression below describes a basic fact in the database:

```
restaurant(la tour d'argent,
          address(quai de grenelle, paris),
          {monday, tuesday},
          {menu(du jour, 390), menu(special,570)}).
```

The way this is written is different from that described for structured values but is equivalent. The attribute symbols are not indicated and the tuple constructor is introduced by opening and closing brackets. The nested structures are marked by blocks and each level of nesting is named, with the exception of the sets. For example, the word **address** introduces a tuple with two fields. A set is introduced by the usual symbols **{...}**. This basic fact corresponds to the general structure of a restaurant predicate which can be described in the following way:

```
restaurant(NAME,
    address(ROAD, TOWN),
    DAYS,
    MENUS))
```

where **NAME, ROAD, TOWN, DAYS** and **MENUS** are variable names.

In order to derive facts from the database all you have to do is write a program made up of a list of rules. For example, the rule below produces the names of the restaurants, with their closing days, which are on the same road as the Musée d'Orsay and which have a menu at less than 100 francs.

```
reply(NAME,DAYS) ←
        restaurant( NAME, address( ROAD, paris), DAYS, MENUS),
        historic-building( musee d'orsay, address( ROAD, paris),
        -,-,-, ),
        member( menu(-, PRICE ), MENUS)), PRICE ≤ 100
```

This rule uses the **member** predefined predicate related to sets. This predicate, which is normally written **member (X, Y)**, expresses the fact that X is a member of set Y. The literal **PRICE ≤ 100** uses one of the predefined functions which corresponds to a comparison operator. Also, a dash in a term indicates an unimportant element, that is, an element that plays no part in the evaluation of the query. When this rule is evaluated on the database it returns a set of values.

One consequence of the introduction of sets is that the rule unification process becomes more complex. LDL provides three low-level primitives for handling sets which extend Horn clause logic to sets and the processing of sets:

- The first is called '*set generation*'. It uses a special function **scons(T,S)** with two arguments T and S which adds the term T to the set S. The set **{a, b, c}** can thus be generated by the expression **scons(a, scons(b, scons (c, {})))**, where **{}** represents the empty set.

- The second primitive is called '*set grouping*'. It is used to group terms together using the **<...>** construction. For example, the following rule produces a relation which groups together all the restaurants in the same town:

```
restaurantsbytown( TOWN, <NAME> ) ←
                   restaurant( NAME, address( -,TOWN),-,-).
```

When writing a rule that uses the grouping constructor, certain
restrictions must be observed: the body of the rule must not contain a
grouping constructor, the head of the rule must only contain one grouping
constructor; the body of the rule must not contain a negative literal.

- The third primitive is called 'partition' and partitions a set into two non-
  empty subsets. The calculation of the cardinality of a set demonstrates a
  possible use for this primitive:

```
cardinality({}, 0).
cardinality({X}, 1).
cardinality(SET, V) ←  partition(SET, S1, S2),
                       cardinality(S1, V1),
                       cardinality(S2, V2),
                       V = V1 + V2.
```

The notation {X} denotes a singleton and refers therefore to any set with
one element. The first rule describes the cardinality of the empty set.
The second rule gives the cardinality of a singleton. Finally, the third
indicates that if a set S is divided into two subsets S1 and S2, then the
cardinality of S is the sum of the cardinalities of the subsets. This
example also shows how literals can be written which use the predefined
functions like arithmetic operators.

Now we will show, in Figure 7.3, how to calculate each restaurant's
average price; the result will give the average prices for all the restaurants.
The cardinality predicate has already been described. The sum predicate
gives the sum of the elements in a set of numbers. We have not shown how
it is written, but it works on the same principle as the cardinality predicate
by using the partition operator. This recursive approach is interesting because
parallelism can be used to calculate the cardinality and the sum of the set of
menu prices generated in the price predicate.

```
price( NAME, <PRICE> ) ←  restaurant(NAME, -, -, MENUS),
                          member( menu( -, PRICE), MENUS).
average( NAME, AVG ) ←    price(NAME, SET),
                          cardinality(SET, CARD),
                          sum(SET,SUM),
                          AVG = SUM/CARD.
```

Figure 7.3 Calculating the average price of a restaurant's menus

To summarize, LDL is an interesting language because it integrates the logical approach well with the important functions of databases. Its main features are as follows:

1. LDL is based on a Horn clause language. In contrast to Prolog, there is no order for executing the rules for the unification of sub-goals.

2. Sets are seen as primitive data structures and are therefore used directly in the language. Remember that in Prolog the concept of the set does not exist directly and has to be simulated by using a list.

3. The way negation is handled differs from Prolog. In LDL, negation is based on set difference while in Prolog negation is based on failure.

4. The language provides schema definition and update facilities.

7.4 Models with object identity

7.4.1 The concept of identity

The concept of identity has always existed in the various models of database systems, but in a more or less visible way. In first-generation network or hierarchical type systems object identity is synonymous with the record key. For the relational system, two tuples are identical if their values are equal. However, the relational systems do use the concept of a key attribute. These attributes are identified by an internal key in the subsystem responsible for storing the tuples. In most semantic models, each unit of information is identified by a name which can be used to distinguish between the entities, independently of the values associated with their attributes. The following example illustrates this concept. Let us consider the two affirmations: peter loves alice and john loves alice. If alice does not designate the same person, a model by value will not allow us to distinguish the two individuals because the model will be equivalent to the logical facts loves("peter", "alice") and loves("john", "alice"), unless we add other characteristics that resolve the ambiguity.

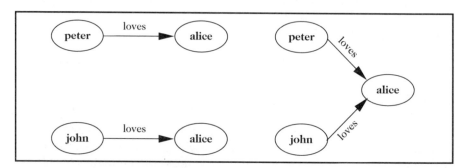

Figure 7.4 Modelling with identity

Figure 7.4 shows how the two cases can be modelled if the concept of identity is introduced: either alice is one person, or alice is the name of two distinct people. Each node in the figure identifies a distinct unit of information. This concept of identity plays an essential role in semantic models, described in Chapter 4, and in object-oriented models because it is one of the intrinsic properties of those models. One consequence of the concept of identity is that it allows data sharing. The examples of historic buildings, used in the section about structured values, Section 7.2, each include a town name. Suppose we had wanted to add other characteristics of the town: the population, the name of the area, the names of the airports, and so on. You can see that redundant information would have to be stored in each historic building in the same town. To remedy this situation all we have to do is introduce object identity for the corresponding town. If we do this for the three historic buildings, Eiffel Tower, Palace of Versailles and Pantheon, we will get the following descriptions:

```
eiffel = [ name: "Eiffel Tower",
     address:    [town: paris,
                  road: "Champ de Mars"],
     days_closed: {"Christmas", "Easter", "Assumption"},
     entrance_fee: 25F]

palace = [ name: "Palace of Versailles",
     address:    [town: versailles,
                  road: "Place d'Armes"],
     days_closed: {"Christmas", "Assumption"},
     entrance_fee: 30F]

pantheon = [ name: "Pantheon",
     address:    [town: paris,
                  road: "Place du Pantheon"],
     days_closed: {"Christmas", "Easter", "Assumption"},
     entrance_fee: 18F]

paris = [name: "Paris",
     population: 3000000,
     airport: {"Orly", "Roissy"}]

versailles = [name: "Versailles",
     population: 100000,
     airport: {}]
```

In this description of objects, identity appears explicitly: a name is given to every object in the database. These names appear in italics so as to distinguish them from the normal values describing the properties of objects. Here we have five objects with the names *eiffel*, *palace*, *pantheon*, *paris* and *versailles*. The structure of the object named *eiffel* is a tuple; its description is analogous to that of a structured value. Among the tuple's components we have the town attribute which refers to the *paris* object.

7.4.2 Formalization

The preceding description has intuitively shown us that the concepts of structured values and object identity can be mixed. This is not new – the Socrates database system developed at the University of Grenoble in the 1970s has a data model that integrates these characteristics. Nevertheless, the first formalization of this type of model appeared in Kuper's work on the LDM language, whose model proposed a richer type system than the relational model but above all a data manipulation language definition which was analogous to the one in that model. The description we give below is based on the work done on the O_2 database system. It has the advantage of being in harmony with our approach and it will serve as an introduction to the description of object-oriented systems in Chapter 9.

In relation to the hypotheses formulated when modelling structured values in Section 7.2, let us assume there is a set of names of *classes* $\{P_1, P_2, ...\}$ which are distinct from the names of relations, and a set of names which identify the objects $O = \{o_1, o_2, ...\}$. The distinction we have introduced between the names of classes and the names of relations is based on the fact that classes are associated with *objects* whereas relations are associated with *values*.

The set of *object values*, written Obj (not to be confused with the set Val) is defined by:

- Any element of $D \cup O$ is a value of Obj (called *atomic*).

- If $v_1, ..., v_n$ are object values and $a_1, ..., a_n$ are distinct attributes, then $[a_1 ; v_1, ..., a_n : v_n]$ is a tuple type object value.

- If $v_1, ..., v_n$ are distinct object values then $\{v_1, ..., v_n\}$ is a set type object value.

An assignment of identifiers to classes is an application π of **P** in the parts of Obj where **P** designates a finite set of class names. Similarly, a set of object values is associated with each relation name using the application ρ.

By extension of the concept of type for structured values, the set of type expressions, written Type, is defined by the following grammar:

$$t ::= \emptyset \mid D \mid P \mid [a_1 : t, ..., a_k : t] \mid \{t\}$$

In this grammar the class names are terminal elements of the language. Examples of types that satisfy this definition and correspond to the objects described above are:

```
[name: string,
address: [town: Town,
             road: string],
   description: string,
   days_closed: {string}
   entrance_fee: float]

[name: string,
population: integer,
airport: {string}]
```

In the first type expression, Town is a class name.

The interpretation of a type t is dependent upon the allocation of identifiers, and for this reason the domain of the interpretation of a type t is written $[\![t]\!]_\pi$. The definition is analogous to that already given and assumes the existence of a finite set of classes **P**:

- $[\![\emptyset]\!]_\pi = \emptyset$

- $[\![D]\!]_\pi = D$

- $[\![P]\!]_\pi = \pi(P)$ for each $P \in \mathbf{P}$

- $[\![a_1 : t_1, ..., a_k : t_k]\!]_\pi = \{[a_1 : v_1, ..., a_k : v_k] \mid v_i \in [\![t_i]\!]_\pi , i = 1, ..., k\}$

- $[\![\{t\}]\!]_\pi = \{\{v_1, ..., v_m\} \mid v_i \in [\![t]\!]_\pi , i = 1, ..., m\}$

By extension, a database *schema* S is a triplet $S = (\mathbf{R}, \mathbf{P}, \mathbf{T})$ where **R**, **P**, **T** are respectively a set of relations, a set of classes and a total application of $\mathbf{R} \cup \mathbf{P}$ in Type.

A schema S can be pictured as a graph G_S made up of five kinds of nodes: the nodes related to tuple type values ($\otimes$), the nodes related to set type values ($\odot$), the nodes related to classes whose structure is of tuple type ($\bigotimes$), the nodes related to set type classes ($\bigodot$) and atomic nodes ($\square$). The arcs in the graph describe the laws for composing a class or a relation. Furthermore, the nodes are labelled with the names of the class or relation that they represent. This representation is analogous to that given in the section describing a structured value.

An *instance* I of a schema S is a triplet (ρ, π, υ) where ρ is an assignment of values to relation names, π is an assignment of identifiers to names of object classes, and υ is a partial application of the set $\cup\{\pi(P) \mid p \in \mathbf{P}\}$ in Obj; the role of υ is to assign an object value to each object O, such that:

1. $\rho(R) \subseteq [\![T(R)]\!]_\pi$, for each R in $\mathbf{R}$

2. $\forall P \in \mathbf{P} \; \forall o \in \pi(P), \; \upsilon(o) \in [\![T(P)]\!]_\pi$

These two conditions guarantee the global consistency of an instance of the schema and particularly that there are no references to objects that do not exist, because the interpretation domain is defined as a function of π.

For the example we have developed during this description the schema is:

($\emptyset$, {Historic_building, Town}, **T**)

---

with

```
T(Historic_building) = [name: string,
                        address: [town: Town,
                                  road: string],
                        description: string,
                        days_closed: {string},
                        entrance_fee: float

T(Town) = [name: string,
           population: integer,
           airport: {string}]
```

An instance $I = (\emptyset, \pi, \upsilon)$ corresponds to:

```
π(Historic_building) = {eiffel, palace, pantheon}
π(Town) = {paris, versailles}

υ(eiffel) = [name: "Eiffel Tower",
             address: [town: paris,
                       road: "Champ de Mars"],
     days_closed: {"Christmas", "Easter", "Assumption"},
     entrance_fee: 25F]

υ(palace) = [name: "Palace of Versailles",
             address: [town: versailles,
                       road: "Place d'Armes"],
     days_closed: {"Christmas", "Assumption"},
     entrance_fee: 30F]

υ(pantheon) = [name: "Pantheon",
               address: [town: paris,
                         road: "Place du Pantheon"],
     days_closed: {"Christmas", "Easter", "Assumption"},
     entrance_fee: 18F]
```

```
v(paris) = [name: "Paris",
    population: 3000000,
    airport: {"Orly", "Roissy"}]

v(versailles) = [name: "Versailles",
    population: 100000,
    airport: {}]
```

7.4.3 Conclusion about the model with identity

The model we have just described is a starting point for more in-depth studies on formal models with object identity. These studies take two main directions.

The first is that of data manipulation languages. Using this model, you can define a logic programming language, analogous to LDL, but which integrates the concept of identity. This has been done in the IQL language which has the following characteristics:

- Set and tuple manipulation at any level of nesting;
- The possibility of creating new objects using an identifier invention mechanism;
- Static typing of the languages rules.

Instead of having a rule-based language, you could also develop algebræ and calculi. All these languages are based on the need for operations that handle the concept of identity. Thus there are at least two equality operators: one based on identity and one on the equality of values. Furthermore, a *differentiation* operator is used to map from an object to its value for any object o this operator returns its value $v(o)$.

The second direction corresponds to extensions of this model which take into account the concept of *inheritance* similar to that in object-oriented languages. Formal studies have highlighted the link between that approach and type interpretation, as we have described it. However, taking inheritance into account involves adding two more constructors: type union and type intersection. This work is beyond the scope of our book and we refer the reader who wishes to study these aspects to the bibliography.

7.5 Extensible systems

7.5.1 Introduction

Relational systems have a relatively simple type system. Atomic types include integers, reals, Booleans and strings of characters and are only used to define the tuple type. A relation is a homogeneous collection of tuples. The commercial systems have added some additional elements, such as dates, currencies or ranges of values and basic operators for manipulating those types. You can, for example, convert a date in English format into a date in French format. You can also calculate the difference between two dates and give the result in days. In spite of these basic extensions, many applications require the use of new types adapted to the specific needs of the application. The concept of an *abstract type* provides a solution to this by allowing you to define new types and the associated operations. Let us recall the essential elements of this concept, as defined in Chapter 5.

An abstract type is defined as a data structure and a set of operations used to recall or to modify the information related to the structure. A type encapsulates the data and the operations that can be executed on that data. The operations are the abstract type's interface.

If we continue in this manner, a relation's attributes may have as a domain values corresponding to an abstract type. The relational model built on this basis is much richer. Nevertheless, we must realize that these types are only attached to a relation's attributes and that they do not constitute a general mechanism for the construction of types, as the following example shows.

Let us consider a geographical application that handles regions. A region is represented by a data item with two elements: a rectangle, which encloses the region, and a convex polygon, which represents the region. To make things simpler we will limit ourselves to convex regions without holes in them. In order to define a region type, we need a definition language. In this case, we have based it on a syntax similar to that seen at the start of this chapter, with tuple and array constructors.

```
type   Region = [
       rec: Rectangle
       contour: Polygon]
type   Rectangle = [
       sw: Point
       ne: Point]
type   Point = [
       x: float
       y: float]
type   Polygon = array of Point
```

A region is a tuple with two fields: rec and contour. Similarly, a rectangle is defined by two opposite points called sw and ne and a point is determined by its coordinates. Finally, a polygon is declared as an array of points. This representation of a region is only one of the possible solutions. The database administrator is responsible for choosing the most appropriate definition for the application. After the data types have been defined, the operations that can be applied to those types must be defined. These operations are seen as functions whose *signatures*, that is, the input and output arguments, have to be defined. We could define the following functions:

```
rec(Region)                                   : Rectangle
contour(Region)                               : Polygon
sw(Rectangle)                                 : Point
ne(Rectangle)                                 : Point
x(Point)                                       : float
y(Point)                                       : float
surface(Region)                               : float
window(Region, Rectangle)                     : Region
intersection(Region, Region)                  : Region
rectintersection(Rectangle, Rectangle)        : Rectangle
isin(Polygon, Point)                          : boolean
inter(Region, Region)                         : boolean
inrect(Rectangle, Rectangle)                  : boolean
interrect(Rectangle, Rectangle)               : boolean
```

The meaning of most of these functions is obvious. The first six illustrate the fact that an attribute can be seen as a function. The `window` function has two arguments: a `region` and a `rectangle` and returns a `rectangle`. The `intersection` function calculates the intersection of two regions and the result is a `region` because the regions are convex. If the regions could be of any kind, the intersection of two regions would not necessarily be a `region`, it could be a `set` of regions. The function `isin` indicates whether a `point` is in a `region`, while `inter` tests to see if the `intersection` between two regions is not empty. Similarly, `inrect` and `interrect` check whether a rectangle is contained within another rectangle and if the intersection between two rectangles is not empty, respectively. Using this information, an *extended* relational schema can be declared using an SQL type syntax:

```
create table Town (townname: string,
                   townplan: Region)
create table Historic_building (hbname: string,
                                place: Point)
create table Forest (forestname: string,
                     forestplan: Region)
```

In this schema the `townplan`, `place` and `forestplan` attributes refer to the new types. If r_1 denotes an instance of the `Region` type, then the tuple [townname: `versailles`, townplan: r_1] is an instance of the `Town` table. Using this schema, a user could express the following queries:

1. Which historic buildings are in the town of Versailles?

2. Which towns have a forest of more than 100 hectares within their boundaries?

3. Which town plans have an intersection with the rectangle '10:20,20:60'?

Without knowing anything about the query language or the reply construction procedure, we can nevertheless note that all these queries use functions associated with the type declarations. For example, a historic building fits the criterion in the first question if its coordinates are inside the town plan of Versailles.

In order to provide an extensible type system, starting from a relational system, you must resolve several problems:

- How can an abstract type be defined? This involves not only the type's structure but also the operations associated with it.

- How can these types be implanted in a relational database system? The relational systems do not provide functions for handling these new types. They can only store the elements required for specifying the types and the values of instances. You must therefore define mechanisms that transform an abstract type into an internal representation suitable for the database.

- In what ways will the relational languages be changed by the extension? In particular, can SQL be extended to incorporate a new typing structure and the operations specific to those types?

- In traditional relational systems, the user can define indices which are built on atomic types such as integers, reals and character strings. Can indices be built on the fields of the new types? For example, can you have a spatial index on historic buildings using the `Point` type?

Answers to these questions will be provided in the following parts of this section. We will discuss them in the order we have just described them. Further, in order to illustrate these new concepts we will use two systems that provide functions like these: Postgres and Sabrina.

7.5.2 Using abstract types

There are two parts to the implementation of an abstract type in a relational system: the first describes how the type's components are represented in the database, and the second defines the functions and/or operations that can be applied to instances of the type. There are different possible solutions to carrying out this task.

The solution used in the Postgres system consists of providing the type's definition and the mechanisms for converting between the external and internal representations of the type at the same time. The internal representation corresponds to the coding of the type in the database, while the external representation is that relating to the application. Thus, the `Rectangle` type can be defined by the command:

```
define type Rectangle is (Internallength = 16,
              InputProc =ChartoRectangle,
              OutProc = RectangletoChar, Default = " ")
```

In this example, it has been decided that the external representation of a rectangle is a string of characters containing the two opposing points of the rectangle. The coding `20,50:10,70` corresponds to a rectangle, the coordinates of whose corners are `(20,50)` and `(10,70)`. The `ChartoRectangle` procedure takes a string of characters in that form as an input and returns an internal representation of the rectangle coded in 16 bytes. Conversely, the `RectangletoChar` procedure takes the internal representation stored in the database and converts it into an external representation which can be accessed by the application program. These conversion procedures are invoked when the query language is interpreted. We will come back to this point in the next section.

Another solution for implementing abstract data types, is to use a language like Lisp. This approach has been used in Sabrina. Lisp is interesting because it allows you to operationally define both a type and the operations. In order to create a new type the user writes a Lisp function. If the function returns **true** when it is called, then the function's argument belongs to the type involved. If it returns **nil** then the argument does not correspond to the type. For example, a **point** can be defined using the following declaration:

```
dd #: t: Point (x)
    ( and (number (car x))
          (number (car (cdr x)))
        ( null (cdr (cdr x))))
```

The name of the function, `Point`, is the name of the new type. The formal parameter `x` is the argument of the function. The body of the function is the code that holds the definition of a point. Here, a point is defined as a list of two numbers. The **and** function ensures the conjunction of the three criteria: the first two guarantee that the elements in the list are numbers, using the function **number**, and the last one checks that the list only contains two elements by using the function `null`. The `Rectangle` type can be defined in a similar way:

```
dd #: t: Rectangle (x)
    (and ( apply': Point (car x)
          (apply': Point (car (cdr X)))
          (null (cdr (cdr x)))
          (distinct (car x) (car (cdr x)))))
```

This definition calls the point definition. The use of the **apply** command is the result of a technical nicety. You must be sure that the (car x) function will be evaluated before the **Point** function. The **distinct** function has been introduced to check that the two points are distinct. These two examples show clearly the advantage of using Lisp functions, in so far as all of a type's properties can be expressed as constraints.

The way in which a tuple from the **Historic_buildings** table is stored corresponds to its definition. It is made up of a string of characters for the historic building's name and a data structure relating to the point. Lisp can accept this structure, that is, a structure using brackets. For example, the tuple relating to the Eiffel tower is represented by:

```
[ hbname: "Eiffel", place: (10 20) ]
```

where (10 20) represents, in the form of a list, the coordinates of the point relating to the Eiffel tower.

In the database system, the Lisp structures are seen as strings of characters. Consequently they cannot be interpreted by the DBMS. Only the Lisp processor can do that. Thus we can see one of the limits of this approach. Each time data has to be selected it cannot be done at DBMS level. The search for historic monuments whose x coordinate is equal to 10, for example, cannot be done simply in the form of a relational selection[2].

7.5.3 Implications for the query language

The introduction of abstract data types into a relational system causes changes to the query language. If we take SQL as a reference language, and limit ourselves to a subset of SQL, we can examine the consequences. Let us consider a general SQL selection expression of the form:

select $X_1.A_1, X_2.A_2, ..., X_k.A_k$
from $R_1X_1, R_2X_2, ..., R_nX_n$
where $F(X_1, X_2, ..., X_n)$

---

2   In this elementary case, it would be possible to consider the character strings of the (10*) form, and to search for this value. This transformation draws our attention to the internal representation of the database.

where F is a Boolean expression built from SQL Boolean terms and the basic logical operators and, or and not, X_i, (i = 1,n) are variables that designate the tuples related to the relations R_i, and A_j, (j = 1,k) are the names of attributes.

We can use the following principles in order to extend the query language:

- Let us consider an operation associated with an abstract type and its signature $f : t \rightarrow t'$. This signature expresses the fact that the function f has as an input argument a variable of type t and returns a result of type t'. If t' is an atomic type, then in any SQL expression where there is an atomic expression compatible with t' we can substitute an expression of the form $f(x)$, where x is of type t, for that expression.

- The second principle is the principle of function composition. If f and g are two functions with the signatures $f : t \rightarrow t'$ and $g : t' \rightarrow t''$ respectively, then $g(f)$ is an expression of the language with the signature $t \rightarrow t''$.

- If the type t' in the function $f : t \rightarrow t'$ is a set of tuples, then, anywhere where a relation expression appears, we can substitute a functional expression with f.

By applying these principles to the query examples given above we get the following.

1. Which historic buildings are in the town of Versailles? In order to construct the reply we check that the coordinates of a historic building are inside the contour of a town.

```
select X.hbname
from Historic_building X Town Y
where Y.townname = "Versailles" and
            isin( contour(Y.townplan), X.place)
```

2. Which towns have a forest of more than 100 hectares within their boundaries?

```
select Y.townname
from Town Y, Forest Z
where surface(intersection(Y.townplan, Z.forestplan)) ≥ 100
```

3. Which town plans have an intersection with the rectangle 10:20,20:60?

```
select Y.townplan
from Town Y
where interrect(rec(Y.townplan), "10:20,20:60")
```

In the example described at the start of this section, the new data types introduced did not explicitly call for a set of tuples constructor. Consequently the examples of queries have not used the third extension principle and the possibility has not been explored here.

7.5.4 Interpretation of the extended language

The interpretation of the query language is not the same for differing implementations of abstract types. In the two situations described, those of Sabrina and Postgres, the first uses the Lisp processor and the second conversions between the internal and external representations of the type. Let us describe the latter.

The operations that can be applied to a type are defined in a programming language; the input and output arguments are also expressed in the language's type system and take no account of the internal representation of those types in the DBMS. When the query language invokes a function f, that function cannot be interpreted by the DBMS and you have to look for the image f_b of f in the DBMS. There are two solutions to constructing the function f_b. The first consists of implementing the code of f on the internal representation of the DBMS. In order to do that, the programmer must know precisely the internal structures of each type. This solution has the advantage of being efficient because it takes the internal representations directly into account. However, it is reserved for specialists. The second solution has two merits: it can be generalized and it does not depend on the use of specialized programmers.

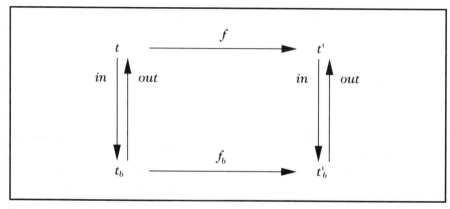

Figure 7.5 Type conversion diagram

The equivalence diagram in Figure 7.5 shows the correspondence between the external types (programming language level) and the internal types (DBMS level). An external type t corresponds to its internal type t_b, the index b signifying that it is at database level. If $in[t]$ and $out[t]$ are the procedures for converting t to t_b and conversely, the conversion diagram shows us that f and f_b are obtained by function composition:

```
f_b = in[t] o f o out[t]
f   = out[t] o f_b o in[t]
```

This approach is simple and only based on the implementation of conversion procedures. For example, the intersection function translates as:

```
intersection_b(aRegion1, aRegion2) =
            in[Region](intersection(out[Region](aRegion1),
                                    out[Region](aRegion2)))
```

where **aRegion1** and **aRegion2** are variables denoting instances of the **Region** type. This approach, based on type conversions, can lead to mediocre performance if the cost of conversion is too high. However, some optimization is possible; in the case of function composition it is not necessary to apply the **in** and **out** transformations systematically.

If **in** and **out** are two basic generic functions used to manage the interface between the database and the application programming language, then it is essential that there is a function associated with the constant expressions in the query language. A constant expression in the query language is an expression that denotes an instance of a type composed of atomic values. For example, the expression **10,20:20,60** is a constant expression which denotes an instance of the **Rectangle** type. We will call the generic function, which associates a constant expression with the internal representation of this type t, **con[t]**.

Using these elements, we can now interpret the query language. For example, let us consider one of the queries given above:

Which town plans have an intersection with the rectangle **10:20,20:60**?

```
select Y.townplan
from Town Y
from interrect(rec(Y.townplan), "10:20,20:60")
```

This query is translated as:

```
select out[Region](Y.townplan)
from Town Y
from interrect_b(rec_b(Y.townplan), con[Rectangle]("10:20,20:60"))
```

The out[Region] expression converts the internal representation of a region into its equivalent at application language level. The functions interrect_b and rec_b are derived from the interrect and rect functions according to the rules defined above. Furthermore, the con[Rectangle] function transforms the constant expression into the internal representation of a rectangle. This approach, based on transformations, requires a complete analysis of the types in the query.

7.5.5 Access methods and extensibility

The preceding sections described the solutions implemented in order to enrich the type system and define the operations associated with the new types. If databases are used to manage new applications, they must also respond to the need for efficient access to the data. One of the consequences of this evolution is the need for specialized access methods. This means that the scope of the concept of extensibility is not limited solely to data types. Indexing facilities, in particular, must be adapted to the new data types.

If we consider the schema introduced at the beginning of this chapter, we can imagine different indexing strategies. In the case of the Town relation, an index on the town name falls into the category of the kind of indexing all database systems can do using a B-tree. On the other hand, if we want an index on the town's surface area the problem is more complicated. To achieve this, all you have to do is to calculate each town's surface area, using the surface function, and use the result as the key to the index. Each time a town is modified or a new town is introduced, the surface areas will have to be recalculated and the index updated. The implementation of these indices, which are based on a function and not on an atomic attribute, can be carried out by using the indexing procedures provided by the DBMS. The extensions that have to be added are limited and only involve a mechanism for starting updates. Finally, much more complicated indexing techniques can be developed to handle geometric data types. Specialized structures have been developed for this purpose, for example R-trees. Using this type of indexing, questions such as: 'which towns are located in a given region?' can be handled efficiently. In this case, much more significant extensions have to be added on to the system. It is no longer a case of adapting or reusing mechanisms that are already up and running; a complete new set of access and memory management procedures has to be provided. The two levels of complexity of the possible extensions are illustrated in Figures 7.6 and 7.7 which highlight the difference between an *autogenous* (first case) and *exogenous* (second case) access method.

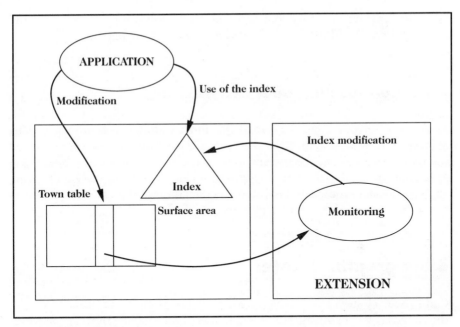

Figure 7.6 Autogenous extension

In the case of an autogenous method, the indexing techniques provided by the DBMS are reused. For example, an index on the surface area will be managed as a B-tree; a monitoring mechanism will simply be added to start updates.

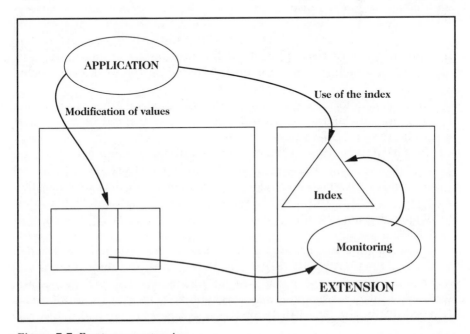

Figure 7.7 Exogenous extension

In the case of an exogenous method, the extension concerns both the access structure and the monitoring system for starting updates.

7.5.6 Conclusions about extensibility

In this section we have described the most important elements of this approach. This is based on the idea that new features can be added to an existing system. These extensions involve the type systems, the query language and the access structures. Other aspects have not been touched on, such as the consequences for the query language optimization techniques or for the concurrency control methods and restarts.

Bibliographical notes

Codd [Cod77] suggested developing the relational model in order to enrich the language's semantics. However, it was Makinouchi [Mak77] who first proposed a model where the first normal form was abandoned. From then on, numerous studies have contained propositions for models based on either the concept of nested relations, called NF2, or on the concept of complex values. The most important were written by Jaeschke and Schek ([JS82]), Thomas and Fisher ([FT83], [TF86]), Korth, Roth and Silber-schatz ([KRS88]) and Abiteboul and Beeri ([AB87a]). This last model is the most complete in the sense that the type system is richer and it discusses the problem of the equivalence between the calculus and the algebra. The Verso project ([BRS82], [AB84], [VAB*86] and [AB86]) undertook the implementation of this type of model on a database machine. Our discussion of structured values is directly based on the work of Abiteboul and Beeri.

The origins of logic programming with structured values are to be found in the work on Datalog. The word Datalog was invented by a group of researchers from Stanford University, MCC and a research centre in Oregon. At the SIGMOD in 1984, Ullman demonstrated the differences between Prolog ([Col82]) and Datalog. The LDL language ([NT89]) is based on theoretical results which give rigorous semantics for dealing with negation ([Naq86], [KP88]) and sets ([BNR*87], [Kup87]). Furthermore, new techniques for implementing recursive clauses efficiently have been used ([CGK*90]).

There are other rule-based languages based on a structured value model: COL ([AG88], [AGVW89]), RDL1 ([KdMS89]). In COL the essential element is the introduction of multi-valued functions which are used as the basic mechanism for handling sets. Negation is dealt with by stratification ([CH85], [ABW86]). The RDL1 rule-based language is non-determinist and works with the Sabrina system ([KdMS89]) which is an extended relational system.

The role of identity, and its various forms, was discussed by Khoshafian and Copeland [KC86]. One of the first formalisms to take account of both the concepts of value and identity is the work of Kuper on LDM ([Kup85], [KV84]). Similarly, Bancilhon and Koshafian have proposed a calculus for complex objects ([BK86]).

The model with object identity we have described is a simplified form of the work done on the O_2 ([LRV88], [LR89c]) and IQL ([AK89]) models. We have used the notation and terminology of IQL. We have adopted this form in order to limit ourselves to essentials and to describe the four developments of relational systems in a homogeneous manner. Furthermore, this type of model is the starting point for the study of object-oriented models and their query languages.

NF2 models with identity have been used in both products and prototypes; the Socrates system ([Abr72]) was probably one of the precursors amongst the first-generation systems. Systems like AIM ([DKA*86]), DASDBS ([SPSW90]) and Damokles ([DGL87]) are in this category. If you add the concept of structural inheritance to this type of model, you have database systems which can be called structurally object-oriented. On the other hand, object-oriented models use a more general form of inheritance which uses not only structural inheritance but also inheritance of object behaviour, that is, of the operations associated with the objects.

The study of query languages that integrate the concepts of complex objects, identity, inheritance and operations is the theme of numerous projects, both theoretical and practical ([GM88], [CDV88], [Bee88], [Kim89], [ASL89]). For example, the Extra/Excess language ([VD90]), developed in the Exodus project, proposes an algebra for complex objects with identity. In the O_2 system, the query language respects the principle of encapsulation and was designed to be integrated into a programming language ([CDLR90], [BCD89]). Osborn ([Osb88]), Beeri and Kornatsky ([BK90]) have developed rewriting rules for optimizing algebraic expressions, Zdonik and Shaw ([SZ89], [SZ90a]) have constructed an algebra that respects the principle of encapsulation of object-oriented languages and, finally, Straube and Özsu ([SO91]) have studied the equivalence between an algebra and a calculus.

The last development we have looked at in this chapter is that of extensible systems. The following projects fall into this class: Exodus ([CDRS86]), Postgres ([SRH90]), Genesis ([Bat86], [BBG*88], [BLW88]), Starburst ([HCM*90]) and Sabrina ([KdMS89], [Kie89]). Even though these projects differ, their common purpose is to explore extensibility. The main aim of our description has been to show how the types that can be handled by a database system can be enriched using the concept of abstract data types ([OT86]). Reality is, of course, much more complicated and the notion of an extensible system covers various aspects. For some people, it means providing basic units from which a system can be constructed and leaving it up to the architect to assemble them, after having fixed certain parameters.

Exodus, Starburst and Genesis follow this approach. From another point of view, extensibility can be seen as a way of extending the capacities of an existing system; for example, by using the data manager of a relational system to extend the data model to complex objects, and consequently the storage modules. This approach is the one taken by Postgres which is largely based on the work done on Ingres. Sabrina follows an identical approach to Postgres but stresses deductive rule-based languages and complex objects. In these extensible systems several extensions of SQL have been put forward which are similar to the propositions advanced for structured values ([Kim82, PA86, GV90]). The interpretation mechanism described in this chapter is based on ([WSSH88]).

Exercises

1. Why do we say that a relation is a 'flat' value and a structured value a 'hierarchical' value?

2. What properties does the calculus for the model with structured values have which make it more powerful than the relational calculus?

3. LDL differs from Prolog in several important ways which make it suited to databases. What are those ways?

4. Relational models cannot distinguish between equality and identity in an intuitive way. What implications does this have for a database and how does the model with identity solve this problem?

5. The extensible system outlined in Section 7.5.1 associates functions with abstract type definitions. Which functions would you use to satisfy queries 2 and 3 in that section?

6. In Sabrina, the Lisp functions are used to implement the abstract types. What is the main advantage of this approach?

7. Describe the differences in the ways Postgres and Sabrina interpret the query language.

8. What is the difference between an autogenous method of indexing and an exogenous one?

8

Database programming languages

*No one has yet invented the language which can express instantly
what you can see in the blink of an eye.*

Natalie Sarraute
The Planetarium

Chapter 7 described solutions which are descended from the relational system or which directly extend the relational system's computing power. Now, in this chapter, we are going to look at systems that have their origins in programming languages or that have data models more powerful than the relational one, and that are also more general and better integrated than the extended relational systems.

After we have described in detail the general principles of this approach, we will look at the idea of extending existing programming languages with a data model (relational or functional). We will then describe those solutions that consist in defining programming languages whose data persists after program execution.

Rather than follow a uniform approach to the treatment of the languages, in each case we will stress the most important or most original points.

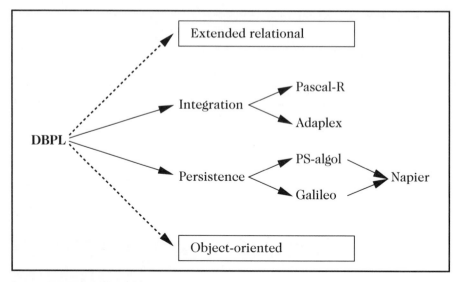

Figure 8.1 The different approaches

8.1 Two approaches

The procedures adopted by the systems or languages described in this chapter are designed to resolve the following problem: how can you make a general programming language's data persist or how can you define a programming language with the same features as a database system? The difference between these two approaches is subtle. In both cases, the end result is an integrated system which can perform general data handling operations (in terms of computing power) in secondary memory.

On the one hand, the approach that consists of integrating DBMS features into a programming language puts the emphasis on manipulating *bulk data*. Therefore, these systems have the following characteristics:

- *Data is structured into collections.*
  The languages that belong to this tendency all introduce the concept of relation or set amongst their constructors. Some of them limit relations to first normal form (the fields can only be atoms) whereas others allow more general constructions.

- *Data can be searched for according to contents.*
  Structuring data into collections is of no interest unless the language provides primitives for search by contents. These primitives may take several forms but they can all be used to construct filters which, when applied to a database, extract a (small) subset of data appropriate for a computation.

- *Multi-user concurrent accesses.*
  This last point is not a particular characteristic of this approach. However, concurrent access management is an essential feature of a DBMS and must always be taken into account in these integrations.

On the other hand, the persistent programming languages approach puts the accent on programming power and making the data the language handles persistent. The characteristic features of this approach are:

- *Types and persistence are orthogonal.*
  In contrast to the preceding approach, the purpose of persistent programming languages is not to provide access to relations (or more generally, packets of data) using a program, but to allow the data (all the data) handled by the programs to persist after program execution terminates. The direct consequence of this is that persistence must not be attached to a particular type of data but must be a property of all the types permitted in the language, whether they are simple or constructed. We then say that the types and persistence are *orthogonal*. All the languages belonging to this tendency (PS-algol, Galileo, Napier) conform to this condition. More specifically, the persistence in persistent programming languages must satisfy the following conditions, set out in [AB87b]:

1. Persistence is a property of data items and not of types.

2. All data items have the same rights to persistence.

3. A data item's description (its type) must persist for as long as that item persists.

The first two points mean that persistence must be independent of data type. An important corollary is that the code used to manipulate a data item is independent of whether that data item persists or not. It is evident that these conditions are not satisfied by standard programming languages. For example, Pascal or C makes data persist by using files; the way data is handled differs depending on whether it is persistent or not.

Violation of the third point is a common source of error. It should not be possible to record a data item using one type and to re-read it using another type.

- *Abstract data types.*
  In relational systems, as well as in most of the database programming languages created by integration, the only abstraction is the relation. Persistent programming languages usually place the emphasis on data abstraction. Examples of this are Galileo and Napier which both provide the concept of an abstract data type.

- *Modular programming.*

  Persistent programming languages usually offer the possibility of building sophisticated name spaces. We will see this in detail when we discuss Galileo and Napier. Usually, these name spaces (often called environments) set up an association between identifiers and type or data definitions in order to check the types in declarations and expressions before they are evaluated. In languages like Galileo and Napier, the environments are also used to define the data's visibility in terms of time and therefore its persistence. The view of persistence granted by this approach is very different from that given by integrating a standard programming language with a database management system.

8.2 Integration into an existing language

8.2.1 Pascal/R

Pascal/R was one of the first database programming languages. It combines a general programming language with a database model in the most consistent way possible. The model is the relational model and the language is Pascal. The first problem met when implementing this integration was integrating the two type systems: the programming language's system and the one inferred from the data model. In Pascal/R the tuple type is identified using the Pascal **record** type without a variant (**case of**). The fields can be any Pascal atomic type. The designers added a new type constructor to the language: **relation**. This constructor is used to define a structure where all the elements are the same kind of **record**. The **relation** constructor also takes as an input the attributes that make up the key. The relations' tuples are similar to Pascal **records** and there are similar restrictions on the types allowed in the tuples. For example, you are not allowed to use **variant** types as tuple components.

In order to manage persistence, Pascal/R introduces the **database** type. This type associates a name with a fixed number of relations built using the **relation** constructor. A relation is not persistent unless it is part of such a declaration. The example below gives an example of a **Tourism** database declaration in Pascal/R which contains the relations **Historic_buildings** and **Restaurants**. The **relation** constructor takes two arguments. The first indicates the subset of attributes that make up the key and the second indicates the type of tuples in the relation.

A Pascal program can declare a variable on that database. This allows you to execute the program on different instances of a given database. One restriction, linked with the implementation, is that a given program can only use a single type of database. As you can define variables on databases, on relations or on tuples, relations can be arguments of procedures.

```
Historic_buildings = relation name, town of
   record name: string;
          town: string;
          road: string;
          day_closed: string;
          entrance_fee: integer;
   end;

Restaurants = relation name, town of
   record name: string;
          town: string;
          road: string;
          day_closed: string;
          menu: string;
          price: integer;
   end;

Tourism = database
          historic_buildings: Historic_buildings;
          restaurants: Restaurants;
          end;
```

Pascal already has operators equivalent to the normal comparators
($\leq$, $\geq$,...). Pascal/R extends them so that relation type values can be compared
and adds set operators specific to those values:

- The **in** operator tests whether a tuple is in a relation.

- The **each** operator specifies the result of a selection operation carried
  out on a relation. For example, the following expression extracts all the
  Parisian historic buildings from the Tourism database:

```
each h in Tourism.historic_buildings: h.town = "Paris";
```

- The instruction **for each** is an iterator which you can use to go through
  the tuples in a relation sequentially and therefore to make a join. Thus,
  to find the names of the restaurants located in the same road as the
  Musée d'Orsay, we would write:

```
for each h in Tourism.historic_buildings: h.name = "Musee
d'Orsay"
    do
    for each r in Tourism.restaurants: r.town = h.town
                                   and r.road = h.road
        do writeln(r.name);
```

Naturally, Pascal/R provides a library of functions and procedures for manipulating relations.

The disadvantages of Pascal/R are essentially those of the relational model. The **record** type only allows you to define tuples with atomic attributes. Similarly it is impossible to define null values concepts. In Pascal/R, types and persistence are not completely orthogonal. Owing to a choice made by the designers of the language, you cannot decide to make a Pascal integer or record persistent other than by using them in a relation. Only relations in a database can persist, and you cannot define complex structures.

On the other hand, the system's chief merit is to have integrated Pascal and the data model completely in a way that seems natural when used. It is a example of a good classical approach which mixes two concepts intelligently: relational databases and the Pascal language.

8.2.2 Adaplex

The approach taken by Adaplex is original in more than one sense. It integrates the Ada programming language and the functional data model Daplex. Ada occupies a separate position amongst the imperative programming languages because it provides high-level concepts: modules, abstract data types, tasks for parallel programming, and so on. Daplex is an interesting model because it differs from more classical models in its use of a functional paradigm and inheritance management. Adaplex, like Pascal/R, is not a simple immersion of Daplex in Ada but a real integration. It is an extension of Ada which incorporates new data types and control structures that correspond to Daplex. Below, we give the Tourism database in Daplex:

```
database Tourism is
type Historic_building is entity
     name: string;
     town: string;
     road: string;
     day_closed: string;
     entrance_fee: integer;
end entity;

type Menu is entity
     name: string;
     price: integer;
end entity;

type Restaurant is entity
     name: string;
     town: string;
```

```
            road: string;
            day_closed: string;
            menus: set of Menu;
        end entity;

        type Historic_restaurant is entity
            entrance_fee: integer;
        end entity;

        include Historic_restaurant in Restaurant;
        end database
```

The types that describe Daplex entities are introduced by the keyword **entity**. These types have a tuple structure but the fields can have any values, which allows you to use structured values. Thus, in the example, the menu attribute is defined as a set of instances of the Menu type. Inheritance is indicated using the **include** keyword. The Historic_restaurant type is defined as a subtype of restaurant. Besides the Restaurant type's attributes it also has the entrance_fee attribute. All the Historic_restaurant type entities are therefore specializations of the Restaurant type.

As in Pascal/R, persistence is the privilege of certain data types. Not all Ada data can persist. An Adaplex database is made up of extensions of the types of entities described in the schema introduced by the keyword **database**. You can handle types of entities whose values are temporary in an Adaplex program, but only the data items declared in the schema persist.

The Adaplex language is a complete language, as it includes Ada. Data is manipulated in a functional way, as in Daplex. Thus menus(restaurant) will return the set of a restaurant's menus.

The **database** constructor constructs an Ada object, similar to a module (**package**), which is stored in persistent memory. In contrast to Pascal/R, Adaplex does not allow you to have multiple instances of the same databases which correspond to the same type. In order to manipulate the data in a database, an Ada program must refer to the package corresponding to the database's schema (Tourism, for example) and define a transaction that contains the actions to be carried out on the database. In Adaplex, a transaction is a sequence of operations enclosed between the clauses atomic and end atomic. The following example shows a procedure which calculates the average prices of the menus of the restaurant 'la Tour d'Argent':

```
use Tourism
*the use clause designates the database involved in the
computation*
atomic *start of transaction*
```

```
procedure average (in a_rest: Restaurant; out: average: pnum);
    declare
        number: pnum:= 0;
        sum: pnum:= 0;
    for each menu in menus(a_rest) loop
        number:= number + 1;
        sum:= sum + price(menu);
    end loop;
    average:= sum/number;
end average

declare average: pnum;
average(a_rest in Restaurant
    where name(a_rest) = "la Tour d'argent", average);
put(average);
end atomic; *end of transaction*
```

As in Pascal/R, the iterator **for each** is used to handle sets. The computation is done by Ada operators. The selection of the restaurant by name (**"la Tour d'argent"**) is done using a Daplex selection clause (**in...where**).

In conclusion, Adaplex is an interesting system because it is the first to have integrated a sophisticated data model into an existing programming language. The approach is, therefore, similar to Pascal/R but it uses a data model that prefigures the high-level models like the object-oriented models.

8.3 Persistent programming languages

8.3.1 PS-algol

The PS-algol (short for *Persistent S-algol*) language is derived from S-algol. This language differs from any of the previous approaches in that it adopts a uniform treatment of persistence. Any value in the language can persist; persistence is therefore independent of type. In contrast to Pascal/R or Adaplex, PS-algol wants to provide persistence (data management in secondary memory) while changing the original language as little as possible. PS-algol definitions and programs are therefore essentially S-algol definitions and programs. Below we give the definition of the **Tourism** database in this language:

```
structure Historic_building (
        string name ;
        string town ;
        string road ;
        string day_closed ;
        int entrance_fee )
```

```
structure Menu (
          string name ;
          int price )

structure Restaurant (
          string name ;
          string town ;
          string road ;
          pntr day_closed ;
          *pntr menus )
```

The data types manipulated by PS-algol are those of S-algol and are made up of:

- *Basic types.*
  Boolean, integer, real, file, character string and pointer.

- *Constructed types.*
  the vector, which is a dynamic array of objects of the same type, and the structure, which is a tuple made up of fields whose types can be either basic types or vector types.

It should be noted that, in contrast to Pascal, the pointer type does not refer to the type of data it points to. Thus the menus field in the `Restaurant` structure is of the **pntr** type, as is the **day_closed** field. In the one case the pointer points to a list of character strings, in the other to an array of menus.

This definition of the pointer type makes it impossible to check statically the types of PS-algol programs, to the detriment of their security and performance. It should be noted, however, that the type is verified on execution, in order to prevent inconsistent changes to the database.

To handle persistence, PS-algol introduces a new type, the *table*, indexed by integer or character string type keys. The elements in a table are pointers to instances of vectors or structures. The table's size is defined dynamically. PS-algol provides a certain number of procedures for handling tables and making them persistent. Even though persistence is not only obtained by means of tables, it is true that any PS-algol data type can be made persistent by being made an element of a table. The table can also be used to group together temporary data.

The following example shows how the calculation of a restaurant's average price is written in PS-algol. The database is assumed to contain a table for the restaurants and a table for the menus of each restaurant:

```
structure Menu(
          string name;
          int price)
```

```
structure Restaurant (
          string name ;
          string town ;
          string road ;
          pntr day_closed ;
          *pntr menus )


!Connecting to the database
let db = open.database("Restaurants", "miam", "read")
if db is error.record do {write "error, database not opened"]


!Reading the list of restaurants and initializing
let restaurants = s.lookup("Restaurants", db)
let rest = s.lookup("la Tour d'argent", restaurants)
let sum:= 0


!Defining the procedure for adding the price of a menu to the sum
let add = proc(pntr val → bool)
begin
    let sum:= sum + val(price)
true
end


!Calculating the sum of the menus' prices and then the average
let number:= s.scan(rest(menus), add)
average:= sum div number
```

The principle of the calculation is to construct a procedure **add** which adds the price of a menu to a global variable **sum**. This procedure is applied to all the entries in a menu table that belongs to a restaurant which has been selected by name. The **s.scan** procedure goes through a collection (in this case a vector) and applies the function to each element as long as the result of that evaluation is the Boolean **true**. It returns as a result the number of entries it has applied the function to. It only remains to divide the sum by the number of entries to obtain the average.

PS-algol has other interesting properties that it inherited from Algol 68. Procedures are values just like any others. A procedure can be assigned, can be the result of an expression or another procedure or can become part of a structure or a vector. All this is also possible in the context of persistence. Therefore, PS-algol allows you to store a procedure in a database, thus providing a form of encapsulation and, therefore, of data abstraction. The following example shows how you can define an abstract type Complex which can only be accessed by the procedures add, print and Complex:

```
let add:= proc(pntr a, b → pntr);nullproc
let print:= proc(pntr a);nullproc
let Complex:= proc(real a, b → pntr);nullproc


!Definition of the abstract type
begin
   structure Complex(real real, imaginary)
   add:= proc(pntr a, b → pntr)
        Complex(a(real)+b(real), a(imaginary)+b(imaginary))
   print:= proc(pntr a)
        write(a(real)),
        if a(imaginary) < 0 write "-" else write "+"
        write rest(a(imaginary)), "i"
   Complex:= proc(real a, b → pntr)
        Complex (a, b)
end


!Examples of manipulations
let a=Complex(-1.0, -2.8)
let b=Complex(2.3, 3.2)
print(add(a,b))
```

The internal representation of the complex number is hidden because it is not visible outside the block in which it is defined. It is still possible for errors to occur on execution because the add, print and Complex procedures are not statically typed and can therefore be invoked with arguments other than complex numbers. PS-algol provides the is and isnt primitives which test a value's type and allow errors to be handled. However, checking remains the responsibility of the programmer.

PS-algol is therefore a very powerful language which provides persistence orthogonal to the types, associative access to collections, procedures which are like assignable values and a form of data abstraction. On the other hand, it has the disadvantages of the old language from which it is descended (Algol). Data manipulation is not as easy as in a DBMS and the type system is permissive, which is not good for program security. The main interest of this language lies in the techniques used for implementing persistence, which we will describe in detail in Part IV.

8.3.2 Galileo

Galileo is another example of a language with a type system designed to make the understanding and manipulation of persistent data easier. This language was developed at the University of Pisa. Its type system is partly derived from that of a primitive version of ML. Galileo has the classic abstraction mechanisms described in Chapter 4, that is:

- *Classification.*
  As in object-oriented languages, entities with the same characteristics are grouped into classes. All the elements of a class have the same type and are represented in a similar way.

- *Aggregation.*
  The elements in classes are aggregates which group together hetero-geneous components which may in turn be elements of other classes. The aggregates' components may be collections (groupings) of the same type of values. This allows you to represent multi-valued associations between entities.

- *Generalization and specialization.*
  The elements in a class may be seen in various ways via *subclasses*. The hierarchy is an inheritance hierarchy. The subclasses are derived from classes using predefined operators. The subclass mechanism is the equivalent of the ISA hierarchy in semantic models (*see* Chapter 4).

- *Modularity.*
  The data and the operations can be partitioned into environments which are interlinked. Thus a complex schema can be broken down into a structure of smaller units. A unit could correspond to a user view or to the description of the schema obtained by successive refinements.

Galileo has other interesting characteristics. It is a language of expressions, which means that any construction in the language returns a value and is evaluated as an expression. It is also an interactive language: the system loops on an input request and returns the result of the evaluation of an expression. Therefore the user can make declarations and write expressions which are immediately evaluated in the current context. As in Lisp or ML, Galileo functions are assignable values of the language and can therefore be used in data structures, passed as parameters or returned as results. Finally, Galileo is a statically typed language. The language has basic types: Booleans, numbers, strings, and so on. It has very varied type constructors: tuple, sequence[1], exclusive union, function, reference. It also allows you to define abstract types. Galileo's types can, therefore, be divided into two categories:

- The concrete types, for which the equivalence rule is structural equiva-lence. Two values with the same structure are compatible.

---

1 In Galileo, a sequence is a list of elements of a given type.

- The abstract types, for which the equivalence rule is nominal equivalence. Two abstract types defined by the user are always distinct and a value of one type cannot be manipulated in the same way as a value of another type.

The type system allows subtyping. If **T** is a subtype of **T'**, then any value of **T** can be an argument for any operation defined on **T'**. For the concrete types, the subtyping relation is inferred by the type controller. For the abstract types, the user must explicitly declare the subtyping relations in the following way:

```
type Historic_restaurant ↔ (Restaurant
                            and entrance_fee : float)
* A historic restaurant is a restaurant and has an entrance fee *
```

In Galileo, a class is a sequence of elements of an abstract type. Each element in a class corresponds, intuitively, to a real-world object and the language provides commands for creating and deleting objects. The elements in classes are the only values in the system that can be modified. Galileo stresses the difference between the extensional aspect (**class**) and the intensional aspect (**type**) of the database. This allows it to have a subclass definition mechanism which is independent of the subtyping mechanism (*see* Chapter 6).

All the expressions evaluated by Galileo's interpretation loop are transactions (atomic actions on the database). Galileo has an exceptions mechanism which allows you to handle easily errors which may occur during transactions. Thus, in the case of nested transactions, the failure of an internal transaction can be detected and an alternative transaction started in order to obtain the desired result. The construction used has a block structure, which is different from the usual structures using **commit** and **abort**:

```
Expression iffails Expression
```

If the first expression fails, all its effects are cancelled and the value returned is that of the second expression.

Here is the Tourism database in Galileo:

```
use Tourism:= (
    and Historic_buildings class
                            Historic_building ↔
                            (name: string
```

```
                              and address: (road: string
                                        and town: string)
                              and day_closed: var string
                              and entrance_fee: var num)
                              key (name)

        and rec Menu ↔

                              (title: string
                              price: var num
                              restaurant: Restaurant)
        and Restaurants class ↔

                              Restaurant
                              (name: string
                              and address: (road: string
                                        and town: string)
                              and day_closed: var string
                              and menus: var seq Menu)

    Historic_restaurants subset of Restaurants class
                  Historic_restaurant "
                  (is Restaurant and entrance_fee: float))
```

The above example shows how Galileo manages structured values (the address attribute of Historic_buildings or Restaurants). The types can mutually reference each other, as in the cases of the Menu and Restaurant types, using the **rec** keyword. A class construction in Galileo is a relatively complex construction. The class operator establishes the following links:

- The identifier that follows the keyword **class** is linked to a new abstract type with a tuple structure. This is the case for the Historic_building and Restaurant types in the Tourism database.

- The class name (the identifier preceding the **class** keyword) is associated with a modifiable sequence of instances of the corresponding abstract class. This sequence represents the set of instances of the class. It can be used in a program just like any other sequence.

- A function is generated automatically with a name constructed from the class' name. This is the function that is used to create a new instance and add it to the class. Thus the function called mk_Restaurant adds a new restaurant to the Restaurants class.

The environment concept is an important concept in Galileo. Environment definitions are created using operators and environment expressions. Every expression is evaluated inside an environment. Initially, there is a global environment which is the default working environment (called the current environment). When you make your declarations you must link them to the global environment, using the **use** instruction, in order to make them persistent. Thus the Tourism database's definitions are grouped together in an environment with the name Tourism which is attached to the persistent global environment.

You can use the **enter** instruction in order to define any previously defined environment as the current environment. You can then evaluate any expression in an interactive way within the context of this new environment:

```
enter Tourism;
number:= 0;
average:= 0;
for x in Restaurants with name of x = "La Tour d'argent" do
    for y in menus of x do
            (average:= average + price of y;
            number:= number + 1;)
average:= average/number;
```

The environment concept is complicated but in compensation it gives you great power of expression. You can construct a current environment from existing environments, using sophisticated operators to combine them. Therefore, you can define schemas and views which are much more general than those in traditional databases. The following example constructs a new environment from the Tourism environment which contains the lists of the historic buildings whose entrance fee is less than 10 francs and of the restaurants located in the same roads as those historic buildings:

```
use Promotions:= (use Tourism in
    Historic_buildings:=
            derived all m in Historic_buildings
                    with entrance_fee < 10;
and
    Restaurants
            derived all r in Restaurants
                    with r.address isin
                    for m in Historic_buildings
                    do m.address)
```

The Promotion environment contains two sequences which are derived from the Tourism environment. This new environment is, therefore, a view (in the relational sense of the term) of the Tourism environment.

In conclusion, Galileo is interesting because it combines a number of possibilities from semantic models with a functional approach (function handling, static typing, interactivity). Its main drawback is its complexity, both syntactic and semantic. The price that has to be paid for its sophistication, which is a result of, amongst other things, its close relationship to ML, is that it is difficult to learn.

8.3.3 Napier88

Napier88 was designed and implemented at St. Andrews University in Scotland by the team that developed PS-algol. This system is the direct descendant of PS-algol and its aim is to find solutions to the problems that its antecedent did not resolve satisfactorily.

Napier88 is a persistent programming language. In contrast to PS-algol, which was built using an old language, Napier88 was built from the ground up. Its main characteristics are as follows:

- Napier88 is statically typed. No type error can occur during program execution.

- An environment mechanism, inspired by Galileo's, provides modularity.

- Napier88 provides parametric polymorphism: functions with a type as a parameter can be defined and used in a persistent environment.

- Napier88 allows abstract data types to be defined in the form of existentially quantified types, in the same way as Cardelli and Wegner's Fun language (*see* Section 5.2.2.2 in Chapter 5).

Along with the traditional basic types, Napier88 provides the `pixel` and `picture` basic types, which are used to handle graphic data, and the `file` basic type, which is used to access the underlying file management system.

In Napier88, the structures are arrays, tuples and variants. The arrays and tuples are similar to those in PS-algol, whereas the variants are used to represent unions of types. As in PS-algol, functions are assignable values. The difference lies in the possibility of defining polymorphic functions:

```
let size = proc[t] ( *t → integer) size(t)
```

The size function is a polymorphic function of the type:

```
proc[t] ( *t → integer)
```

It takes as input an array of any type and returns the size of that array. In order to use this function, the programmer must name the type with which the function is instantiated, then enter the parameter. Thus you can write size[string](vector of("one", "two")) which returns the value 2.

The abstract types in Napier88 are existentially quantified types. Therefore, an abstract type is defined in the following way:

```
type Test is abstype[ref](a: ref; b: proc(ref → ref))
```

The ref identifier is the reference type of the Test abstract type. In order to create an object of this type, you must instantiate the reference type, as you do in Fun, by writing:

```
let three = Test[integer](3, proc (x: integer → integer); x +1;);
let half = Test[real](0,5, proc (x: real → real); x + 1.0;);
```

The values associated with the identifiers three and half are of the same type, that is, the Test type. This way of defining abstract types in Napier88 has the same advantages and the same drawbacks as the way of defining existential types in Fun. These existential types have a simple interpretation in type theory in terms of infinite unions of ideals but they are difficult to handle and often not very intuitive.

In contrast to PS-algol, in Napier88 type checking is static. However, feedback from the users of PS-algol led the designers of Napier88 to introduce a way for the programmer to take control of checking, if they so wish. Thus the **any** type is defined as the union of all the other types in the language. Where the **any** type is expected, you can assign any assignable value in Napier88. In order to preserve a consistent type system, the operations that can be implemented on **any** type values are very restricted (assignment, projection and equality). An **any** type value can be *projected* on another type in the following way:

```
let quid = any(34);
project quid on x: integer in
    x - 30
```

The above expression will evaluate correctly and return the integer 4. This projection of the **any** type onto another type is a form of controlled dynamic typing which allows you to retain great flexibility in certain cases where a value's type cannot be determined in advance, while at the same time pinpointing the places in the program where this dynamic typing occurs and therefore where a typing error may occur during execution. In Napier88, such errors cause a predefined exception to be raised and the program halts.

Napier88's environment mechanism is derived from that of Galileo, but differs on one important point: a Napier88 environment is an assignable value in the language, which is not the case in Galileo. Therefore, Napier88's type system contains the **env** type whose instances are environments. One particular value of this type is the global persistent environment which is written **ps**. Data persistence is defined as in Galileo, which means that a value persists if it is attached to this persistent environment. There is a predefined function for creating new environments. The following example creates a new environment containing three values:

```
let e = env()
in e let one:= 1
in e let two:= 2
in e let three = 3
```

The evaluation of these four expressions causes a new environment to be created which is attached to the identifier **e** of the global environment (**ps**). Three identifiers (**one**, **two**, **three**) are defined in this new environment and associated with the integers 1, 2 and 3. In order to use the definitions contained in the environment **e**, you must use the **use** clause in the following way:

```
use e with one: integer, two: integer
   in let modify = proc() one:= one + 1; two:= two + 1;
```

As environments are assignable values, whether a definition exists in a particular environment or not can only be checked on execution. The **use...with...** clause allows these checks to be located in certain places while guaranteeing the correctness of the rest of the program.

The last important aspect of Napier88 is that an application can be broken down into parallel processes. A process is an assignable value in the language, which is defined in a similar manner to functions but evaluated differently. The main reasons for introducing process management into such a language are the improvements in performance achieved by executing code in parallel and the exploitation of the inherent parallelism in applications. The designers of Napier88 specify this method of process-oriented design in the context of database systems, graphic systems and generally for all complex applications. We will not explain this procedure in more detail here as it is beyond the scope of this book. Nevertheless, the idea of providing a persistent programming language with a process management mechanism is very interesting, the more so because the mechanism is well integrated with the rest of the system.

In conclusion, this language has many high-level features. In the context that interests us, we regret the fact that it has no query language, as this makes data manipulation rather cumbersome, and no subtyping.

8.4 Conclusion

The systems we have described in this chapter represent the two main approaches to database programming, that is, the complete integration of a DBMS (relational in Pascal/R or functional in Adaplex) into an existing language and the definition of a persistent language.

Pascal/R and Adaplex successfully resolve the problem of integrating a language and a database, which was one of the main problems we stressed in Chapter 3. However, Pascal/R's data model is the relational model, which significantly reduces its power of expression. Adaplex goes a bit further than Pascal/R from this point of view because Daplex is a more sophisticated model, providing subtyping in particular.

PS-algol and Napier88 were created by programming language designers. Their main objective is to program general applications while handling data in secondary memory. This language orientation explains the principle of persistence and types being orthogonal, because you do not have a database model on the one hand and a language, with its own type system for handling data on the other.

Galileo is a persistent language, as any assignable value can persist if it is attached to a persistent environment. However, the language provides constructions belonging to semantic models which are absent from PS-algol and Napier88, and in particular the concepts of abstract types, subtyping, transaction, class and inheritance. Galileo corresponds closely to the principles for integrating a data model and a type system that we defined in Chapter 6. The only feature it does not have is parametric polymorphism.

We have seen that these languages provide the programmer with all the necessary computing power, as opposed to the relational systems which only have a query language. However, there is a problem writing queries in these languages. Any database manipulation has to be done by a program, which is impossibly cumbersome for anyone who simply wants to consult the data. Furthermore, it requires learning the language. To put it simply, from the point of view of *ad hoc* queries these systems are a step backwards from the relational systems. In the following chapters, we will see that the designers of the database programming languages that succeeded them (mainly the designers of object-oriented systems) have found solutions to the query problem, often by adapting the relational query languages.

Another problem is that of optimization, which is vital in a context where large quantities of data are being manipulated in a multi-user environment. The relational languages benefited from a large amount of research into optimization. These efforts resulted in efficient solutions which were implemented in relational database management systems. This was possible because the simple structures (algebra or calculus) of the relational query languages lent themselves to optimization. In a general programming context the problem becomes immensely more complicated. Optimization, in the sense used for databases, has never been investigated by the programming languages research community. A program written in a given language is much more complex than a query. It is therefore very difficult, if not impossible, to deduce the structural properties necessary for optimization.

Bibliographical notes

Pascal/R is described in an article by J. W. Schmidt ([SM80]). Ada is described in ([Ich79]), Daplex in ([Shi81]) and Adaplex in ([SFL80]). The underlying principles for designing a database programming language were first set out in M. Atkinson and P. Buneman's manifesto ([AB87b]). The persistent approach is represented by PS-algol ([ACC81]), which installs persistence in S-algol ([Mor79]). Galileo was developed at the University of Pisa ([ACO85]) and was heavily influenced by ML ([Har86]). Napier88 is fully described in [MBC*88a], [MBC88b].

Exercises

1. Persistence and types are said to be orthogonal in persistent programming languages. What does this mean?

2. In later examples of the tourism database, Historic buildings may be closed on more than one day and Restaurants may have more than one menu. Why would it be difficult to express this in Pascal-R without creating new relations?

3. In the example at the end of Section 8.2.2, the procedure declaration uses the Ada **for..each** iterator to handle the menu set and the Daplex **in...where** selection clause to select a Restaurant. The difference between these two operators highlights the difference between the programming language and the data model. Explain.

4. Describe the new type PS-algol introduces to manage persistence.

5. By contrast, Galileo uses the concept of environment to handle persistence. How does this work?

6. Napier88 introduces several new concepts into persistent languages. Amongst other things, it provides types for handling graphic data and it allows you to define polymorphic functions and abstract types. Describe how you can define these functions and types.

7. Why are the languages described in this chapter unsuitable for the end users of database systems?

9

Object-oriented systems

Humans find themselves when they are confronted by objects.
Antoine de Saint-Exupéry
Terre des hommes

In this chapter we will describe the object-oriented approach to databases. This is the third approach to database programming languages. First, we will summarize the origins and the principles of object-oriented languages, then we will describe three systems representing that approach. The O_2 system, which also stems from that tradition, will be described in greater detail in Chapter 10.

9.1 The object-oriented world

The principles of object-oriented programming originate in two schools of thought founded in the 1960s. The first found expression in the concept of structured programming. Programs were becoming larger and larger and more and more complicated. They were difficult to use and practically impossible to reuse. In this approach the emphasis was on the processing. A program is structured into independent subprograms. By contrast, the other school of thought concentrated on data. The data that had to be handled was also growing in both complexity and volume so it had to be structured and grouped together according to shared characteristics. This school of thought gave rise to data driven-programming.

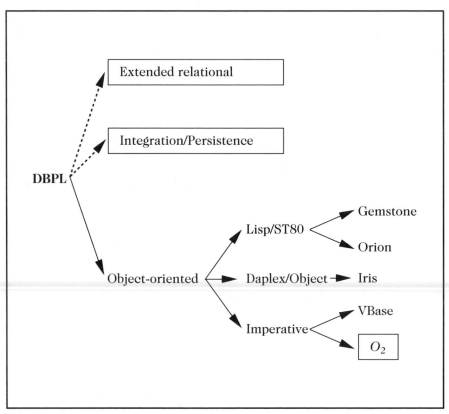

Figure 9.1 The different approaches

The first attempt to reconcile these trends was the result of dealing with the problems of simulation. Simula-66 and then Simula-67 prepared the ground for object-oriented programming. In Simula, the concept of a class, which groups together a data structure and the procedure for manipulating it, is already apparent. Smalltalk is directly descended from Simula, in so far as the main concepts are concerned. It adopts and expands this approach by making the programming environment, where everything is an object, uniform. Smalltalk also provides interactivity, directly inspired by the Lisp approach. Lisp and artificial intelligence generated other approaches, in parallel to Smalltalk. In the wake of Smalltalk, we find other languages that provide object-oriented programming features, while preserving the traditional control structures of imperative languages. This approach is mainly represented by the object-oriented layers imposed on C, namely: C++ and Objective-C, or complete languages such as Trellis/Owl and Eiffel.

Another approach which interests the database community is the marriage of objects and logic programming. This approach is particularly favoured by the Japanese, following their choice of Prolog as the basic language for their fifth-generation machines.

9.2 Object-oriented principles and terminology

In this section we describe the main features of object-oriented programming languages as they appear in the Smalltalk school of languages. Object-oriented database systems have mostly taken that approach and adapted it to the specific needs of databases.

The main aim of object-oriented programming is to create software that is flexible, extensible, reusable and easy to maintain. As we demonstrated in Chapters 4 and 6, the quality of a database application software package, just like that of any other software package, depends in the main on the design methodology used and on adherence to certain programming rules. We saw that semantic models on the one hand, and certain type systems on the other, were used to that purpose. We also showed the importance of the concepts of abstract types and modules. Object-oriented languages were designed to incite (strongly) the programmer to use a form of abstraction and modularity. They provide the necessary tools as well as the control and security mechanisms. We will describe these points in the rest of the section.

9.2.1 Object identity

Object identity is a very important point in object-oriented database systems. As we saw in previous chapters, identity is often defined by the value, the properties or the name associated with the data item. However, this identity is not always sufficient. It is derived from the value and can therefore be changed if there are any updates. This phenomenon is aptly illustrated by the following dialog which we have borrowed from P. Wegner [Weg90].

'Smith, how you've changed. You used to be tall and now you are short. You used to be thin and now you are fat. You used to have blue eyes and now you have brown eyes.
But my name isn't Smith.
Oh, so you have changed your name too.'

An object identifier must, therefore, be independent of the associated value. It must not be directly managed by the programmer and should not be confused with the various names that the programmer may use to refer to the object. Therefore, object identity is generally implemented using a unique *internal* identifier which is independent of the object's value or its address in memory. This is the case for object-oriented languages like Smalltalk. This concept of a unique internal identifier is even more important in the context of object-oriented databases. The objects manipulated by these systems are persistent and may change over time in a way that neither the user nor the program that created them can control. Therefore, that identity must be managed, at system level, independently of the application that generates the objects. In object-oriented databases, the programmer is provided with means for comparing objects on the basis of both identity and equality.

Let us consider the following two objects:

```
id₁ → [name: R4, make: Renault, year: 1978]
id₂ → [name: R4, make: Renault, year: 1978]
```

For the system, there are two distinct objects. But their values are equal and you could say that the objects are equal (*value equal* in object-oriented database terminology). In systems such as O_2, there are even more subtle distinctions. For example, the two following objects are neither identical nor equal:

```
id₁ → [name: R4, make: Renault, year: 1978, chassis: id₃]
id₂ → [name: R4, make: Renault, year: 1978, chassis: id₄]
```

Their values differ on the chassis attribute whose value is an object represented by its identifier. The chassis are represented as follows:

```
id₃ → [type: XF330, weight: 200]
id₄ → [type: XF330, weight: 200]
```

The chassis, which are not identical, are equal. In some systems, objects id_1 and id_2 would be said to be *deep equal* (the standard terminology). This equality means that values may differ but that when you develop them by replacing the identifiers by the values of the objects they represent, you get two equal values.

If we had represented the two cars as follows:

```
id₁ → [name: R4, make: Renault, year: 1978, chassis: id₃]
id₂ → [name: R4, make: Renault, year: 1978, chassis: id₃]
```

their values would have been equal. Notice that in this case, the two cars would have to share the same chassis! This kind of distinction can be easily expressed in object-oriented languages or databases. But it is much more difficult to express the same thing in a relational database.

The above example brings us to another important aspect of object identity for databases: sharing. We have seen that an object can reference another object directly by its identifier. The direct consequence of this is that any modification of the referred object is directly visible if you access it from the referring object. Once again, this feature is not directly available in relational systems and application programmers must handle it themselves.

9.2.2 Encapsulation

Object-oriented programming puts the emphasis on data. Therefore, a software package is a set of *objects*. An object is characterized by a structure and an interface.

The structure is generally identified by a unique identifier, and has a state which generally groups together the fields which contain the information to be processed. The values in these fields can be atomic values, as traditionally in programming languages, or other objects represented by their identifiers. In certain languages, such as Smalltalk, all values are considered to be objects for reasons of uniformity.

The visible part of an object is the object's interface, which is made up of *method selectors*. The object's structure is only known to the object itself and cannot be accessed from outside. An object can only be manipulated using the methods that have been associated with it by its creator. This is the principle of *encapsulation*. Therefore, we can see that an object-oriented programming language imposes modular programming, where each object does not know how the other objects are implemented but only knows their interfaces. This takes us back to the principles of programming using abstract types described in Section 5.2. Figure 9.2 shows an example of an object whose structure contains five attributes which describe a person's surname, christian name, date of birth, spouse and children. The values of the spouse and children attributes are objects represented by their identifiers (id_1 and id_2). The id_1 identifier represents an object (a person) whose implementation is unknown. The interface is made up of four method selectors, `name`, `name_of_spouse`, `names_of_children` and `age`. The object user only knows these selectors. This amounts to saying that from outside the object it is possible to find out the person's name, age, spouse's name, and children's names but that it is immaterial how these data items are obtained. Any program that uses these method selectors remains valid even if the implementation changes.

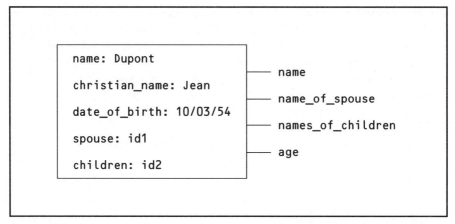

Figure 9.2 An object that describes a person and his or her family

9.2.3 Classes

We saw above that an object is characterized by its structure and its interface. Usually, a software package contains a number of objects that have the same structure and the same behaviour. Therefore it is useful to group them together. A *class* describes all the objects that have the same characteristics and how they behave. Owing to the principle of encapsulation, the concept of class is reminiscent of the concept of an abstract type described in Chapter 5. However, it differs greatly because even though a class describes the structure and the behaviour of its *instances* it is not necessarily used for type checking. Furthermore, in object-oriented languages class has an *extensional* connotation. In other words, it is used to designate and to manipulate the set of its instances in a similar way to relations in relational databases. The concept of class in object-oriented languages is reminiscent of the concept of class in semantic models, described in Chapter 4. However, in semantic models, classes only describe the structures and do not use methods to describe the behaviour of instances. To summarize, we can say that types are used to define assertions used for checking, statically and dynamically, expressions written in the language, whereas classes are moulds used for generating and manipulating objects with common properties and behaviour. Therefore, an object-oriented language can have a concept of class and be untyped. A language such as Smalltalk does no static type checking. It is a very flexible language, suitable for rapid prototyping, but does not guarantee program security. Typing is also useful because it allows certain parts of programs to be optimized during compilation. This is why certain object-oriented languages have a concept of type more or less linked to the concept of class (C++).

Figure 9.3 shows an example of a class that describes people, in a hypothetical language. The `Class` clause introduces the name of the class. The `Attributes` clause gives the list of attributes or instance variables and the `Methods` clause gives the list of selectors and the associated method. The set of pairs (selector, method) is often called the *methods dictionary*. The distinction between selector and method is important because you can have several methods for the same selector which is used with different classes. We will describe this point in Section 9.2.5.

```
Class
    Person

Attributes
    name
    christian_name
    date_of_birth
    spouse
    children

Methods
    name
            return(self.name)
    name_of_spouse
            return(self.name_of_spouse)
    ...
```

Figure 9.3 The `Person` class

We saw that a class is used to describe objects. Usually, an object is created via an expression of the `my_person = new(Person)` type, where **new** is an expression that uses a class to generate an object that corresponds to the description given by that class. The object has its own attribute values, whereas the list of attributes and the methods dictionary are managed by the class. In most object-oriented languages, the set of instances of a class is assembled in a collection which usually has the same name as the class and is called the *extension* of the class.

9.2.4 Inheritance

We have already introduced the concept of inheritance in Chapter 4, devoted to semantic models, and in Chapter 5, devoted to type systems. All the object-oriented languages implement the concept of inheritance between classes. The principle is to specialize and to factorize. This allows you to share information efficiently so that you get both a more compact code and a finer-grain representation of the problem you want to resolve. Therefore, in an object-oriented language, application design consists of grouping the most general information into classes which are then specialized step by step into subclasses, specifying more specific behaviour with each step. Figure 9.4 shows an example where the **Person** class is specialized into the **Employee** subclass.

```
Class
    Employee

SuperClass
    Person

Attributes
    salary
    manager
    department
    bonus
    length_of_service

Methods
    salary
            return self.salary
    name_of_manager
            return(self.name_of_manager)
    ...
```

Figure 9.4 An example of specialization

The **Employee** subclass inherits the attributes and the methods dictionary of the **Person** class (which is called the superclass) and defines its own new attributes and new methods. Therefore, the instances of the **Employee** class can be used in place of instances of the **Person** class and have additional properties. Another facility, which is usually provided, allows a subclass to redefine the implementation (that is, the method) associated with a selector of the superclass.

Classes are placed on an inheritance graph which allows us to visualize the links between them. Figure 9.5 is an example of an inheritance graph.

We have put the classes defined in this section, along with some predefined classes found in languages such as Smalltalk, into a graph. These classes make up a library of utilities provided with the language. The **Object** class is present in most object-oriented languages. It groups together the functions which are common to all classes, that inherit them systematically.

The **Measurable** class represents any measurable quantity and can be refined into the **Number** class, then the **Float** class, and so on.

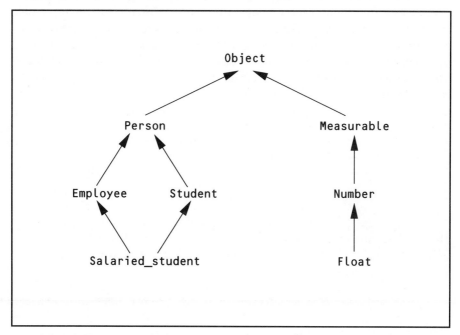

Figure 9.5 An inheritance graph

Multiple inheritance allows you to model an application in a more flexible way by avoiding the proliferation of useless classes. The drawback is that this form of inheritance can introduce conflicts of definition. A class can have incompatible superclasses (such as the **Employee** and **Student** classes). Therefore there can be a conflict of inheritance between attributes and/or method selectors with the same names in incompatible superclasses. For example, in the case of the **Salaried_student** class, the **Employee** superclass defines a department attribute which indicates the department in which an employee works, whereas the **Student** superclass defines an attribute with the same name which defines the teaching department to which the student is attached. There is a conflict of inheritance for the **Salaried_student** class because no decision can be made about the path in the graph that should be followed to find the department attribute. There is no universal technique for resolving this type of conflict and there are very varied solutions to this problem in the various object-oriented languages and database systems. These solutions range from inheriting from the superclasses in a particular order, which indicates priority inheritance from a given class, to renaming the attributes or methods so as to inherit all the attributes and methods from the superclasses. We will examine some of these solutions when we describe selected systems below.

9.2.5 Message sending and late binding

In standard programming languages, a call to a procedure is bound during compilation. In object-oriented languages such as Smalltalk, the executable method is dynamically linked to the selector, according to the class of the object to which it is applied (the receiver of the message). The application of a method to an object is called *message-sending*. In order to highlight this process of selection by the receiver, the message sending syntax usually differs from that of procedure calls. For example, to get the name of an employee, you would write `my_employee name` where `my_employee` designates an object in the class `Employee` and `name` is a selector.

Therefore, you can see that the receiver of the method is an implicit and privileged argument of it. In the method's body the receiver is generally designated by the keyword **self**. Thus, in the `Person` class, the `name` method's body contains the expression **self.name**. This expression means that the value of the object `name` is extracted from the object referred to on execution by **self**. The `name_of_spouse` method is a little more complicated. Firstly, the value of the `spouse` attribute is extracted. This is a `Person` class object. Then the `name` method is applied to that object which returns the spouse's name.

We have seen that for any given selector, there can be several methods in several distinct classes which correspond to so many different implementations. It is impossible to know, when message sending is compiled, which code should be executed because the code is a function both of the method selector and of the receiver's class. This is very dynamic because the same message sending can produce a completely different result depending on the receiver's class at the time of execution. This process whereby the method is selected on execution is called *late binding* or *dynamic linking*. To paraphrase a classic saying of the object-oriented community, late binding avoids having to correct the existing code and add another case to a **case** statement in order to handle the new data type you need. Thanks to late binding, all you have to do is create the new class with methods belonging to the same selector and the system will automatically use the new methods in the existing code.

Let us presume that in the `Employee` class we have a `higher_than(limit: integer)` method which compares the salary of the receiver with the limit given as an argument and returns the Boolean **true** if the salary is higher than the limit. The following code will print the name of all the employees with a salary higher than 250,000F:

```
for(x in Employee when (x higher_than(250,000)))
    print(x name);
```

Owing to the semantics of inheritance, salaried students are also employees and are part of the extension of the `Employee` class. Let us now assume that the method associated with the `higher_than` selector in the `Salaried_student` class is different from that of the `Employee` class and applies a coefficient of reduction. In this case, late binding will allow this difference to be taken into account without us having to modify the iterative loop as we would have to do in a traditional language. Similarly, if you add new subclasses to the `Employee` class, the iteration can be used without being recompiled. Therefore, late binding makes the language very dynamic. The drawback is that it reduces performance because late binding can take a long time. It may be necessary to examine all the classes in order to find the method to apply during execution, because a class can inherit its method from any class above it in the inheritance hierarchy.

9.2.6 Other trends

In the preceding sections, we have described the main characteristics of object-oriented languages from a particular viewpoint. We have been mainly interested in the characteristic aspects of the 'Smalltalk school' of languages. This is because object-oriented databases have followed that school. However, there are numerous other approaches to object-oriented programming which are considered to be part of the object-oriented mainstream but which differ strongly from the languages based on classes. We will briefly outline them here. The objects we described previously were characterized by an internal identity independent of their value. This value is often called a 'state', in opposition to another approach where the objects do not have an associated value: functional objects. In the latter case, the objects are characterized by a set of functions but have no internal identity. Therefore, we encounter the principles of functional programming once again in an object-oriented context. These languages do not allow side-effects and do not use variables. One representative language is OBJ2, which is principally a theoretical prototype. It allows you to specify objects of a given type in an axiomatic way using equations. This approach uses techniques similar to those of abstract data types.

Another trend is languages with *actors*. This trend originated from the requirements of parallel programming and multi-processor architectures. In these languages, we find the concept of an *active* object. In the previous languages, when a message arrived at an object it was executed immediately. Languages with actors allow you to specify a message queue for an object (called an actor in this case). The queue can be located in the object's interface or at queuing points inside the object. An actor can have several queues which act as letter boxes in which the waiting messages are saved. The operating principle of these languages with actors differs in a significant way from that of languages with classes. In this case, we are concerned with modelling parallel programming. An actor can implement three main actions:

create a new actor, send a message to other actors whose addresses it knows and change state, using a primitive called **become**. The actor can use this primitive to become another actor whose state is the new state. The important point is that, as in functional programming, the state is not modified by assignment but nevertheless the state changes. During this operation, arriving messages are queued for execution. This technique is used to manage concurrency of access and protect an attribute against concurrent accesses.

9.3 Object-oriented databases

The area of object-oriented databases systems is vast and varied. The name object-oriented has many meanings in this context. Some designers consider that a system is object-oriented if it manipulates complex objects in the way defined in Chapter 7, with a concept of identity and maybe an inheritance mechanism. In this case we call them *structurally object-oriented* systems, because these systems do not effectively implement encapsulation (object + methods). One example of this approach is the Damokles system. Usually, the name object-oriented is given to systems that adapt the characteristics we have described in the previous section to the context of databases. Therefore, in these systems we will find both the concept of objects and the concept of methods.

Before describing the various features of a certain number of prototypes and products, it would be useful if we set out in detail the particularities of the object-oriented approach to databases in relation to its original context. Databases need the most reliable programming environment possible. Data items are both large in size and large in quantity and must be protected. This means that types must be checked before execution. As we saw in Chapter 5, this implies the definition of a type system strict enough to enable the programs to be typed during compilation. This may seem to contradict the object-oriented approach, which emphasizes flexibility of use and an interpreted approach. In a number of object-oriented database systems, the designers have striven to define a typing framework that allows the greatest possible number of errors to be detected during compilation yet preserves the flexibility of the object-oriented approach. Thus, systems such as O_2 associate a type with the classes of objects, the instance variables, the parameters and the results of methods. In the O_2 system, the Person class is defined as follows:

```
add class Person
   type tuple (name: string,
               christian_name: string,
               date_of_birth: Date,
```

```
                spouse: Person,
                children: set(Person))
methods

                name return string
                name_of_spouse return string
```

In contrast to Figure 9.3, you can see that each attribute and each method has an associated type, which is used to statically type the programs. However, this preoccupation with typing must not be allowed to cancel out the benefits of the object-oriented approach. If you insist that the compiler knows exactly which method will be invoked when a message is sent you lose the benefits of late binding. This is why, in most object-oriented database systems, if the compiler can ensure that the search for a method will succeed (that is, in the hierarchy of superclasses of the receiver's class, there is a selector corresponding to that of the message), effective binding is only carried out on execution, while being optimized as far as possible.

One consequence of this is that object-oriented databases make a distinction between classes and objects that does not exist in most of the languages inspired by Smalltalk. We said earlier that these languages represent all the concepts in terms of objects, including the classes themselves which are object instances of meta-classes. This meta-circularity cannot be preserved if you want to statically type programs because, as we saw in Chapter 5, most type systems distinguish types from their instances.

In the remaining part of this chapter, we describe the main characteristics of the systems that we consider to be the most representative. The idea of an object-oriented database first really appeared in 1984 with the Gemstone system. As we shall see in the next section, the approach followed can be loosely described as the extension of Smalltalk to database functions. Orion follows a slightly different path. This system, based on Lisp, places the accent on dynamic and evolutionary capabilities. Ontos, on the other hand, is a system based on an object-oriented extension of C and therefore uses an imperative paradigm.

9.4 Gemstone

Gemstone is a direct extension of the Smalltalk object-oriented language. Consequently the syntax of Gemstone's data definition and manipulation languages is exactly the same as that of Smalltalk. In particular, the Tourism database is created by sending a **subclass** message to the **Object** class. This means that Tourism is automatically a subclass of **Object**. We could, of course, put a user-defined class in the place of the **Object** class. In Gemstone, the way classes are created only allows for simple inheritance, because the subclass message can only be sent to one class. Therefore, the Gemstone system does not allow for multiple inheritance. Here is the Tourism database in Gemstone:

```
Object subclass: #Tourism
  instVars: 'historic_buildings restaurants'
  classVars: ''
  immutable: false
  constraints: #[#[historic_buildings Historic_buildings]
                #[restaurants Restaurants]]

Object subclass: #Historic_building
  instVars: 'name road town days_closed entrance_fee'
  classVars: ''
  immutable: false
  constraints: #[#[name String]
                #[road String]
                #[town String]
                #[days_closed Days]
                #[entrance_fee Float]]

Object subclass: #Restaurant
  instVars: 'name road town days_closed menus'
  classVars: ''
  immutable: false
  constraints: #[#[name String]
                #[road String]
                #[town String]
                #[days_closed Days]
                #[menus Menus]]

Object subclass: #Menu
  instVars: 'title price'
  classVars: ''
  immutable: false
  constraints: #[#[title String]
                #[price Float]]
```

The tuples are represented by objects, and the instance variables play the roles of attributes. Sets are represented by objects which are instances of subclasses of the Set class. This representational mode, inherited from Smalltalk, does not allow complex structures, like those described in Chapter 7 to be defined simply. For each set type (set of restaurants, set of historic buildings, and so on) there has to be a corresponding class in the schema that is a subclass of the Set class.

The typing of the Gemstone program is entirely dynamic and carried out using the `constraints` clauses described in the class definitions. These clauses associate a class name with each instance variable and every time an instance variable is updated, the system checks that the object belongs to that class or one of its subclasses. There is no static typing.

To calculate the average price of a restaurant's menus you write a method in the `Restaurant` class:

```
Restaurant averageMenus
    | menuSet sum |
    menuSet:= self menus.
    sum:= 0.
    menuSet do[:menu | price |
          price:= menu price.
          sum:= sum + price.]
    ^(sum / (menuSet size))
```

The calculation itself is done by applying this `averageMenus` method to a particular restaurant. Variable declarations are made between two | (`menuSet` and `sum` in this case). The Smalltalk block that performs the iteration comes after the **do** keyword. Notice that you can use the same identifiers for names of methods and variables (for example, price on the left- and right-hand sides of the first instruction in the block). The ^ symbol is the Smalltalk equivalent of the **print** instruction in an imperative programming language. Here, it returns the value of the `sum` variable divided by the cardinality of the `menuSet` set, which is obtained by applying the `size` method to it. Notice that this method could be a method of a Smalltalk class. The Gemstone language is, as you can see, completely integrated into Smalltalk.

Gemstone's designers defined a query language, with a syntax close to that of SQL, so that queries can be written in a non-procedural language. This language can be seen as a short cut which can be used to perform those operations that do not require the whole Smalltalk program. Let us remember that one of the essential characteristics of databases, which we recalled in Chapters 1 and 3, is this facility for writing simple queries simply.

You can use Gemstone's query language to search for objects according to selection criteria. These selection operations work on classes that inherit from the **Set** or **Bag** classes. The selection conditions are conjunctions of comparisons. A comparison expression operates either on two paths in the database or on one path and a literal. A path is an expression such as `aRest.road` which you use to access an object's component via its instance variables. The example below is a query which returns the restaurants located in the rue de Lille that have menus whose average price is less than 150F:

```
Restaurant select:
   {aRest | aRest.road = 'rue de Lille' &
   aRest averageMenus < 150 }
```

Gemstone was the first object-oriented DBMS to be developed into a commercial product. The approach taken had the merit of blazing a trail for the object-oriented approach to databases. Unfortunately the results, above all in performance terms, were disappointing for the first prototype. Gemstone paid the price for too close a relationship with Smalltalk and its interpreted environment.

9.5 Orion

Orion was also one of the pioneers of the object-oriented approach to databases. The procedure followed is very different from that of Gemstone. The target domains are CAD, AI and office integration. The computing style is functional and uses Lisp. In Orion, the emphasis is on queries that use predicates and on version management, composite objects, dynamic evolution of the schema and the handling of multimedia data.

Orion's data model takes an 'all objects' approach, similar to that of Gemstone. Thus everything from an integer to a restaurant is an object with an identifier and a value. An object is either atomic or composite, that is, structured as a tuple. An object cannot be a set, but the value of a composite object's attribute can be a set of objects. Orion provides the concepts of multiple inheritance, class and method. We will not go into these concepts, which correspond to their common interpretation in object-oriented theory, but we will take a closer look at the data model and the programming. The following example describes the Tourism database in the Orion formalism:

```
Historic_building [name: string,
                   address: Address,
                   day_closed: string,
                   entrance_fee: num]

Restaurant [name: string,
            address: Address,
            day_closed: setof string,
            menu: dependent setof Menus]
```

```
Address [road: string, town: string]

Menu [title: string, price: int]
```

In Orion, you can define links of several kinds between objects and their components. Intuitively, the link between a person and his or her spouse is different from that between a restaurant and its menus. Two spouses exist independently of each other but a restaurant's menus only exist relative to that restaurant. In order to represent that difference in Orion you can define *dependent* objects. A restaurant's set of menus is an object that depends on the restaurant. The existence of a dependent object is conditional upon the object on which it depends. Furthermore, a dependent object cannot be referenced by several objects.

Orion's designers carried out a very thorough study of all the possible schema modifications in this context. The study showed that allowing dynamic schema modifications in a high-level environment such as this is extremely complex. The authors established a taxonomy of around 20 critical cases of schema modifications when Orion was used in a CAD context; we can cite, as examples, moving a class in the inheritance graph or deleting a class from the list of superclasses of a given class. They then defined the semantics of these schema modifications and isolated a set of invariants which must be preserved in the database during schema modifications. Such complexity would not be justified in the context of a database programming language dedicated to management applications, but it seems inevitable for CAD applications which, as we said in Chapter 3, require a very dynamic environment.

Orion's query language is based on the select message. This message can be applied to the extension of a class. The following query returns the set of restaurants located in the rue du Bac in Paris that have a menu whose price is less than 150F:

```
(Restaurant select :R
   (:R address road = "rue du Bac") and
   (:R address town = "Paris") and
   (:R menu some:M (:M price ≤ 150)))
```

In this example the variable :R iterates over the objects in the restaurant class. The some clause is like the select clause. It applies to a set (the value of a restaurant's menu attribute) and sends a message to each element. It returns the Boolean true if the application of the message to at least one of the elements returns the Boolean true.

Orion's query language is strongly influenced by Smalltalk and Lisp, at the expense of readability. It gives priority to navigating in complex objects and does not provide a means of making a query about two classes that are not correlated by composition. This is due to the fact that a query is a **select** clause which is applied to the extension of one, and only one, class. Therefore, the result of a query is always a subset of the objects in an existing class. You cannot return either a projection of those objects on certain attributes or new objects obtained by composition from existing objects. In Orion, using the Tourism example database, you cannot write a query that returns the historic building and restaurants in the same road or even all the historic buildings that are in the same road as at least one restaurant. The reasons for these limitations are (1) Orion was targeted at CAD applications and it seems that in this context queries that cover several classes are unusual and (2) as a query does not construct a class, it cannot produce objects that do not correspond to already existing classes[1].

In conclusion, the Orion system is interesting because it is aimed at CAD applications. The concept of the dependent object and the in-depth study of schema modifications are results of this orientation. On the other hand, as we have seen, the query language is quite limited if you want to use it in a context other than CAD. Furthermore, the fact that Orion is implemented in Lisp does not allow static typing.

9.6 Iris

Iris is an object-oriented database management system developed by Hewlett-Packard laboratories. It was designed to fulfil the same objectives as the other systems described in this chapter, that is, to increase programmer productivity in the context of the new database applications. Iris is interesting because its data model has been very strongly influenced by the semantic models such as Daplex (*see* Section 4.2.10) and by TAXIS [Bor85]. The Iris system's architecture is described in Figure 9.6.

The data model and the query and update processors are installed in the *Iris Kernel*. The updates and queries are written in a functional format. The functions are either stored in memory in the form of tables or calculated. These calculations can be written either as Iris functions or as foreign functions in a general language such as C. Iris can be used via *ad hoc* interfaces or via a programming language. These interfaces are client processors of the kernel which express a query in the form of an Iris expression. Figure 9.6 shows that there are four interfaces. The two interfaces on the left are interactive. Object SQL is an object-oriented extension of SQL adapted to the Iris data model. The second is a graphical interface based on X-Windows

---

1 Later versions of Orion apparently correct this limitation.

which allows users to search for and to update the values in Iris functions. The next two interfaces are used to define application programs. The first, CLI (*C Language Interface*), allows Iris data with an object-oriented paradigm to be manipulated using C. The second is an immersion of standard OSQL in various programming languages.

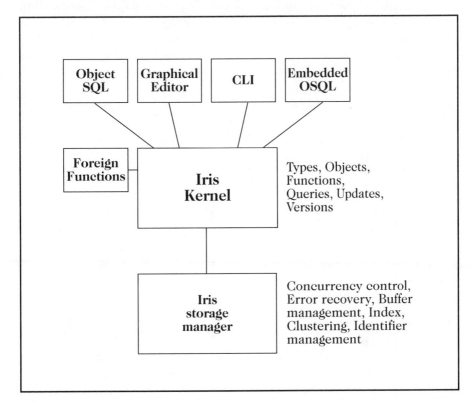

Figure 9.6 The Iris system's components

Iris differentiates between 'literal' objects and identified objects. The first category covers objects whose identity is defined by their value, such as character strings, integers or lists. The second category covers the usual objects in object-oriented systems, that is, those with internal identifiers independent of their values. Amongst these objects there are system objects, such as types and functions, and user objects, such as people and restaurants. The concept of type is used to group together those objects to which a specific set of functions can be applied. Iris does not have static typing and the concept of type in Iris is close to that of class in object-oriented languages. Types in Iris are organized into an acyclic inheritance graph. A function defined for a supertype can be applied to all the instances of subtypes. One original feature of Iris is that objects can acquire or lose types dynamically. This allows the evolution of the database to be managed more flexibly than in most object-oriented systems, but at the cost of static checking. Figure 9.7 shows Iris's inheritance graph. This graph is typical of most object-oriented languages and systems. The types and the functions are both present in the graph. Therefore the meta-data is represented in the same way as the data itself. Once again, this is possible because Iris programs are dynamically typed. You find the same kind of approach in Orion, in contrast to systems such as O_2 (*see* Chapter 10) where types and classes are not objects.

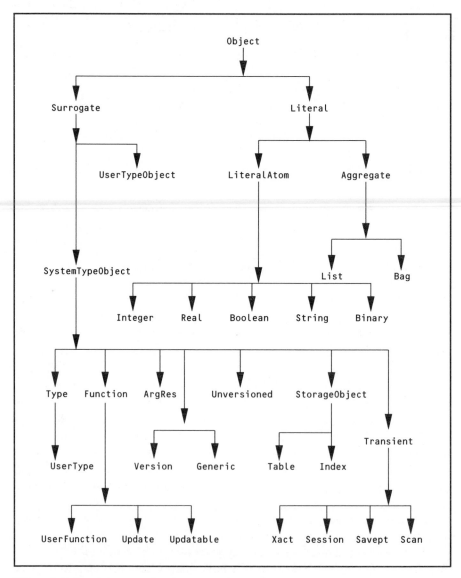

Figure 9.7 The Iris system's inheritance hierarchy

You can trace the links between different types of objects in the inheritance graph. For example, the types defined by users are instances of the UserTypeObject, and are therefore objects with identity, whereas the collections are instances of literal types (Bag and List). The function type is a subtype of the SystemTypeObject type, which allows it to inherit the system functions that can be applied to that type. The advantage of this approach is that it uses inheritance to model the implementation of system objects and therefore to describe the system itself.

A type is characterized by a set of functions. Below, we give the example of the Historic_building type in Iris:

```
name: Historic_building              → Charstring
address: Historic_building           → Address
days_closed: Historic_building       →→ Charstring
entrance_fee: Historic_building      → integer
```

Notice that you can define multi-valued functions. Thus the days_closed function returns a sequence of character strings. A function can also return a result that takes its values from a Cartesian product of types.

We will now give a few examples of how Iris is used *via* the OSQL interface. OSQL is an object-oriented extension of SQL whose main points of difference are:

1. In OSQL you can refer to objects directly rather than accessing them by keys. This means you can use the object identifiers which by definition do not exist in the SQL world.

2. The OSQL query can use user-defined functions or Iris system functions in the **where** and **from** clauses.

Below, we show how to create types and frame queries in OSQL. The types created are the same ones shown above, but the syntax differs because we are using OSQL.

```
create type Historic_building
  (name Charstring required,
  address Address,
  days_closed Charstring many,
  entrance_fee Integer);
```

```
create type Historic_restaurant subtype of Historic_building
  (menus Menus many);
```

We have created two types in OSQL. The first describes the historic buildings characterized by the functions name, address, days_closed and entrance_fee. Notice that the days_closed function is multi-valued (**many** keyword). The Historic_restaurant type is declared as a subtype of Historic_building. Therefore it has all the functions of that type plus the multi-valued menus function. We assume that the Address and Menus types have been declared. It is, therefore, possible to create stored functions that correspond to relations between objects. Thus if we presume that a Guide type exists, we can define the rating function:

```
create function rating (Historic_restaurant, Guide) → Integer;
```

If we assume that r references a restaurant and g references a guide, we can associate the rating 4 with the restaurant in the following way:

```
set rating(r,g) = 4;
```

The stored functions are implemented as arrays which associate input values with output values. The other two main types of functions are derived functions and foreign functions. Derived functions are built from other functions and OSQL. They are compiled by the object manager in algebraic form and interpreted every time they are called.

Foreign functions are used in the same way as in extended relational systems (*see* Chapter 7). That is to say, they are used as an interface for the abstract data types that are added to Iris. In practice, you can add to the Iris basic types by writing definitions of new abstract types in C, for example, which will be used in Iris functions.

If we assume the database has been populated, we can now select all the historic restaurants whose Michelin guide rating is 4:

```
select name(r)
for each Historic_restaurant r
where rating(r, Michelin) = 4
```

In the above example, we assume that `Michelin` is a variable that refers to a Guide type object; it is not a character string type value. Therefore OSQL is, because of its paradigm (functions are applied to objects; in the example `name` and `rating`), a functional language whose syntax is taken directly from SQL but which also allows you to manipulate object references.

9.7 Ontos

Ontos is the product that succeeded Vbase and is described as a distributed object-oriented database management system. It contains mechanisms for version management, nesting transactions and exception handling. The DBMS's present interfaces are a C++ type interface and an object-oriented SQL. In relation to Vbase, which adopted a philosophy like that of object-oriented systems such as O_2 or Iris which provide interfaces with a high level of abstraction and emphasize user-friendliness and security, Ontos has deliberately chosen to situate itself at a lower programming level, so that programming is closer to system level, in the hope of attaining better application performance. Ontos's main interface, which is very similar to C++, allows you to take the underlying hardware into account, just like C++. Therefore, Ontos is closer to a persistent object manager, with C++ or object SQL type interfaces, than a complete object-oriented database management system. The designers intend to provide interfaces to other programming languages in the future.

Ontos, like other object-oriented systems such as O_2, is based on a client–server type distributed architecture where a local area network links the servers and the workstations. Naturally, data and task distribution is transparent to users.

The database schema is defined directly, using C++ class definitions. Therefore the programmer does not need to use two different languages for defining data and manipulating it. As C++ does not itself provide all the facilities expected of a database management system in modelling terms, Ontos has chosen to extend it by providing a library of classes that fulfils that role. For example, the library contains classes which can be used to define aggregation concepts, such as dictionaries, sets, arrays and lists.

In order to optimize access to interlinked data items, Ontos allows the programmer to define *clusterings* on disk. As Ontos has chosen to emphasize performance, programmers can control the transfer of objects from disk into memory. Therefore they can choose to transfer one object, a logical group of objects or the closure of an object, that is, all the objects that can be accessed by reference from the given object. In most of the other object-oriented systems, the programmer is not responsible for these choices and the system usually transfers the closure or automatically manages the default objects.

Ontos provides a nested transactions facility which allows you to comfortably manage long transactions, such as those found in applications like CAD. If you nest a sequence of short transactions inside a long transaction, you can then test conflicts progressively and, therefore, limit the effects of aborts caused by data access conflicts. Ontos can manage cooperating processes and allows several processes to share the same transaction. A typical case of this type of configuration is that of applications using several windows in which different processes are active.

Ontos can manage any number of versions of the same object. All the versions of the object are gathered together in an object called a *Configuration* object. Configurations are linked to each other by derivation links. Each configuration (except the first) has a parent and any number of children, which allows either alternative or serial versions to be managed.

In C++, the description of the classes can only be accessed by the compiler, it cannot be accessed during execution. This is incompatible with the requirements of persistent object manipulation. Ontos solves this problem by providing five classes called schema classes which are used to represent the definition of classes in a way which is independent of the hardware and can be accessed during execution. These classes are: **Type**, **Property**, **Procedure**, **ArgumentList** and **Argument**. **Type** is used to represent the definition of a user class, **Property** describes the types of the properties associated with the classes, **Procedure** represents the *member functions* (C++ terminology), **ArgumentList** represents the list of a member function's arguments, so that the arguments can be transmitted during execution, and **Argument** describes the types and the default values of a member function's arguments. Therefore, the role of these classes is to provide the system with the database schema information it needs for execution.

The object-oriented interface to SQL mainly consists of extending the kinds of arguments allowed in the three SQL clauses (**select**, **from**, **where**). The **select** clause can accept not only names of properties (whose role is analogous to that of the attributes in the relational model) but also calls to member functions and paths to an object (as in the models with complex objects described in Chapter 7). The same is true for the **from** clause, which accepts any argument whose evaluation returns a collection of objects, and the **where** clause, which accepts Boolean expressions that contain calls to member functions.

In conclusion, Ontos is a system designed according to the same principles that guided the definition of C++, that is, it incorporates the strong points of the object-oriented approach but in a very pragmatic way and chooses performance criteria at the expense of certain important aspects of that approach, such as security, the reuse of data via encapsulation and the homogeneity of the programming interface.

9.8 Conclusion

In this chapter, we have described four object-oriented systems which represent the main trends in object-oriented database research. If we look at the historic evolution of these systems we can draw several conclusions:

- The first systems were based on untyped interpreted languages. The present tendency is to define languages with object-oriented functions but which are compiled (for performance) and statically typed (for security).

- All the systems provide object identity. However, we have seen that it is also desirable to be able to handle structures (tuples, sets, and so on) without identity. Defining and manipulating `Address` and `Menu` type objects in some of the systems described is cumbersome because every data type is abstract and every value is an object with identity. In Chapter 10, we will see that the O_2 system allows you to manipulate both objects and values without identity.

- Most current systems have a more or less complete query language. Others only provide a general programming language. It seems clear to us that both are necessary in order to avoid making simple manipulations too cumbersome and to make it easy for users to query the database.

- Finally, very few systems offer the whole set of database management system functions described in Chapter 1. In particular, the problems of concurrency and recovery become more difficult in this context, and the traditional solutions are sometimes awkward to use, as we shall see in Part IV.

Bibliographical notes

Many books have been written about object-oriented languages. Among the most interesting are [Mey88], [Str89], [Cox86] and [GR83]. The reader can also refer to articles which synthesize the various approaches. Simula is described in [DN66] and [BDMN73]. Languages based on a Lisp approach are presented in [BS83b], [MW80] and [Hul84]. In [Min75] there is a proposition for a knowledge representation system. ESP ([Chi84]) is a language that comes from that tradition. Other object-oriented languages are described in [SCB*86], [Mey85], [Lie86] and [FGJM85].

A compilation of the main articles about the systems described in this chapter can be found in [ZM90]. The Gemstone system is described in

[CM84]. The main articles about Orion are [KBC*88] and [BK87]. Iris is described in [WLH90]. Ontos is described in [AHD90]. Finally, a book dedicated to object-oriented database systems has been published by ACM Press ([KL89]).

Exercises

1. The increasing complexity and size of programs and data in the 1960s led to the development of two schools of thought. Describe them.

2. The concept of object identity is essential in object-oriented languages. How does it differ from the way objects are defined in other types of languages?

3. The principle of encapsulation dictates that an object should have a structure and an interface. Explain these terms.

4. Why is it that an object-oriented language, such as Smalltalk, can have a concept of class yet be untyped?

5. In the context of an object-oriented language, what do we mean by an inheritance conflict?

6. Explain the connection between message sending and late binding.

7. How do the requirements of databases affect the implementation of object-oriented principles in database systems?

8. The way objects are created in Gemstone prevents you from using multiple inheritance and defining complex structures easily. Why is this?

9. Describe the characteristics of dependent objects in Orion?

10. Suppose we create the following types in Orion, using OSQL:

```
create type Town
    (name Charstring required,
    county Charstring required,
    std_code Integer);
create type Market_town subtype of Town
    (market_days Integer many);
```

Explain why it would be possible to find the STD code for a market town.

11. In many ways Ontos seems more like a persistent object manager with an SQL interface tacked onto C++ than a database management system. Explain why this opinion could be sustained.

10

The O_2 system

In order to talk about yourself, you have to talk about everything else.

Simone de Beauvoir
The prime of life

10.1 Origins and objectives

The O_2 system is an object-oriented database management system which was designed and implemented between September 1986 and September 1989 by the Altaïr non-profit making public body. This group was founded by INRIA (Institut National de Recherche en Informatique et en Automatique), IN2 (a Siemens group subsidiary) and the University of Paris-Sud, Orsay campus. Its personnel includes researchers from INRIA, engineers from IN2 and teaching staff from the University of Paris-Sud. The prototype was validated in September 1989 and a commercial product was launched at the start of 1991.

In contrast to research prototypes, such as Galileo, the primary aim of O_2 was not to develop new techniques and original solutions to the problem of database programming. The Altaïr group's objective was to develop within five years a *complete* database management system which would be an advance on relational systems. Consequently, work was not concentrated on a particular aspect of the problem, such as, for example, the language (*see* Galileo), the evolution of the schema (*see* Orion) or data persistence (*see* PS-algol). In order to create a complete system, we had to find solutions to problems as varied as the data model, the programming and query languages, the user interfaces, the programming environment and transaction management in a non-traditional context. Therefore, the work was more the 'horizontal' kind, consisting of integrating solutions that already existed in isolation into a complete system, than the 'vertical' kind, concentrating on a particular problem.

The O_2 system was designed to be as general as possible. It can be used to run traditional management applications but is also capable of providing solutions for new applications such as CAD or geographical databases.

10.2 Data model

O_2 is an object-oriented system. The objects have an identity and encapsulate data and behaviour. Objects can only be manipulated using their interfaces, that is, the methods. The objects are defined via classes which are organized in a multiple inheritance hierarchy.

10.2.1 Objects and values in O_2

An original feature of the O_2 model, in relation to those of the systems we have studied in the previous chapters, is that you can have both the concept of objects and the concept of values. In object-oriented database management systems, the value encapsulated in an object is usually a tuple composed of other objects represented by their identifiers. This implies that the value is always 'flat', in contrast to what is possible in relational systems extended to handle complex objects. Here, we will only present examples of such objects; if you want a formal description of these concepts please refer to Chapter 7. In O_2, you can define not only objects but also complex (or structured) values, as in the following example:

```
i₀: tuple(name: "Eiffel tower",
          address: i5,
          description: "Famous Parisian historic building",
          days_closed: list("Christmas", "Easter",
                            "Assumption"),
          entrance_fee: 50)

i₁: tuple(name: "Paris",
      map: i2,
      hotels: set(i3, i4))
```

```
i₅: tuple(town: i1,
    road: "Champ de Mars",
    number: 1)
```

The objects are pairs (identifiers, values). Thus, the first object has an identifier i_0 and a **tuple** type value which is made up of atomic values (Eiffel tower), complex values (the days_closed attribute) or objects (i_1, i_2, and so on). As opposed to Chapter 7, we have adopted the convention of referring to objects using the notation i_j in order to emphasize the fact that these identifiers are internal to the system and not known to the application programmer. O_2 objects are encapsulated, that is, their values can only be accessed by the methods associated with them.

10.2.2 Types and classes

The instances of a type are values, as in an ordinary programming language. The instances of a class are objects and the class is characterized by a name, a type and methods. The type describes the structure of the values encapsulated by the objects in the class and the methods define the external interface of those objects. The types in O_2 are constructed recursively using the traditional atomic types (**integer**, **float**, **double**, **string**, **char**, **boolean**, **bits**), class names and **set**, **list** and **tuple** constructors. The expression:

```
tuple (name: string,
    map: Bitmap,
    hotels: set(Hotel))
```

describes a tuple type which is used to define the structure of objects in the Town class. Notice that the map attribute's domain is the instances of a class and the hotel attribute's domain is the sets of objects in the Hotel class. The following commands define the five classes:

```
add class Town
        type tuple (name: string,
                    map: Bitmap,
                    hotels: set(Hotel))

add class Historic_building
        type tuple (name: string,
```

```
                        address: Address,
                        description: string,
                        days_closed: list(string),
                        entrance_fee: integer)

add class Address
        type tuple (road: string,
                    town: Town)

add class Hotel
        type tuple (name: string,
                    address: Address,
                    facilities: list(string),
                    stars: integer,
                    price: float)

add class Restaurant
        type tuple (name: string,
                    address: Address,
                    menus: set(tuple(name: string,
                                     price: float)))
```

Notice that you can define classes that refer to each other, as in the cases of Town, Hotel and Address.

10.2.3 Persistence

The O_2 system allows you to name objects or values individually. To do this you use data definition language commands, such as:

```
add name Eiffel_tower: Historic_building
add name Paris: Town
add name Parisian_historic_buildings: set(Historic_building)
```

The name Eiffel_tower is then a global name for an object in the Historic_building class. These names are global variables linked dynamically to objects or values.

In the O_2 system, persistence is defined using these names. They are 'handles' you can use to find objects or values after the program that created them has finished executing. More precisely, the persistence rules are as follows:

- any named object or value is persistent,

- any object or value referred to by a persistent object is persistent.

If the name `Eiffel_tower` is associated with object i_0 which was defined previously, then object i_1 and the values `Eiffel tower` and `Famous Parisian historic building` will be persistent because they are attributes of object i_0. Notice that this rule is similar to the one used in Galileo. The definition of the classes and their associated methods is persistent.

10.2.4 Methods

Methods are defined in two stages. First, you specify the method's signature, using a schema definition language command:

```
add method check_price(): boolean in class Hotel
add method increase_fee(amount: integer) in class Historic_building
```

The first method is attached to the `Hotel` class and has no other parameters than the (implicit) receiver. The second method is attached to the `Historic_building` class and is used to increase the entrance fee. We will describe how these methods are implemented in Section 10.3.1.

10.2.5 Subtyping and inheritance

Inheritance allows you to define classes incrementally by reusing the classes that already exist. Because it is an object-oriented database system, O_2 stresses data structure. This is why, in O_2, inheritance is based on subtyping.

Subtyping for tuple types is defined as indicated in Chapter 5, that is, a tuple type t is a subtype of t' if and only if t contains at least all the attributes of t'; eventually these attributes may be refined. Thus, for example:

```
tuple(name: string,
      address: Address,
      description: Text,
      days_closed: list(string),
      entrance_fee: integer,
```

```
        facilities: list(string),
        stars: integer,
        price: float)

is a subtype of:

tuple(name: string,
      address: Address,
      description: Text,
      days_closed: list(string),
      entrance_fee: integer)
```

There are similar conditions for sets and lists: a **set(T)** type is a subtype of a **set(T')** if and only if T is a subtype of T'. The O_2 system infers this subtyping relation from the inheritance relations between the classes declared by the user. For example, you can define a historic hotels class as follows:

add class Historic_hotel **inherits,** Historic_building, Hotel

You use this command to declare that the Historic_hotel class inherits from the two classes Historic_building and Hotel. The command interpreter infers the associated type from the superclasses' types and checks that it is compatible with the subtyping conditions. If the type is suitable, the class is created and placed in the inheritance graph. The class inherits all the methods from the superclasses but you can still define new ones or redefine the inherited methods.

The O_2 system has a predefined Object class. As in Smalltalk, this class is the root of the inheritance graph and every class inherits from it. Its purpose is to define the methods that are common to all the objects in the system, such as those that test identity and equality or make copies.

10.3 Data manipulation

Methods are implemented using standard programming languages supplemented by an object-oriented layer. In the first version of the prototype, C and Basic were used to create CO_2 and BasicO$_2$. We will only describe CO_2 in this section because BasicO$_2$ follows a similar procedure. We will then describe the query language, which can be used as a query interface by the end user or as an easy short cut for writing CO_2 programs.

10.3.1 The CO_2 language

CO_2's design principle is to respect, as far as possible, the style and philosophy of C. Therefore the object-oriented layer provides set and tuple manipulation with a similar syntax to operations that already exist in C. For example, the union of two sets is written x+y, just like adding two integers in C; similarly, the extraction of an attribute is written **self**.a, just like extracting a field from a C structure. We will illustrate the most interesting points of CO_2 with the help of examples.

A method's body is implemented in the following way:

```
body increase_fee(amount: integer) in class Historic_building
     co2{ *self.entrance_fee += amount; }
```

The value of the object to which the method is applied is written ***self**. Just as in Smalltalk, **self** designates the receiver of the method and ***** is the de-referencing operator which returns the object's value rather than the object (in this case a tuple). In order to respect the principle of encapsulation, O_2 only allows that operator to be used on the receiver or on an object in the class where the method is defined. The **entrance_fee** attribute's value is an integer and therefore we can use the C **+=** operator to increase it.

You apply a method to an object by sending a message, as in Smalltalk. The syntax for sending a message is:

```
[receiver selector (arguments)].
```

Objects are created using the **new** command, which takes the name of a class as its argument: Eiffel_tower = **new**(Historic_building). The object is created with a default value which depends upon the type associated with its class.

In CO_2, you can construct and manipulate complex values which correspond to the constructors mentioned in Section 10.2. To assign a value to a newly created object, you would write:

```
*Eiffel_tower = tuple (name: "Eiffel tower",
                       address: Eiffel_address,
                       description: "Famous Parisian historic
                          building",
                       days_closed: list("Christmas", "Easter"),
                       entrance_fee: 50);
```

To add an element to a list or a set, you use the += operator, as in:

```
*Eiffel_tower.days_closed += List("6th June");
```

You can run through the lists and sets using the **for** iterator, as follows:

```
for (x in Parisian_historic_buildings when (*x.entrance_fee <= 40))
    [x increase_fee(3)];
```

The above code increases the entrance fees for all the historic buildings in the value `Parisian_historic_buildings` if they satisfy the condition introduced by the keyword **when**.

10.3.2 The query language

In contrast to the query languages of relational systems, which are limited, O_2 has a general programming language which provides the computing power of programming languages such as C. The disadvantage is that CO_2 does not provide the same flexibility as query languages. Therefore, the O_2 system provides a query language which can be used either by the end user or to write CO_2 programs easily. The main characteristics of the query language are as follows:

- The result of the evaluation of a query can be either a value or an object. A value result can be constructed from the query definition but an object result is always an object that exists in the database. The query language does not create new objects, and does not perform updates.

- The query language is of the functional type. Queries are constructed from basic functions, composition operators and iterators. The syntax is of the SQL type.

- In contrast to CO_2, the query language is typed dynamically and can access freely the values encapsulated in objects. In other words, this language does not have to respect the principle of encapsulation.

The following examples illustrate the main constructions in the language:

```
Add 2 + 2: 2 + 2.
Days when the Eiffel tower is closed: Eiffel_tower.days_closed.
```

In this example, we are extracting the value of the **days_closed** attribute from the object denoted by **Eiffel_tower**.

Names of the hotels in Paris with air-conditioning:

```
select h.name
from h in Paris.hotels
where "air-conditioning" in h.facilities
```

In this example, we have a query which is very similar to one in SQL for databases with structured values. You describe the paths to follow in order to access the values of the attributes you are interested in.

The Eiffel tower's entrance fee and the days it is closed:

```
tuple(entrance_fee: Eiffel_tower.entrance_fee,
      days_closed: Eiffel_tower.days_closed)
```

Both this query, and the following one, illustrate how the constructors (in this case the tuple) can be used to structure the result.

Menus and names of the restaurants in Paris where you can eat for less than 100 francs:

```
select tuple(restaurant: r.name, menu: m.name)
from r in Restaurant,
     m in r.menus
where m.price < 100 and r.address.town.name = "Paris"
```

The O_2 query language is therefore very flexible because it can filter lists and sets using an SQL syntax, while allowing you to construct and manipulate complex values without the limitations of the relational query languages.

10.3.3 Applications programming

In the preceding paragraphs, we saw how the programmer can define classes and methods and manipulate objects and values using the query language or CO_2. Now we will show how to construct and execute an application in the O_2 system.

An O_2 application is made up of *programs*. Each program represents a specific task in the application. An application can also define global variables which are used to store the data used by various programs. These variables are temporary and only exist during the session when the application is executed.

A program's body is written in CO_2. The difference between a program and a method is that a program is not attached to any particular class and contains transaction management commands. Furthermore, a program can call methods by *sending* messages but cannot call other programs.

In the example of an application definition below, we assume that there is a database made up of the Historic_building, Town, Restaurant and Hotel classes and the names Eiffel_tower and Parisian_historic_buildings. The Tourist_agency application is constructed as follows:

```
add application Tourist_agency
    variable buildings_visited: list(Historic_building),
             total_price: float
    program consult(list(Town)),
            consult_restaurant(restaurants: list(Restaurant)),
            book_restaurant
```

You can add new programs or new variables to an existing application at any time:

```
add program book_tour in Tourist_agency
add variable towns_visited: list(Town) in Tourist_agency
```

10.4 Interface generator

Programming a database application consists not only of manipulating data on disk but also in writing code that generates communications between the user and the application. It is reckoned that 60% of the code in an application is dedicated to managing its interface. Designing and implementing graphical user interfaces requires not only time but a thorough knowledge of interface-writing software. Usually, database application programmers find that interface-writing toolboxes do not satisfy their requirements, such as: displaying and editing structured objects, navigating the database and searching for objects by contents. In this section we will describe the O_2

interface generator, called Looks. Looks is a toolbox designed to fulfil the following objectives:

- To allow simple interfaces to be written quickly using predefined components that manage the dialog.

- To make it easy to change these components so that they match the users' precise requirements.

- To manage the dialog with the end user, that is, to display information about the database on-screen in a user-friendly way in order to make it easy to interact with the application.

Looks provides creation and deletion facilities and facilities for editing O_2 objects and values. It is inserted in Le_Lisp above the Aïda toolbox.

10.4.1 Generic display algorithms

As we saw in Section 10.2, the objects and values manipulated by O_2 have complex structures. The display of a data item is controlled using two parameters called *expansion* and *positioning*. A value in the O_2 system is seen as a graph that connects the atoms (the atomic values) and the constructors (**tuple**, **set**, **list**). Each value in the O_2 system can be displayed at a depth chosen by programmers according to their needs and the space available. This choice corresponds to the expansion parameter. Figure 10.1 illustrates the three predefined types of expansion: **icon**, **level_one** and **all_you_can_show**.

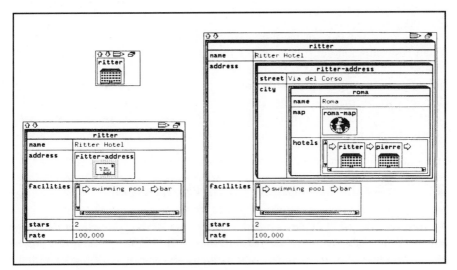

Figure 10.1 Three representations of the same object

The Looks tool provides the programmer with several options for positioning windows on the screen. The O_2 system provides specific representations for certain classes, such as the diagram, bitmap and text classes. Each type of value has specific editing facilities based on the **cut**, **paste**, **create** and **copy** operations. These operations are executed directly, using the mouse. Looks controls the editing operations interactively in order to prevent structural inconsistencies and impose respect for O_2's type system.

10.4.2 Navigation and interrogation

The database can be consulted in two ways. The first consists of following the composition links of each object. For example, starting from the representation of a list object, you could go down the list to find a given person.

The second way of consulting the database is to use the graphical interface for a subset of the query language. This interface allows you to filter the extension of a class, a set or a list of objects using the partial description of an object.

10.4.3 Dialog control

One of the most important problems that human–computer interface software must manage is the transfer of control from the application to users and vice versa. When the application has control it asks questions to which the users must respond. Users do not control the running of the application. The users have control when they address queries to the application and control the execution.

Generally, the two forms of control must coexist in an application. Thus, when reserving a hotel room, clients must enter the specification of a hotel, but they may also want to obtain information about that hotel from the application. This presumes that the application will suspend its activity to display the information requested. Therefore, two forms of control may be nested in a randomly complex way. Looks provides the programmer with control transfer primitives which automatically manage dialog consistency.

10.5 The programming environment

In this section we will describe the O_2 programming environment. This programming environment has been designed like an O_2 application and is therefore written in CO_2 and Looks. It is an illustration of the possibilities of the system. The features of this environment are as follows:

- Navigation in, interrogation of and printing of the database and the schema.

- Printing, testing and updating of the methods and the application programs.

- Use of a toolbox of predefined classes and objects and reusable programs for programming applications.

- User help for *ad hoc* interrogation and printing of the database.

The approach chosen for the design of OOPE (Object-Oriented Programming Environment) is based on the Smalltalk programming environment. It makes extensive use of graphics and is entirely object-oriented.

10.5.1 Design principles

As we will see in Section 10.6, all the data items manipulated by the O_2 system are seen as objects by the object management system. From data items to methods, everything, including the classes, is an object from the point of view of data storage. This is in contrast to the language level where a distinction is made between classes, objects and methods for static typing reasons and security purposes.

At OOPE level, the designers have chosen to represent everything in terms of objects, in the same way as at the storage system level. The advantage of this approach is that it provides a simple and uniform interface. Therefore, the programmer using OOPE manipulates classes and methods as database objects, which reduces working and learning time. Similarly, all the development tools are seen as objects by OOPE. This is the case for the **log**, the **navigator** and the **O_2_shell**. The **debugger** is not itself an object but is made up of several objects.

When OOPE is initialized, a set of objects is displayed on the screen, as shown in Figure 10.2.

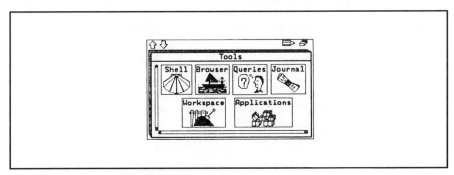

Figure 10.2 The OOPE tools

10.5.2 Defining classes

Seen from OOPE, a class is a tuple structured object which contains structural information about the class: its name, its associated type, its position in the inheritance graph and its methods. An Infos attribute contains additional comments about the class. An example is shown in Figure 10.3.

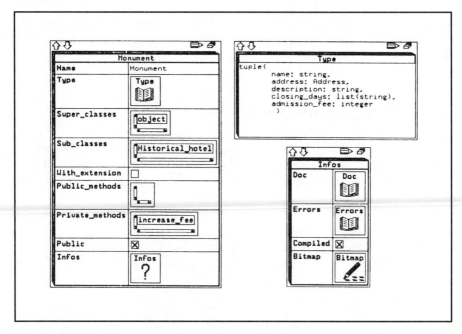

Figure 10.3 The Historic_building class

The methods associated with OOPE objects that represent classes can be used to add a subclass or methods, to display the hierarchy of classes (*see* Figure 10.4) and to validate or delete a class.

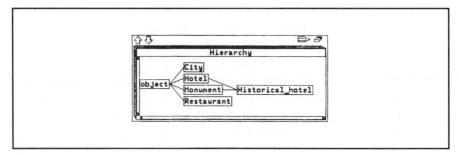

Figure 10.4 The inheritance graph

10.5.3 Methods

Like classes, methods are represented by tuple structured objects which contain the method's signature (its name, parameters, result and the receiver's class), the language the code is written in, the body and additional information. Figure 10.5 represents the method that increases the entrance fee of a historic building.

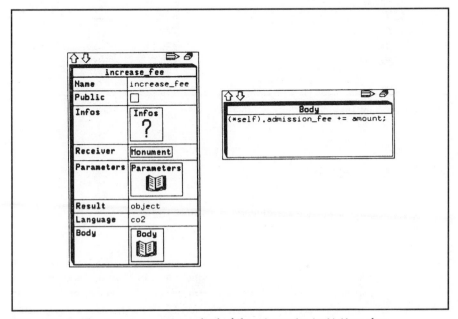

Figure 10.5 The increase_fee method of the Historic_building class

The methods associated with the **methods** objects can be used to compile, create or delete a **method**. OOPE also allows you to execute a method immediately after creating it, so that you can test it.

10.5.4 Applications and programs

OOPE sees an application as a tuple structured object (*see* Figure 10.6) whose methods are its programs. Therefore to execute a program you send a message to the application object with the name of the required program as the selector. The applications are grouped together in a named object, which is one component of the **Tools** set of objects shown in Figure 10.2. Like the methods, programs are described by tuple structured objects (*see* Figure 10.6).

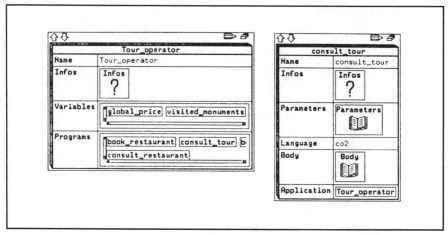

Figure 10.6 The Tourist agency application and one of its programs

10.5.5 Debugger

In O_2 debugging is done by navigating around the objects in the database and editing them. The operation is therefore uniform with the OOPE interface.

The O_2 debugger is *symbolic, interactive* and *graphical*. The operational principle is very simple. Under the debugger, a program updates a set of objects that describe its state. The programmer uses the execution manager, which is one of the programming environment's named objects, to modify the way the program executes.

As well as the usual functions of traditional debuggers (that is, interactive display and modification of variables, execution of program functions and instructions), the O_2 debugger also provides functions that are characteristic of the object-oriented approach. For example, the programmer can interactively control the sending of messages, or replace one message by another or by the value it returns. The O_2 debugger is written in CO_2 and is made up of the following four objects:

- The *execution manager*, which is displayed in the form of a control panel. The functions provided are the interactive setting and removal of halt points on program lines and methods, the display of the list of halt points, the execution in a chosen mode (step by step or another option) and the control of message sending.

- The *symbol table* contains static information about the methods' code. A symbol table is created for each method when it is compiled and stored in memory with the method.

- The *execution stack* is a pile of symbol tables. It is created and managed when a program is executed under the debugger. This object is used to display the calls to methods. In order to do this, the symbol table for the method called is pushed onto the stack each time a message is sent. When execution terminates, the table is popped off the stack.

- The *editor* is a text class object which is used to display the source text of the method being debugged.

In Figure 10.7, we show a debugging session. The code being debugged is the code for the `increase_fee` method, whose body is shown in the **body** window.

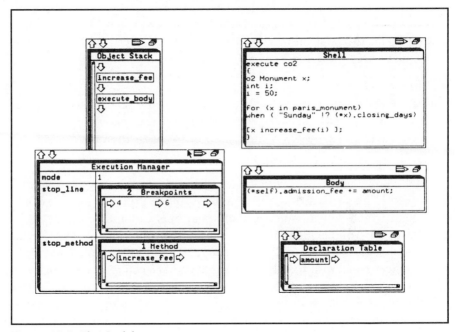

Figure 10.7 The O_2 debugger

10.5.6 Other tools

OOPE also provides the following tools:

- *The toolbox.*
  One of the aims of the object-oriented approach in general and O_2 in particular is to increase programmer productivity. One of the corner-stones of this is the reuse of software components. Therefore, the O_2

system provides the application programmer with a control-oriented toolbox which contains a number of classes of objects already used for control. The O_2 system's toolbox was generated after consulting the libraries provided by object-oriented languages such as Smalltalk-80, C++, Eiffel, MacApp and the features of spreadsheets like Excel. The main classes in the toolbox are Date, Quantity, Currency and Money. There are a total of 34 classes organized into a three-level hierarchy with 450 methods.

- *The navigator.*
  The objects in the O_2 system are linked to each other by composition links. Therefore, starting from one object, you can explore the part of the database accessible by that object by navigating along the links between objects. This feature also allows you to explore the inheritance graph and the applications, starting from the object class, as all these elements are OOPE objects.

- *The O_2 shell.*
  One of the OOPE objects is the Text class whose objects are displayed as full-screen editors. The O_2_shell object is a Text class object which is used to edit and execute O_2 commands or to access the Unix system.

- *The work space.*
  OOPE provides the user with a work space object, whose type is a set of objects. The work space object allows you to group together several objects which you then use to build your application (*see* Figure 10.8). This avoids you having to use the navigator several times to look for the same object. Furthermore, a work space object can be named and made persistent along with the objects it contains. You can create and name as many work space objects as you need. Once they are named, these objects will appear in the Tools object and will, therefore, be immediately accessible.

Figure 10.8 A work space

- *The log.*
  The log carries out the traditional database management system log functions. It records all the important operations implemented on an OOPE object and stores a version of the object once an operation has terminated. You can retrieve a version of the object from the log at any time. The log is a named object with the set of objects type, as you can see in Figure 10.9.

Figure 10.9 The log

10.6 Implementation of the O_2 system

In this section we will discuss the implementation of the O_2 system. Because it is an object-oriented system, O_2 provides the concepts of objects, complex values, classes, methods, inheritance, subtyping, overloading of method names and late binding. Because it is a database management system, O_2 provides mechanisms for accessing and updating large quantities of persistent data as well as concurrent access and transaction mechanisms.

10.6.1 General description of the system

As you can see in Figure 10.10, the O_2 system is made up of seven modules: the programming environment (OOPE), the interface generator (Looks), the language processor, the query interpreter, the schema manager, the object manager and the disk manager.

The disk manager is responsible for disk I/O, placing the data on disk, addressing and buffer management. The object manager converts the abstract objects in the O_2 data model to their representation on disk, and vice versa. The schema manager is responsible for managing the information about classes and methods. The language processor handles the data definition language commands, updates the schema via the schema manager and compiles the methods. The query interpreter handles queries written in the query language and executes them using the object and schema managers. The interface generator is responsible for managing the screen, the display of objects and interactions with the object manager. The programming environment provides the programmer with the tools necessary for developing applications. It is, therefore, the normal interface with the system.

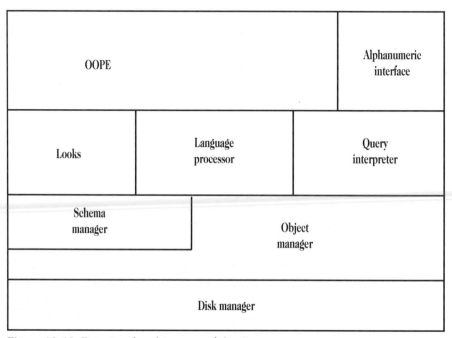

Figure 10.10 Functional architecture of the O_2 system

In development mode, the seven modules are present and the application programmer works interactively using OOPE. In execution mode, only the object manager, the schema manager and Looks are used because the application has been compiled into object code which only contains calls to those three modules.

O_2 is installed on a hardware architecture comprising a server and several workstations. Therefore, there is a workstation version and a server version of the system. The two systems have an identical interface but differ in their implementations. The workstation version is single-user and main-memory oriented, whereas the server version is multi-user and disk oriented. In development mode, Looks, the language processor, the query interpreter and OOPE are resident on the workstation, whereas the server is only responsible for disk management. The schema and object managers are present in two different versions on both the workstation and the server.

10.6.2 The language processor

The language processor is made up of five modules: the command interpreter, the compiler selector, the CO_2 and $BasicO_2$ compilers and the query interpreter.

The command interpreter is the highest-level layer. These commands are the ones we saw in Section 10.2. They are divided into schema definition and modification commands, method or program code definition commands (**body** commands) and code interpretation commands (**query** and **execute** commands).

The schema definition and modification commands are analysed and the corresponding operations executed by schema manager primitives.

The method or program code definition commands are passed, via the compiler selector, to the corresponding compiler (CO_2 or $BasicO_2$). The compiler produces C source code containing calls to the object manager. The C source code is compiled by the standard C compiler.

10.6.3 System architecture

The system is composed of three layers. The highest is the schema manager which is responsible for installing the primitives for creating, searching for, updating and deleting classes, methods and persistent names. The schema manager is also responsible for checking the subtypes and the consistency of the schema. The second layer is the object manager which is responsible for implementing persistence, garbage collection, index management and clustering strategies. This layer uses the third layer, which is the WiSS system (Wisconsin Storage System) or the disk management system. This layer provides persistence and concurrency management for flat records (as opposed to the complex structures handled by O_2).

The main reason for installing the schema manager above the object manager is the desire for uniformity. Schema data access and storage are managed in the same way as for database objects. Furthermore, this solution offers the advantage that the object manager's error recovery mechanisms can be used for the schema.

10.6.4 Schema manager

As the classes and methods are managed as system objects, the schema contains a **Class** class and a **Method** class. The objects in these classes contain the data that allows classes and methods to be defined.

The schema manager provides facilities that allow you to define classes incompletely. Therefore, you do not have to follow a given order of creation when defining a set of classes that reference each other. For example, you can create a class with an attribute that references a class that has not yet been created. The class will be called 'phantom' and consistency checking will not be completed. When the referenced class is created, the schema manager will restart the consistency checking process for the 'phantom' class, which is now completely specified. These features also exist for method signatures, which can also be 'phantom'.

Deletion of classes is managed in a more restrictive way. A class can only be deleted if it is an end node of the inheritance tree and it is not used in the definition of another class' type or methods. In a case where classes reference each other, you can destroy several classes simultaneously.

10.6.5 The object manager

The object manager is made up of three layers. One of the layers is the module responsible for managing complex objects on disk, clustering and indexing, basic support for transactions and message sending. Another layer manages the object buffer and the third manages the queries that come from the workstations and distributes them to the corresponding modules.

10.6.5.1 The complex object manager

This object's role is to provide the primitives for the creation and deletion of objects, the search for objects by name, the `Object` class' predefined methods and the implementation of the object constructors (tuple, set and list).

In the O_2 system, we chose to use physical object identifiers which contain the object's address on disk. We could have chosen to use logical identifiers as in the Gemstone, Orion and ObServer systems, but his would have meant managing a correspondence table for physical and logical addresses. Such a choice can quickly prove to be expensive, since accessing an object would require two disk accesses. On the other hand, O_2 faces the problem of how to preserve objects' identities when they are moved on disk. In order to solve this problem, the complex object manager uses a forward pointer mechanism, provided by WiSS, similar to the solutions found in relational systems such as System-R.

In contrast to the O_2 model, which distinguishes objects from their values, the object manager manages values as objects and, therefore, associates an identifier to them, for reasons of uniformity. The distinction between objects and values is made by the primitives that implement message passing or value manipulation. For example, the primitive that adds an identifier to a set uses a different membership test according to whether the identifier represents an object or a value. In the first case, it would use identity whereas in the second it would use equality of values. Further, as, by definition, values are not shared, a copy of the value would be added to the set in place of the value itself.

10.6.5.2 The message sending mechanism

This module exists on both the workstation and the server. As the methods are implemented as objects, resolving the sending of a message amounts to searching for a method object according to the class of its receiver. The information about inherited methods is duplicated for each class. Resolving the name of the method does not, therefore, entail going through all a class' ancestors and is done in constant time, which is crucial for the system performance of an object-oriented database management system.

10.6.5.3 Transaction support

The system is used either by an application in execution mode or by a programmer working in development mode. In both cases, the database is accessed by transactions. In the O_2 system, the concept of a transaction takes the specific nature of object-oriented systems into account and differs from the traditional idea of a transaction in database management systems:

- There are two different concurrency mechanisms for the schema and the objects. For example, in execution mode, you can choose to have concurrency for the objects but not for the schema.

- Error recovery can be de-activated. A programmer who is prototyping may wish to sacrifice security for performance, given that the data manipulated is test data.

- A transaction can choose to work in 'missing objects' mode or 'resident' mode. The first mode is the normal operational mode of most data managers. The 'resident' mode corresponds to those applications that run entirely in main memory, where the system loads all the data the application may need into main memory. It is possible to combine an application's operational mode (development or execution) with the transaction modes. Transaction modes are specified on execution.

10.6.5.4 Communications manager

We said that the O_2 system operates on a distributed architecture made up of a server and several workstations. A communications manager is therefore needed to manage remote execution.

When an application is started on a workstation, a 'mirror' application is started on the server. This mirror application's role is to manage the interactions with the lower layers of the system; it is re-activated each time control of execution is passed to the server.

The application processes on the workstation and on the server do not operate in the same way. The process on the workstation executes the application code as a transaction and the server process is passive. It is re-activated when a message is sent, handles it by calling the appropriate primitive and then becomes dormant until the next message arrives or until the application terminates.

In the first version of the system, the execution site to which a message is to be sent is specified statically by the application programmer. You can have nested execution transfers. For example, although a selection operation is executed on the server the display is on the workstation. Therefore the two sites are alternately in the roles of client and server. The O_2 system execution migration protocol is, therefore, more than just a uni-directional call to a remote procedure.

10.6.5.5 Persistence

We saw that, from a logical point of view, persistence of an object in O_2 is determined according to whether it can be accessed from persistent roots (see Section 10.2.3). Persistence is implemented by associating a reference counter with each object. As long as its reference counter is not zero, an object persists. When an object becomes persistent, the reference counters of all its components are incremented. The space occupied by the objects in memory and on the disk is only liberated when the transaction is validated. An object's reference counter may be zero but it may still be referenced by program variables and methods. Therefore the object must exist as long as these references exist. An alternative, more complicated solution, which was not implemented, is to have temporary reference counters.

10.6.5.6 The buffer manager

The buffer manager is responsible for the translation of the object identifiers into memory addresses. It is also responsible for the management of missing objects and the memory area. O_2 has dual management of the disk buffers, implemented by WiSS. and a pool of memory buffers. The objects in the disk buffers are in disk format and in the pool of O_2 buffers they are in memory format.

On the server, a missing object causes a WiSS record to be read and transferred from the disk buffer to the server's O_2 buffer. All the records in the same page are transferred along with the object. This strategy is based on the fact that strongly correlated objects are normally placed on the same page and, by transferring the whole page, which does not cost much more than transferring the object, other missing objects can be avoided. As the applications can share certain data items, the server's O_2 buffer is implemented in the form of a data segment shared by several processes. Shared memory management is the equivalent of the Unix *malloc* shared memory. In contrast to the server, on the workstation the O_2 buffer is private to each application.

10.6.5.7 Clustering

The clustering of objects on disk is managed according to information provided by the database administrator. This information is known as a *cluster tree*. A cluster tree for a class C can be seen as a subtree of C's hierarchy of composition. For example, the cluster tree for the `Historic_building` class can be defined as follows:

```
add cluster tree for class Historic_building
   desc tuple(address: tuple(town: tuple(hotels: set(Hotel)))
              days_closed: list(string))
```

The cluster tree defined above indicates that the value of the address attribute, as well as the hotel attribute of the historic building's town and its list of days closed, should be placed as near as possible to the `Historic_building` object. By default, the clustering manager generates a cluster tree in which all of the object's complex values will appear as branches (in this case the `address` and `days_closed` values).

The clustering strategy is used to place the objects that represent the schema as close to each other as possible. Another cluster tree is defined for the system classes that represent the classes and the methods.

The approach taken by O_2 is very different from that of Orion in that it is more dynamic and the cluster trees can be modified and are separate from the schema information.

Bibliographical notes

The whole of the O_2 system is described in [Deu90]. O_2's data model has been the subject of several articles ([LRV88], [LR88], [LR89a], [LR89b], [LR89c] and [LR89d]).

The schema definition language and the CO_2 language are described in [LR89d]. You should refer to [VDB89] for a detailed description of the O_2 object management system. The query language is described in [BCD89]. The object clustering is the subject of a doctoral thesis ([Ben90b]) as well as an article ([Ben89]). The debugger was also the subject of a thesis ([Pfe91]) and is described along with OOPE in [DP89], [DP90] and [BDPT90]. The structured object editor is described in [PCP89]. An interesting experiment, carried out in parallel to the development of the O_2 system, consisted in creating a persistent object-oriented Lisp which implemented the O_2 model. The implementation principles differ strongly due to the specific characteristics of Lisp which have been preserved. You can find a description of LispO$_2$ in [Bar90] and [Bar91].

Exercises

1. What is the difference between an instance of a type and an instance of a class in O_2 and how are they related?

2. Describe the domains of the following O_2 type definition:

```
type tuple (name: string,
         address: Address,
         menus: set(tuple(name: string,
                          price: float)))
```

3. Summarize the rules for persistence in O_2.

4. Under what conditions would a lunch_menus set be a subtype of the menus set?

5. What are the restrictions on O_2's query language?

6. What is the difference between the way OOPE and the object manager see the data manipulated by O_2 and the way it is seen at language level? What advantages does this confer?

7. The O_2 debugger is made up of four objects. What are they and what are their functions?

8. What features of the O_2 system does the navigator use?

9. The O_2 system is made up of seven components. Name them and describe their functions.

10. Why is it important that the schema manager allows you to define classes incompletely?

11. Describe the role of the reference counter in implementing persistence in O_2.

Part IV

Implementation techniques

The last part of this book deals with implementation problems. The relational database systems developed a reliable and efficient technology for handling large amounts of data in central and secondary memory. This was the result of fundamental research on data representation, transaction management, query language optimization, indexing and so on. They also introduced software architectures where a clear distinction was established between the logical level and the physical level. The aim of this part of the book is to describe the main components of software packages responsible for managing data structured according to a model that conforms to the properties of those described in Chapters 7, 8 and 9. Very often, the software packages that carry out these functions are known as the *object manager*.

Actually, the term 'object manager' has been used in two different contexts. In the programming language and software engineering world it means the DBMS or the repository, which is often dedicated, around which the computer based software development environments are organized. From this point of view, the object manager is designed to handle objects produced by various stages of the software development cycle: specification and design documents, modules, procedures, generated code and so on.

In the DBMS domain, most often when referring to those DBMSs whose underlying data model provides very varied data types, the term data manager means the lower layer of the DBMS which is primarily responsible for storing and accessing objects. The need to handle complex data types for new applications and the progressive integration of programming language and database technologies have led language and DBMS designers to rethink the design of object managers. In the past few years products or prototypes that propose solutions for the outstanding problems have appeared. All these systems have in common the capacity to manage complex objects (object is used here in the loosest possible sense). The objects to be stored may just as easily be data items as programs. However, depending on the features of the system, the kind of data model and the possible architectures, these systems do not focus on the same objectives.

Building a system to manage objects is a complex task which can naturally be divided into several coherent parts. Each part is often intimately linked and intertwined with the neighbouring parts. Nevertheless, each part is responsible for a principal function. These functions can grouped together around the following themes:

1. *Language environment management.*
   This is anything concerned with managing the names, classes, types and modules. The object manager must be able to understand and interpret the model's basic concepts. For example, if object identity is part of the model, the object manager must provide the corresponding mechanisms or a means for simulating them. Similarly, message sending is one of the basic principles of object-oriented programming languages so the system must provide the mechanisms for executing it.

2. *Object representation.*
   This aspect depends on the data model used. First-generation DBMSs provided relatively simple models for small objects. The appearance of new applications has made it necessary to remove these limits in two main directions: representing structured objects and managing very large objects. These two factors are not independent because the complexity of structures has repercussions on the size of the object.

3. *Managing persistence in the programming language.*
   This means providing a uniform means within the language for handling permanent data in the same way as temporary data. There are various possible solutions for achieving this result: *persistence by typing* (only certain types of data can become persistent), *persistence by connection* (only objects that are connected, directly or indirectly, to persistent objects become persistent themselves), *persistence by storage* (there is an explicitly declared storage area and any object placed in that area becomes persistent).

4. *Memory and addressing mechanism management.*
The hierarchy of memories available in a system includes magnetic tapes, disks and main memory. Generally, permanent data is located on the disk or tape, whereas temporary data resides in main memory. Depending on the architecture, main memory is not necessarily monolithic; there may be several levels of main memory with 'cache' memories or, in the case of the workstation/server architecture, main memory is distributed between the workstation and the server. The purpose of memory and addressing mechanism management is to handle the problems posed by locating the information and transferring it from level to level in the hierarchy. The data storage mechanisms also deal with allocating and releasing areas in main memory or on disk, accessing objects, input/output and page management. Obviously, object identity is a key element in these addressing mechanisms. Object identity can be logical or physical. A logical identifier gives no information about the location of the object, whereas a physical identifier does. Similarly, we will discuss the problems arising from preserving the way identity is represented during transfer between main and secondary memory. In order to guarantee optimal performance, memory management aims to cluster objects that are logically accessed at the same time in the same physical storage units. Similarly, data accesses by association must be prioritized; this can be implemented using indexing techniques.

5. *Extensibility.*
The object manager must be designed in such a way that new storage and access structures can be added easily. These extensions must also cover the addition of new data types, so that new application domains can be serviced.

6. *Distribution.*
In the past few years, database technology has evolved from the provision of a centralized resource to the provision of a distributed resource. Furthermore, the new applications require increasing computing power of the kind provided by workstations. If we take a CAD application as being typical of these new applications, we observe that the way of interacting with the database has changed. In the first phase the users load all the objects they need for their design work into main memory. They then work on the structure in main memory and, in the last phase, return the updated information to the database. During the processing in the main memory phase, they make few accesses to the database but consume a vast amount of computing power. This way of working tends to separate the processing and storage functions. Processing is done by the workstations and storage by the server.

7. *Management of traditional database functions.*
Indexing, data sharing, reliability and security are features that must still be guaranteed. However, this can only happen if current techniques are

fundamentally questioned, leading to a search for new solutions to these problems.

8. *Version management.*

   In most new applications, such as CAD, for example, it is important to preserve the successive states of an object and a history of its evolution. This problem is called *version management*. The archiving system must take responsibility for this new phenomenon.

This part is divided into two chapters. The first is mainly concerned with the overall software architecture and the addressing mechanisms. The second deals with the management of data on disk. These two chapters are based on the analysis of several systems. Those we have chosen present fundamental and complementary characteristics. In these chapters we will develop the themes set out in this introduction.

11

Object manager architecture

There is an architecture that works.
Paul Claudel
Conversations in the Loir-et-Cher

11.1 Introduction

Many projects have built object managers. They can be classified roughly into three main categories: virtual memory systems, extensible systems and systems for object-oriented models.

One of the first systems to use the concept of virtual memory was probably Socrate. The basic idea in Socrate was that any data unit that made up an object could be known by a name and that the name corresponded to an address in the virtual space. This DBMS was far from possessing the characteristics of an object-oriented model, but certain concepts used are fundamental. Another example in this first category is the LOOM system developed at Xerox Parc. This system provides a virtual memory support for Smalltalk. The basic idea is to bring the objects into main memory as and when they are needed; in the same way as there can be a missing page in a paging mechanism there can be a missing object in LOOM.

The Exodus, Postgres, Genesis and Starburst projects can be put in the extensible systems category, described in Chapter 7. Even though these projects are different, they have a common aim, which is to do with extensibility. The extensible system concept covers several aspects. On the one hand, it is concerned with providing the basic modules out of which an object manager can be built, and leaving the actual assembly to an architect who can construct an appropriate system after setting certain parameters. Exodus, Genesis and Starburst take this approach. On the other hand, extensibility can be seen as a way of extending the features of an existing system; for example, using the data manager of a relational system and extending the data model to complex objects and, consequently, extending the storage modules. This last approach is the one used by Postgres, which is largely based on the work done on Ingres. Similarly, extensions have been built onto System-R in order to take the management of complex objects, or the composition links of an object that appears explicitly in CAD applications, into account. Similar work has been done in the DASDBS, Damokles and Prima projects, which can be seen as extensions of relational systems with non-normalized tuples.

The last category includes managers specially developed for object-oriented database systems (*see* Chapter 9): Gemstone, Orion, Encore-ObServer, O_2. In relation to the previous category, these object managers have been built to satisfy the needs of object-oriented models. In particular, they make it possible to represent complex data structures, but above all the properties of objects are taken into account from the very lowest layers of the system.

11.2 Problems encountered

11.2.1 Overall system architecture

So as to make the concept of an object manager less abstract, let us consider a hypothetical architecture whose main modules are shown in Figure 11.1:

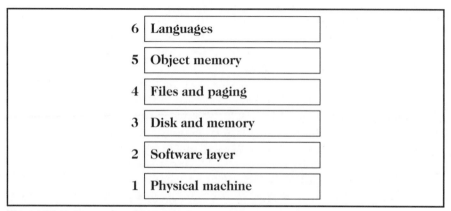

6	Languages
5	Object memory
4	Files and paging
3	Disk and memory
2	Software layer
1	Physical machine

Figure 11.1 Layered architecture

1. The physical machine provides the main memory, a stable secondary memory and a communications interface.

2. The software layer is an interface for accessing the various components of the physical machine.

3. The third layer corresponds to the representation of the stable memory (the disk) as a set of fixed-size blocks. The organization of these blocks into units of contiguous or disparate clusters is an aspect that depends on the nature of the system.

4. The paging mechanism is responsible for transferring blocks between the main memory and the disk. The techniques used to guarantee the security of this mechanism in case of error are once again a function of the system involved.

5. The *object memory* is the crucial layer of the object manager because it implements the DBMS's data model. For example, in an object-oriented model it will implement the message sending mechanism and the execution of the appropriate code for that message, according to the nature of the object. It will also undertake other functions, such as managing temporary objects, accessing objects' values and updating them, creating new objects and so on. You can see the object manager as an abstract machine based on a predetermined list of primitives which communicates with the language layer.

6. The top layer in the figure is the language layer. It is not part of the object manager. Its function is to compile the expressions in the language and to maintain the database's logical schema.

You can interpret Figure 11.1 as a succession of steps which, starting with an object name defined at language level, lead to the location of the object on the memory device. At each step repeaters, with associated tables called *descriptors*, are used. These descriptors are used to find the input parameters for the next step. In this modular architecture, each module is responsible for a system function. The last stage is the system that physically accesses the data, whereas the start of the process is the logical analysis stage, with the interpreter or compiler mechanisms.

The architecture described in Figure 11.1 is typical of a large number of object managers. If it seems clear that the upper boundary of the object manager is the interface between the language layer and the object memory, it is more difficult to locate the lower boundary. Some implementations have reused all or part of an existing DBMS to create an object manager. Others, by contrast, have assumed the existence of a file management system that guarantees functions in layers 3 and 4. One such file management system is WiSS, which was used to implement the Exodus, Orion and O_2 database systems. These examples would tend to suggest that an object manager should limit itself to layer 5: the object memory. However, in the light of the most recent experiences, it seems to us that creating efficient object memories has important repercussions for layers 3 and 4. In what follows, we will take the term object manager to include all or part of layers 3, 4 and 5.

For completeness, we ought to indicate the situation of the traditional DBMS functions in each of the layers: transaction management, concurrency, recovery, access rights, indexing and clustering. We will be able to do this later when we describe these aspects. Relational systems are also divided into modules in a way that closely resembles what we have described. In System-R, the RDS module carries out logical data management, security and query optimization functions, whereas the RSS module implements the data access and storage functions. Section 11.4.1 summarizes these features.

The last important aspect of an object manager's architecture is allocation and distribution. The schema in Figure 11.1 refers to a single machine or single site configuration. The situation is much more complicated in a distributed environment.

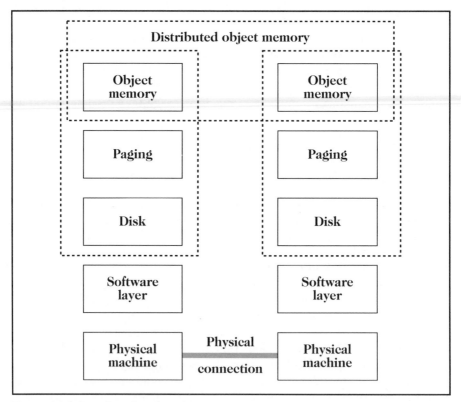

Figure 11.2 Distributed architecture

An increasingly common architecture is that of *workstations* connected to one or more *servers*; the name 'server' refers to the machine where the permanent data is archived and managed. The first level of complexity corresponds to a single server and several workstations. The fact that there is only one server implies that there is only one reference space for objects. The problems that arise are simpler because you only have to look at the distribution of tasks between the workstation and the server. The second level of complexity corresponds to a multi-server configuration, where each server defines its own object space. In this situation, it is necessary to define a global object space. Figure 11.2 shows an example of a distributed architecture. We will come back to this aspect in Section 11.6 and look at the problems caused by distribution.

11.2.2 The object manager and persistence

The concept of the *persistence* of an object was introduced by persistent programming in PS-algol. In programming languages, such as Pascal and Cobol, the lifetime of a variable, and of its contents, cannot extend beyond the program's execution time. In order to save a variable, you have to make a call to the file manager. You have to call it explicitly and you can only do it for certain types of values. For example, in Pascal, you can save the contents of a `record` type value in a `file` type file.

In database systems, the notion of persistence has always been accepted implicitly. Any instance associated with the database's schema is automatically persistent. The problem is that only the objects in the schema can persist. For example, in the relational model, declaring a relation causes all the tuples related to that relation to be stored when they are created. As you cannot declare an array of values or a function in a relational schema, those elements cannot be made persistent either. The basic idea in persistent programming is to consider that, in a programming language, the means of getting an object permanently stored must be independent of the object's type.

In databases, another aspect of persistence is that the DBMS not only guarantees the preservation of permanent data but also maintains its integrity if there is a fault. Several techniques have been developed to deal with incidents; these are called *recovery after fault* techniques. These incidents may be due to three distinct phenomena:

- Transaction abandoned following concurrent accesses to a shared object, leading to a deadly embrace situation;

- Error during execution of a transaction after an anomalous operation; for example, a fault during an input/output operation after an abnormal read/write;

- Power supply to the system or disk cut off.

In order to remedy these situations, the actions carried out on a database are divided into units called *transactions*. The effects of a transaction, particularly updates, must persist if the transaction is completed. If it is not completed, the effects of the transaction must not alter the database. Recovery and concurrency control techniques are used to ensure that transactions are atomic and to guarantee the persistence and integrity of the data.

The object manager is involved in two aspects of persistence: allowing any type of data to be stored and guaranteeing the quality and integrity of the storage. Nevertheless, DBMS terminology tends to favour a specific vocabulary which uses the concepts of transaction, access concurrency and recovery. We will reserve the term persistence for the programming languages approach or for when we are studying techniques for detecting persistent data, as opposed to temporary data.

11.2.3 The object manager and the model

In Chapters 4 and 7, the concept of the data model is explained at length. Let us just remember that a data model is a set of concepts that you use to translate your application's knowledge into a database schema and programs. Each schema is specific to a data model and uses the basic mechanisms found in most models: aggregation, generalization, specialization, classification and association. Whatever type of model is used, the object manager must reflect it faithfully. Though the list of object manager functions we have drawn up in the introduction to this last part of the book is general enough to be valid whatever the model, it is, nevertheless, particularly applicable to object-oriented systems and the role of each function must be situated in relation to the data model. Consequently, one of the key problems is finding out how much the object manager must know about the data model. In some systems, such as Encore-ObServer, it does not have to know much because the object manager is mainly responsible for storing the data as strings of characters. In other systems, such as Gemstone, it has to know a great deal because the object manager has complete information about the objects' structures and behaviours.

Finally, to conclude this general introduction, let us look at the object manager's situation in relation to the module responsible for managing the database schema. The schema itself contains permanent data about the types, the classes and the programs. A first possibility is to handle the information contained in the schema in a totally different way from the rest of the system data; therefore this aspect is located outside the object manager. Another solution is to consider the types, classes and programs to be objects. This recursive type of definition is used in some systems, in which case schema modifications are handled just like modifications of ordinary data. Schema management is then a specific application for the object manager.

11.3 Addressing mechanisms

The aim of this section is to describe the main addressing mechanisms used in the implementation of the new database management systems. We will start by discussing the general problems, such as the nature of the address space and the implementation of the concept of object identity, before reviewing several systems.

Let us remember that the role of an addressing mechanism can be broken down into two main stages. The first stage consists of transforming an external name (which exists at programming language level) into an internal name[1]. This is closely interlinked with the language compiling or interpreting phase. If we look back at Figure 11.1, this stage corresponds to the first layer. It leads to the building of a directory which is managed by the system and defines the association between the external name and the internal name. The internal names may themselves be transformed before the object is eventually located. Therefore, the second stage corresponds to the location of the object which, at the required moment, may be anywhere in a hierarchy of memory stretching from the main memory to the secondary memory on disk. The main problems that arise are the following.

11.3.1 Systems with one or two levels

As we have already explained, one of the fundamental objectives of the new generation of systems is to resolve the mismatch between a programming language and a database management system. The former have always emphasized the richness of data structures in main memory, whereas the second have looked for efficient accesses to secondary memory, often at the expense of the structure richness. The consequences of these two approaches are that the data structures used in databases are relatively inefficient when used in main memory while the structures used by programming languages are badly adapted for persistent data.

Another factor is that the nature of applications has changed or at least the scope of applications has broadened. In a traditional management application, a process interacts with a group of objects for a relatively short period of time during which the objects may be updated. In an application such as CAD, the profile of accesses to the database is fundamentally different. In a first phase, a large number of logically interlinked objects are extracted from the database. In a second phase, a program works on this set in main memory and then, in a final phase, the objects are all copied back to the disk. In the processing phase, the accesses are unpredictable, because they depend on the designer's needs. The objective is to provide the most efficient accesses possible. Similarly, it is pointless to back up an

---

1   In the compiled mode, this directory disappears during execution.

object every time it is modified, because these modifications may be rendered obsolete by later modifications.

From the point of view of the integration of the two technologies on the one hand and the evolution of applications on the other, we can distinguish two main categories of systems:

- *Systems with two levels of representation.*
  In this approach the data is represented in a different way on disk and in main memory. Furthermore, the references between objects on disk and in main memory belong to two distinct reference sets. These references between objects are based on the concept of object identity, which we will analyse in the next section. Each time a data item is transferred from one level to the other, not only is the data item itself converted into the correct format but its references are also transformed. The advantage of this system, for the language interpreter or compiler, is that the data appears in a homogeneous form, whether it is permanent or temporary. The disadvantages are obvious: the costs of converting from one format to another, and the necessity of making copies in main memory between the input/output area and the data heap. Finally, components or sub-components of objects can only be accessed after numerous indirections.

- *Systems with one level of representation.*
  Several systems have solved the problem of multiple representation by adopting a single format for the main memory and the disk. This approach is often based on a virtual memory mechanism. The following have often been cited as the major disadvantages of a virtual memory mechanism for a database environment:

  - This approach does not take data integrity in the case of fault into account because a virtual memory mechanism does not provide control over the writing of pages to disk. Nowadays, the developments in operating systems allow this kind of control to be exercised.

  - The virtual addressing space is too small for large amounts of data. This argument is less cogent for systems with 32-bit or even 64-bit addresses.

  - The page replacement strategy is not adapted to database transactions. This can be remedied by implementing strategies that either force a page into memory for a certain period of time or anticipate the pages that need to be loaded, if they are being accessed sequentially.

The advantages of this solution are obvious: no copies, no format conversions.

Apart from the advantages and disadvantages discussed briefly above, we must admit that these systems have only been developed relatively recently and few experiments or performance measurements have been carried out and compared. Later, we will illustrate these two approaches by presenting systems that take either one or the other.

11.3.2 The concept of object identity

In programming languages, in file management systems and in databases it is necessary to distinguish between, and name, all the data items. Without explicitly referring to a data model, we can say that *object identity* designates the unique name that allows us to handle a data item and to find it in a given environment.

As [KC86] points out, the notion of object identity covers different concepts depending on the angle of approach: structural or temporal. From the structural point of view, identity can be represented by its value (as in the case of a social security number for identifying people), by a name given by the user (as in the case of a variable name in a program, or a file name), or as an intrinsic value of the model (as in the case of object-oriented models). From the temporal point of view, the important factor is the period of time during which an object retains its identity. In a database, it is essential that an object's identity remains the same throughout its existence, so as to preserve data consistency.

In the relational model, the notion of identity does not exist at model level. It is the schema designer who decides on the set of attributes that will be used as the key to a relation. The anomalies linked to this approach are well known and were listed long ago (*see* Chapter 2).

The notion of identity may be an explicit concept in the data model. In the models described in Chapter 9, the concept of identity is an integral part of the model. This approach is used in object-oriented systems. The advantages are well known: object sharing, building of complex objects (an object can be built from other objects, at any depth) and the representation of a set of objects in the form of a graph.

At system level, we consider that any data item is identified by an identifier symbolically designated by the term `id`, `oid` or `pid`, if we wish to express the permanence of that identifier. A data item is therefore a pair (`id`, `data item`) as shown in Figure 11.3.

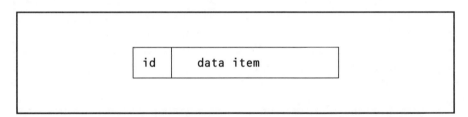

Figure 11.3 Representation of a data item

Similarly, the data item can be seen as an uninterpretable byte string, or as a value whose structure, and consequently components, is known. The way in which the identifier is implemented is an indicator of the kind of addressing mechanism used to find the object. The analysis of how that identifier behaves in relation to structure or value modifications or changes in the object's location is an essential element in the choice of a suitable implementation. Numerous techniques have been implemented for representing the identifier, which we can classify as follows:

1. *Physical address in main memory.*
   This is probably the most common and has been used in programming languages to identify an object in main memory. This address may be real or virtual. In the case of a real address, it is obvious that the object cannot be moved. Using a virtual address only allows whole pages to be moved. If, in addition, the virtual space represents objects on the heap, they cannot be shared by several programs. These two comments are not at odds with the fact of having a virtual memory mechanism and a single level of representation. All it means is that the virtual addressing space for permanent data must be shared by all the transactions.

2. *Physical address in secondary memory.*
   This mechanism is widely used for permanent data. Once again, it may be a real or virtual address. In the case of a real address, the identifier's structure is based on the fact that the secondary memory is divided up into abstract units according to the following hierarchy: `volume`, `segment` or `file`, `page` and `object`. If we take the page, the identifier is in the form (p, o) where p is a page number and o is the offset in the page header, as shown in Figure 11.4.

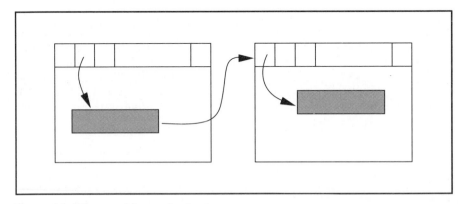

Figure 11.4 Page and forward pointer

This technique is used in several relational systems. It allows the object to be moved within the page without changing its identifier, but if a value is modified and causes a change of page a *forward pointer* must be used. Should there be another overflow, indirection can always be limited to one pointer. With a virtual mechanism, each object's virtual address is found in a virtual space for all the objects in the database. This virtual space is itself applied to the disk space by transforming the virtual address into the physical address. In Section 11.4.2 we will describe a system that implements this type of solution.

3. *Indirection.*

In this approach, the identifier is an entry in an *object table*; this table may be global, including all the objects in the system, or local, including only the objects present in main memory. Each entry in the table contains the real address of an object. This solution has been used in several systems such as LOOM and Encore. The use of this technique leads to good independence between an object's identity and its physical location. The cost is the time taken to search the table. We will come back to this technique later in the chapter.

4. *Structured identifier.*

The idea is to code part of the access path to the object, or certain information about that path, into the identifier. For example, the identifier may include a code representing the object's class. Similarly, in a distributed environment, the identifier may contain certain data about the site where the object was created and where it permanently resides. With such an approach, objects can move from one site to another. Nevertheless, if the identifier contains some semantic data, such as class, the object cannot migrate from one class to another without certain precautions being taken.

5. *Key.*

In most file management systems, objects are manipulated using a key specified by the user. In order to get efficient access to the records in the file, a supplementary access structure is built using indices. These indices are mostly implemented in the form of B-trees. This solution provides total independence between the key and the location. Nevertheless, if you change the key's structure or if you decide to split the file into subfiles the system is not sufficiently adaptable.

6. *Internal identifier.*

The internal identifier technique consists of generating an internal identifier when the object is created that is completely independent of any location and known only to the system. This identifier is never reused, even after the object has disappeared from the system. This solution is ideal from the point of view of independence, but from the point of view of performance it is the same thing as the solution by indirection.

11.4 Virtual memory

Many database systems have tried to achieve a homogeneous view of data by adopting a single representation for the objects in main and secondary memory. This is the idea of a single-level representation, which we discussed previously. It goes back more than 20 years, when virtual memory systems were first developed. In the database domain, this principle has been applied in different ways. One of the first database systems to use this principle was the Socrate system developed at the University of Grenoble. This technique was also extensively implemented in relational systems, in particular in System-R. We should indicate however that these two systems limited it to the management of permanent data. The principle has been generalized to deal with permanent and temporary data at the same time in projects such as Bubba and Cricket.

11.4.1 The RSS system of System-R

We have chosen to describe some parts of System-R because it covers the most traditional features of relational systems and is in the class of systems with segments and paging. In System-R, the RSS (Research Storage System) module is responsible for storage, using the access paths and controlling concurrency (locking, recovery after fault). All the data in RSS (user data, access paths, information about the internal catalogue, temporary data) is stored in segments divided into fixed-length pages (4 Kbytes). The main objects manipulated by RSS are the model's concepts: the relations, the lists, the indices, the binary links and the tuples in the relations, each of which has its own internal identifier called `rid`, `lid`, `iid`, `blid` and `tid` respectively.

Notice that RSS does not take responsibility for the correspondence between the external name and the internal name. RSS locates the objects in the following way, as shown in Figure 11.4.

For any given segment, the tuple identifier `tid` is a data pair (p,o) where p is the page number and o is the offset. This offset is an offset from the bottom of the page and the area it points to contains the address of the record corresponding to `tid`. This location technique allows for efficient management of the space in the page. The space can be compacted and the records moved without their identifiers being changed, only the addresses in the area at the bottom of the page are changed. Furthermore, if there is a capacity overflow, a new page can be allocated and the record corresponding to `tid` then points to a record called an overflow record. This guarantees that accessing a record and secondary usually only calls for one access to a page and never more than two (assuming that a record can be entirely contained on one page).

One particular component of RSS, the *page manager*, is responsible for locating a page of a given segment in main memory. In order to do this, it has a locating function and pool of page frames, which is a contiguous memory area whose size can vary at every system start-up. In order to search for a page address (s, p) where s is a segment number, it proceeds in the following manner: it applies a *hashing* function to the page and segment numbers which returns the address of a page frame as a result. So as to take possible collisions into account, all it has to do is to go through the chained list of page frames corresponding to the same hashing class. If it does not find the page, it means that it is not in main memory and it must be transferred from secondary memory into main memory. In order to do this, a frame in main memory is allocated and assigned to the same hashing class; the space required is released using the LRU (Least Recently Used) technique.

11.4.2 Virtual space and paging: Socrate

In the Socrate system, the set of data items relating to the database schema is stored in a *virtual space* which is a set of one machine word (32 bits) cells. Each cell is referenced by its *Absolute Virtual Address* (AVA) which is used as the internal name of the object. If the object is stored in several words, it follows naturally that the absolute virtual address given is the absolute virtual address of the start of the object. These virtual addresses are also used to reference other objects. In a system such as Socrate, the correspondence between the external name space and the absolute virtual address space is established statically when the database schema is created. The objects have a fixed size and the maximum number of instances of each type is known. This means that each object, even if it has yet to be created, has a preallocated place.

The structure of the external names depends on the data model used. Let us consider a schema containing the `Restaurant`, `Historic_building` and `Town` entity types declared in the following way:

```
entity 1000 Restaurant begin
            name: string(12)
            town: Town
            dayclosed: string(8)
            entity 10 Menu begin
                       name: string(12)
                       price: integer
                       end
            end

entity 100 Historic_building begin
            name: string(12)
            town: Town
            entrancefee: integer
            end
```

```
entity 50 Town begin
            name: string(12)
            department: string(12)
            end
```

If you refer to the analysis carried out in Chapter 5, you will see that the database's schema is built using the tuple and set constructors[2]. This schema's declaration corresponds to a hierarchy. The entities Historic_building, Restaurant and Town are at level 0 and the Menu entity is at level 1. The level 0 entities can be seen as classes, and can therefore be referenced. For example, this is true for the town attribute whose domain is Town. The type of an instance of the database is:

```
[ Restaurant: { [ name: string(12)
                  town: Town
                  dayclosed: string(8)
                  Menu: { [ name: string(12)
                            price: integer ] } ] }
  Historic_building: { [ name: string(12)
                         town: Town
                         entrancefee: integer ] }
  Town: { [ name: string(12)
            county: string(12) ] }
]
```

The external names, which are manipulated by the language, refer to the objects by their rank. You can talk about Restaurant 10 (the tenth restaurant), Menu 5 of Restaurant 10 (the 5th menu of the 10th restaurant), and so on. When the schema is compiled, a table that mirrors the objects' structures and the links between them is built. Thus the type and the location of any object in the virtual space is known.

NAME	TYPE	PARENT	NUMBER	LG	RVA
Restaurant	{[ ]}	0	1000	47	32
name	string	1		3	0
town	Town	1		1	3
dayclosed	string	1		2	4
Menu	{[ ]}	1	10	4	7
name	string	5		3	0
price	integer	5		1	3

Figure 11.5 Directory of names and representation of the virtual space

---

2   The set constructor is introduced by the word 'entity' in Socrate's syntax.

Figure 11.5 is an illustration of the table for the example's schema. The first column contains the element's name and the second indicates the type constructor (tuple or set of tuples), and, in the case of a set of tuples, we note the maximum number of elements. The third column shows the hierarchical composition rule for the names. For example, the name attribute is the second row of the table and is attached to the Restaurant class, which is the first row of the table. If the element is a set, the fourth column shows the maximum number of instances. The fifth shows the length of the element. This length is calculated recursively, starting from the atomic elements. In this example, the strings are counted in bytes and rounded up to words (4 bytes), integers occupy a word and the classes are referenced by a virtual address, which is a word. The last column indicates an element's relative virtual address (RVA). This address is in fact an offset from the parent entity's address. Each set type element is preceded by a bit string whose length is equal to the maximum cardinality of the set, rounded up to the nearest word, in order to calculate the space occupied. The bit in position i in the bit stream represents the ith instance of the corresponding entity: if the instance exists the bit is set to 1, if not it is set to 0. This is why the RVA of Menu is 7 and that of Restaurant is 32. Figure 11.6 illustrates the virtual space for the Restaurant class.

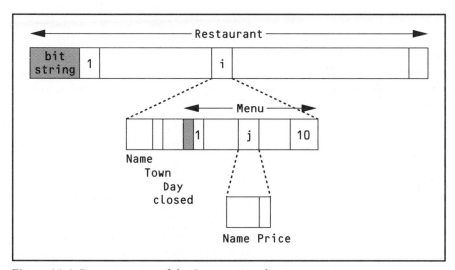

Figure 11.6 Representation of the Socrate virtual space

This method has the advantage of giving a very compact table of names in which you can find the absolute virtual address of the object associated with a name by consulting the table and doing a simple calculation. Let us consider the following Socrate expression:

```
price of Menu i of Restaurant j
```

where i and j refer to a **Menu** and a **Restaurant** respectively. The absolute virtual address of the object is given by the formula:

RVA(price) + RVA(Menu) + (i–1) × LG(Menu) + RVA(Restaurant) + (j–1) × LG(Restaurant).

The method where there is a correspondence between the objects' names and the virtual space has the enormous advantage of simplicity. It does however have major disadvantages:

- As allocation is static, any modification of the schema cannot be reflected easily. It means objects have to be re-allocated in virtual space.

- The virtual space has holes in it relating to objects that do not exist (the situation is analogous to that of a sparse array). In order to remedy this situation, the virtual space must be projected onto disk space.

The second part of the addressing process, which takes an absolute virtual address and gives its location on disk, is done by paging. Generally speaking, a paging mechanism is a mechanism whereby the virtual space is divided into fixed-size pages, 512 words, for example. Thus, you can calculate the address of the corresponding page from the virtual address. These pages are stored in secondary memory on disk and are brought into main memory on demand. The table of the pages present in main memory is maintained by the database system and the algorithm for accessing a virtual address is classic:

1. Calculate the page's address on disk from the virtual address;

2. If the page is in main memory then read it from there, if not load the corresponding page from disk.

In fact, the process is a little more complicated if you want to recover the empty spaces in the virtual space. In order to do this you must establish a correspondence between the virtual space and the disk space. In Socrate, this correspondence is established by hashing, which of course immediately brings with it all the problems associated with that kind of access, and in particular the collision factor. One of the consequences is that, if the page you are looking for is not in main memory, you may need more than one disk access to find the right page. Statistical and theoretical studies on Socrate have shown that the increase in accesses is very small. Figure 11.7 summarizes the set of successive transformations. Starting from a name used in the programming language, the figure shows the access path to the information.

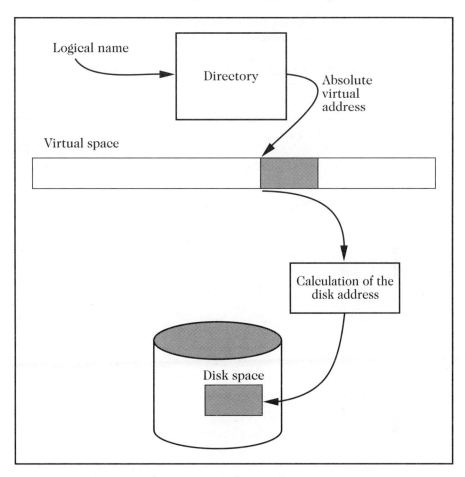

Figure 11.7 Locating an object in a virtual space system

11.4.3 **Temporary and persistent data**

The main objective of the Bubba and Cricket projects is to find a way of managing persistent and temporary objects homogeneously with a single addressing level. The temporary data items are only visible inside the transaction that creates them. The persistent data items are visible inside several transactions (subject to the problem of concurrent accesses), and they continue to exist after the transactions terminate.

Data management takes place in a partition of each transaction's virtual execution space. In fact, there are two partitions: (1) the persistent partition, for persistent data items, which is shared by all the transactions and (2) a temporary partition, for the temporary data items, which is private to each transaction. At the end of each transaction, the data items in the temporary partition that become permanent are transferred to the persistent partition. The operations that handle persistence, clustering and space recovery are carried out during this phase.

When implementing this kind of mechanism the following constraints must be respected:

- An object can only have one virtual address. If its length is modified and it has to be moved to another address a forward pointer mechanism must be used; this is an analogous technique to that described in Section 11.3.2. This means that the object's header must contain an indication of this situation.

- As long as the transaction has not terminated, the effects of object updates on the state of the indices cannot be taken into account. This means there is a problem with any set type data item. A permanent set can be composed of permanent objects and temporary objects. When an iterative process is executed on the elements in the set, this distinction must not be apparent. However, if the transaction does not terminate, the set must be restored to its initial state. Therefore, specific management and an adequate data structure must be provided for sets.

- Concurrency and recovery control are key points in this approach. A process can only access a virtual address after being assured that the access is authorized. Therefore, a mechanism for exercising these controls must be installed in the system's kernel.

- Generally, a correspondence is established between the virtual space and the disk space. In order to reduce the number of input/output operations and the size of the correspondence table for the virtual page and the disk page, it is important to use large pages for the persistent partition, for example the size of a track on the disk, from 16K to 64K. By contrast, a small page size should be chosen for the temporary partitions. This means managing pages of varying sizes.

This approach is relatively new. It calls for more or less radical changes to operating system kernels,. This is why the Cricket project uses the Mach system, which is an extension of Unix. The Bubba project also uses a dedicated operating system.

11.5 Two address levels

The other approach uses two address levels in order to respond to the needs of new database features. In the main, this point of view has been favoured by the designers of persistent languages, such as PS-algol. Nevertheless, the techniques used can be applied in a database system. Let us start by recalling the reasons behind a persistent language.

In programming languages, where the notion of type predominates, data management in main memory is dynamic. This is necessary in order to handle several problems: calls to functions (or even to recursive functions), message sending (a special case of a call to a function) and the fact that an object's size is not always know at compilation time. Though dynamic allocation has advantages it also imposes disadvantages, linked to the recovery of the space taken up by objects that become redundant during the execution of a program. *Garbage collection* must be implemented. In the case of a persistent language that incorporates the features of a conventional database, data management in main memory is further complicated by the fact that it has to manage both temporary variables and persistent variables. The main problems are:

- The number of data types that have to be managed is larger (consisting of all those provided by the programming language);

- The temporary or permanent objects must appear homogeneous to the compiler or interpreter;

- The capabilities of the manager of the programming language heap (held in main memory) must be extended so that it can access database objects held on disk. In order to do this, the garbage collection control principle must be extended according to the rule: 'No object that can be reached from identifiers that are still visible must be collected'.

These principles are implemented in systems with two levels of addressing and representation: one for main memory and one for the disk. We have chosen two systems from this category which are particularly representative: the PS-algol object manager and the LOOM system which is responsible for managing the objects in Smalltalk.

11.5.1 The PS-algol object manager

11.5.1.1 General principles

When any database is opened, in order to handle persistence, an access is given to a specific object which is the root of the database. This object is copied to the local heap and associated with a pointer type local variable. This object contains pointers to the other objects in the database. PS-algol uses a strategy of incremental loading/storage during program execution (in contrast to persistent Lisp or Prolog where the heap is copied at the end of execution). This incremental strategy means that two separate heaps must be managed, one on disk and one in main memory, as must two types of address. The existence and the interaction of these two types of address is central to the system and all the operations it carries out.

We can classify the PS-algol persistence management model in the category of data models that use a space with two addresses. This describes the fact that the method itself takes responsibility for moving the objects from one space to another, by dint of which the objects acquire multiple forms of addresses. When an object is in secondary memory, its external address is its *persistent identifier*, called a **pid**. When the object is stored in main memory, its address is said to be local, denoting the fact that the validity of that address is localized in time and space, inside the specific machine and the process where it was created. This address is called the *local number*, written **Lon**. Depending on the PS-algol implementation, the **Lon** may be a direct address in main memory or an index in a table of objects residing in memory, the entries in the table being the objects' real addresses (a case of indirect addressing). In the rest of our discussion we will assume indirect addressing.

The representation of an object o can contain pointers to other objects, and vice versa. In order to avoid confusion, henceforth we call the first case the *pointer fields* of o and the second case the *references* to o.

During program execution, when an object is in secondary memory all its pointer fields are **pid**s. When an object is in main memory, its pointer fields may be **pid**s or **Lon**s. For objects in main memory, one of whose pointer fields is a **pid**, a problem occurs when the program wants to do something with the object pointed at by this field. A special operation called *de-referencing* is then executed, in which normal program execution is diverted to a dedicated sequence responsible for converting persistent identifiers into local addresses. The execution of this de-referencing operation is the responsibility of the POMS (Persistent Object Management System) kernel, whose role is to execute the following algorithm schematically:

De-reference the **pid** of object o
  if o is not in memory
      then load o at address a
      else look for local address a of o
  replace the **pid** of o by a

Using this de-referencing technique, objects are only brought into main memory when they are required. However, this operation requires knowledge of the objects present in memory. In order to find out if an object is already in main memory and at what address, a table of the objects in memory is used. The characteristics of this table are described below and Figure 11.8 illustrates the principle.

To see whether o is in memory, the system keeps a table of the correspondences between **pid**s and **Lon**s, in both directions. This table of *resident objects* is called the PIDLAM (Persistent IDentifier to Local Address Map).

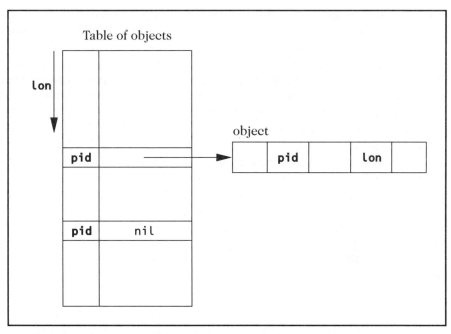

Figure 11.8 The PS-algol table of resident objects

Any object brought from secondary memory onto the heap in main memory has a corresponding entry in the PIDLAM and there are two symmetric partial functions provided for consulting the PIDLAM:

- loca-of-**pid**(**int pid**) → **int** ;

- **pid**-of-loca(**int lon**) → **int**.

The first function returns the **pid**'s local address if the object o is already in main memory and the value nil if not, whereas the second returns the **pid** of an object o whose local address is known. The logical structure of PIDLAM can be seen as a table with double entries; each entry corresponds to one of the two arguments of the two functions. The rank of an entry in the table corresponds to the object's indirect address or to its **lon**. An entry in the table is always a pair made up of an object's real address in main memory and its **pid**. These two functions are implemented using data structures that use hashed access and direct access respectively. The hashing function is applied to a **pid** and returns an entry in the table. This hashing table is managed in the traditional way. Let us briefly recall the principle involved.

When you know an object's **pid** and you want to find out if it is present in the table, you apply the hashing function to the **pid** and it returns an entry in the table. If the corresponding entry contains an identical **pid** value, the object has been found, if not you go through the list of collisions until you find the object or until you reach the end of the list, in which case the object is not in memory. The process used to create an entry in the table is similar: you start with the **pid** and you apply the hashing function which returns an entry. If the corresponding entry in the table is empty, you put the **pid** into that space, if not you look for the first empty space by going through the list of collisions. An entry in the table is created immediately an object is brought from disk into main memory.

At any given moment, the table contains an image of all the objects present in main memory and of those that were in main memory at a certain instant or must be brought from disk. These last two cases correspond to those of objects that are not in main memory, but whose entries must still be retained to preserve the consistency of the references. The real address corresponding to these entries is then the nil address. The justification for this situation is compatible with the algorithm described above.

In the next sections we will describe the algorithms that control the movement of data items from secondary memory to main memory (during de-referencing) and vice versa.

11.5.1.2 Transfer from secondary memory to main memory

When an object *o* is transferred from secondary memory, its pointer fields are all **pid**s. Two strategies can be used to convert the **pid**s into **lon**s. The first consists of not converting any of them and waiting until the system needs the value of a pointer field. A de-referencing operation must then be executed. The second systematically converts the pointer fields to local addresses on loading. This latter situation implies executing the transfer operation recursively and can, in the worst possible case, mean transferring the whole database.

If the pointer field is a **pid**, when an instruction attempts to access one of the pointer fields of *o*, the instruction is diverted. If the pointer field is found in the PIDLAM the instruction's pointer is replaced by the corresponding **lon** found in the PIDLAM and the instruction continues. If the object has to be loaded, the object is brought onto the heap in main memory, the PIDLAM table is updated, the instruction's pointer is replaced by the corresponding **lon** and the instruction continues.

In the second strategy, when an object *o* is transferred from disk onto the heap, all its pointers are automatically translated into **lon**s. The following algorithm gives the sequence of operations carried out when an object is transferred from secondary memory to main memory.

```
forany object x related to the pointer field cx of o do
    begin (*Note that cx is a pid*)
        if x is in the PIDLAM
        (*the PIDLAM contains the pid of x and the corresponding lon*)
```

```
        then replace the cx in o by the lon of x = loca-of-pid(cx)
        else
        allocate a new lon l to x
        (*next index in the PIDLAM*)
        enter the correspondence lon l ↔ pid cx in the PIDLAM
        set the corresponding entry to nil
        replace cx in o by l
    endif
end
```

In this strategy, the objects to be brought from disk are anticipated, and an entry is prepared for them in the PIDLAM. When an object is de-referenced, the fact that it is not in main memory is indicated by its entry which contains the nil value. It must then be found on disk, using the **pid**, and allocated a place in main memory. The corresponding entry must then be modified by replacing the nil value with the object's address in memory.

11.5.1.3 Transfer from main memory to secondary memory

When an object o is transferred to secondary memory, its pointer fields are gone through, to replace any **lon**s by **pid**s, before it is written to disk. This operation is activated in two cases: at the end of a transaction, because all modifications must be saved to disk, or when main memory is full and space needs to be released. We will not explain how the objects to be transferred to disk are selected here; this is the role of garbage collection. If o is the object to be transferred to disk, the following algorithm can be applied:

```
begin
    forany object x related to the pointer field cx of o do
        begin
            if cx is a lon then
                if cx is a lon in the PIDLAM (*object from disk*)
                    then (*there is a corresponding pid*)
                        replace cx by pid-of-loca(cx)
                    else (*an object created during the session*)
                        allocate a new pid p to x
                        enter p in the PIDLAM
                        enter p in secondary memory's index of objects
                        replace cx in o with the pid p
            endif
        endif
        endfor
    write o
    set the entry for o in the PIDLAM to nil
end
```

We can make the following comments about this algorithm:

- The pointer fields of object *o* that are **Lon**s are converted into **pid**s.

- It is during the execution of this algorithm that you find out if an object should persist: if *o* references a temporary object then that object is converted into a persistent object.

- At the end of the procedure **nil** is written into the corresponding entry in the PIDLAM. When object *o* is transferred to disk the corresponding entry is left in the PIDLAM. Only the area relating to the real local address is set to **nil** (absent from memory).

- Because all the references to object *o* pass indirectly via the **Lon**s in the PIDLAM, it is not necessary to go through all the objects in memory to update the object pointers. If an object *o'* references object *o* which has just been transferred to disk, the link from *o'* to *o* is not cut, the reference from *o'* to *o* still exists in the PIDLAM.

11.5.1.4 Locating objects on disk

In the first implementation of PS-algol, the location of objects on disk was the responsibility of the POMS module, using the object's internal identifier. This system uses some of the techniques of the systems previously described. However, it has an interesting feature, which is incremental allocation of physical space.

An object is located according to its internal identifier, using a **pid** structured in the following way: a **pid** is made up of three fields. The first field is 1 bit with the value 1, meaning that it is a disk address. The second field represents an offset, and the third field, called LBN, represents the logical block number. The object is identified in the block by an offset which locates the start of the object's position.

The memory management system performs three successive transformations before locating the object:

- correspondence from **pid** → logical block number and offset;
- logical block number (LBN) → relative block number (RBN);
- relative block number → physical block number.

The first transformation is needed in order to allocate a new **pid** to a new object. This allocation is done using additional information, in particular the object's class, so that objects of the same kind can be clustered in the same block or consecutive blocks. The second transformation is performed to ensure the security (or more properly the atomicity) of transactions according to the duplicate pages technique. During a transaction, changes made to an object are not reflected onto the initial relative block corresponding to the logical block but onto an new relative block. The old and the new relative blocks are swapped over at the end of the transaction. Usually, when managing a duplicate pages mechanism, a direct correspondence can be established between the logical block and the physical block. Here, there is a third transformation whose sole justification seems to be dynamic and incremental management of physical space. The database is divided into physical areas whose size increases by powers of 2.

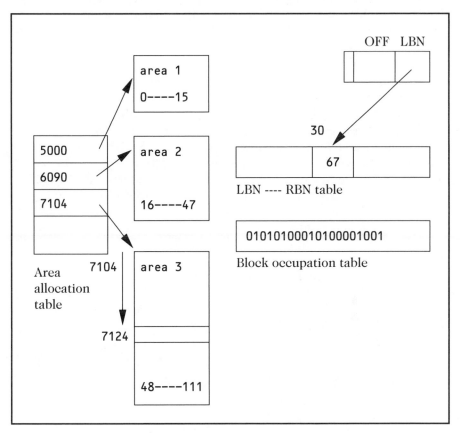

Figure 11.9 Locating an object using its **pid**

Figure 11.9 summarizes the main parts and shows how an object whose **pid** contains the logical block number 30 is located. The LBN → RBN table provides the relative block number. In order to determine the physical block number, the area allocation table must be used. The system manages 12 physical areas numbered z1, z2, ..., z12. The size of area zj is 2^{3+j}. Thus the first area can contain the relative blocks from 0 to 15 and starts at the physical block whose address is 5000, **area 2**: from 16 to 47 starts at 6090, **area 3**: from 48 to 111 starts at 7104, and so on.

If logical block 30 corresponds to relative block 67, it is in **area 3** with an offset of 20 from the area start address. The area start address is given by the area allocation table, from which its physical location, 7124 = 7104 + 20, is derived. In the figure, we have not indicated that the table of correspondences between LBN and RBN and the relative block occupation table are duplicated to ensure physical data security.

Finally, we must mention the fact that management of these tables is incremental, in so far as their lengths are proportionate to the amount of physical space actually used. On creation of the database, their length is 16, because the physical space is initialized with 16 blocks; when it is full, an additional area twice as large is allocated, multiplying the length of the tables by 2.

With this solution, the total number of objects that can be addressed depends on the number of bits reserved for coding the offset and those reserved for coding the blocks. If the offset area is coded in i bits, then a maximum of 2^i objects can be addressed per block. There are then $32 - i$ bits left for coding the blocks. But the number of objects that can actually be contained in a block depends on their average size. When objects are of different lengths, it is very difficult to find the right average. If the objects are small a large offset area is needed, in order to address all the objects, and there is less space for addressing the blocks. Conversely, when objects are large, the number per block is small and a larger area for blocks is needed. This type of difficulty is well known. In order to remedy it and allow for a mixture of large and small objects, the designers of PS-algol proposed another solution.

The physical database is divided into segments, each of which corresponds to a type of object. Each segment is subdivided into partitions, each of which is a set of blocks. The **pid** is coded using the partition number and an object number inside the partition. Persistent objects are addressed in several stages using a table that records the correspondences between the partitions and the segments, as shown in Figure 11.10, according to the following procedure:

1. The persistent address is split into two parts, a partition number and an object number in the partition.

2. The table of the correspondences between the partitions and the segments is indexed on the partition number. Thus accesses are to information about the segment's address and the number of the first object in the partition.

3. The object number in the partition is added to the number of the first object in the partition in order to obtain the rank of the object in the segment's addressing space.

4. Inside a segment, objects are located using an index.

In this section, we have described, in order, the main points of the PS-algol system used to ensure data persistence. We have particularly stressed the management of duplicate addresses and the problems of conversion when an object migrates from disk space to main memory, and vice versa. This identifier conversion aspect is the crucial point for system performance. The basic principle is similar for the system that we are now going to describe. The main differences are a summary of an object can exist in memory without the whole object being present and that objects that have become redundant are eliminated by a reference counter technique.

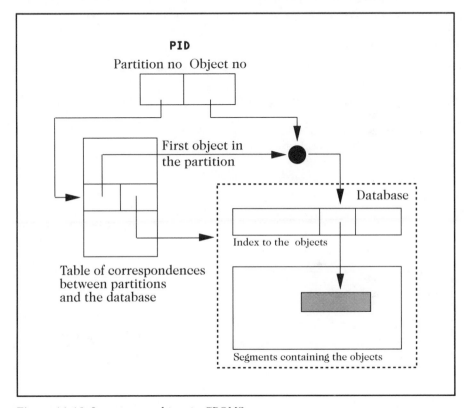

Figure 11.10 Locating an object in CPOMS

11.5.2 The virtual object: from OOZE to LOOM

The successive implementations of Smalltalk have caused its designers to implement mechanisms that manage objects in main and secondary memory. Whether it be in the OOZE system, associated with Smalltalk-76, or in LOOM, associated with Smalltalk-80, the idea is the same. It is to create a *virtual memory of objects*. The technique, in such a mechanism, is identical to a paging system. Objects are transferred from disk to main memory according to need, and if an object is not already present in main memory there is an object missing. In the two systems the basic principle is the same. The difference between OOZE and LOOM is the number of objects managed, 2^{15} for the first and 2^{31} for the second. This basic principle is illustrated by Figure 11.11 which refers to the OOZE system.

The objects in memory have an identity, which is an identifier coded in 16 bits. The objects resident in main memory are recorded in a table called the *resident object table*. An entry in the table contains the real address in memory of the corresponding object. The correspondence between the persistent identifier (**pid**) and an entry is established by a hashing function. In order to find an object o using its **pid** identifier, the system applies the following algorithm:

```
Looking for an object o
    Calculate index = f(pid)
    found = false
    while o not found do
            if table[index] contains pid
                then
                    found = not found
                    note the address of o
                else take the next index
                    % there is a collisions list %
    Go and find o on the disk
```

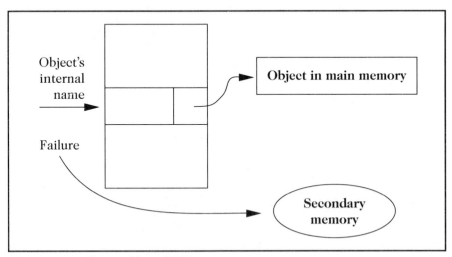

Figure 11.11 Object table in OOZE

This algorithm corresponds to the following steps:

1. Apply the hashing function to the identifier. Check that the entry (index) in the table obtained corresponds to the correct identifier;

2. if yes, follow the pointer to locate the object in memory;

3. if not, look for any collision that may have taken place due to the hashing function and repeat until you succeed or fail;

4. if you fail, the object is not in main memory and you will have to look for it on the disk.

When an object is loaded into main memory, an entry is created in the table. Conversely, when an object is removed from main memory, because there is not enough room, that object disappears from the table. This hashing function is used frequently and performance depends to a large extent on how the function is installed. In OOZE, the function is microcoded and a dedicated architecture has even been suggested. The main weakness of the system is the small number of objects managed. The solution proposed for LOOM remedies this major disadvantage.

The main idea in LOOM is to have two addressing spaces: the main memory space in which identifiers are 16 bits long and the disk space in which identifiers are 32 bits long. This means that a large storage space is available on disk and the objects are handled normally in main memory. The same object is identified by two different names depending on the storage space, there is a *short identifier* and a *long identifier*. As in OOZE, the central element is the table of objects resident in main memory. This is what establishes the correspondence between short identifiers and long identifiers. Figure 11.12 illustrates the main components of the system.

An entry in the table is indexed by the value of a short identifier. It contains information about the reference counter, the nature of the entry (this bit is set to 0 or 1 and is used to indicate whether the corresponding object has been modified in memory) and the object's address in main memory. The normal structure of an object in memory is an *object header* and an *object body*, made up of various fields; some of these fields contain atomic values and others identifiers. The header contains the value of the object's long identifier, the length of the object and a field called *delta* linked to managing the reference counter. The object body includes the object's class and its fields.

When an object is transferred from disk to main memory two main problems arise: the assignment of a short identifier and the conversion of the fields containing the long identifiers. In the case of the first problem, a hashing function on the long identifier is used to obtain the short identifier (always assuming there is no collision on the corresponding entry). The same hashing function is used to find out if an object is present in main memory, using its long identifier. If there is a collision, the fact that the long identifier is present in the object's header means that you can differentiate between entries. In the case of the second problem, the long identifiers have to be converted into short identifiers. The principle of the algorithm described in Section 11.5.1.2 for PS-algol remains valid. If the object referenced by the identifier is already in memory, it is allocated the corresponding short identifier. For those that are not in memory, the object can be replaced either by a *leaf object* or by an *empty object*.

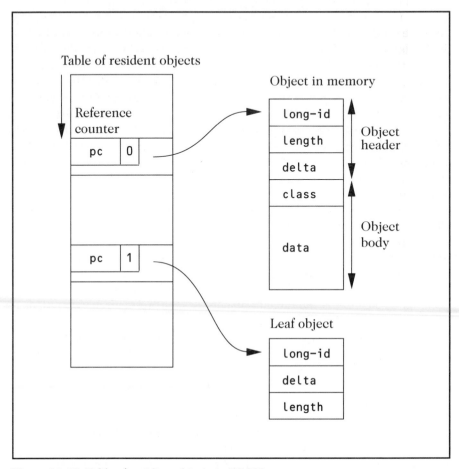

Figure 11.12 Table of resident objects in LOOM

A leaf object is an incomplete object that represents an object in secondary memory. It has a short identifier which corresponds to the result of applying the hashing function to the long identifier, an entry in the object table and a memory representation limited to the header. As long as there is no need to handle the data related to the object, these leaves can be manipulated like real objects. They can be referenced by other objects and you can send them messages.

An empty object corresponds to the case when the object has been totally withdrawn from memory but retains its entry in the object table. In this case, its identifier is replaced by a null reference. This technique is used to save time and space when the transfer occurs, but if you need the value of the corresponding field you will have to read from the disk later.

The decision as to whether to create a leaf object or an empty object is a difficult one and all you have to go on are statistics on the objects accessed. We met a similar problem in the PS-algol system.

The table of resident objects tends to fill up pretty quickly. Therefore, it must be purged of all the useless objects. A *garbage collection process* must be implemented. In LOOM this process is based on an algorithmic principle linked to the *reference counter*. An object's reference counter is a field associated with the object that indicates the number of times that object is referenced by other objects. When the value of an object's reference counter reaches zero, that object is no longer referenced and therefore the space taken up by that object can be recovered. Because of the double addressing, two reference counters are involved: a primary counter (pc) associated with main memory and a secondary counter (sc) associated with secondary memory. The global counter (c) is the sum of pc and sc. However, every time an object's long identifier is converted into a short identifier (the object is then in main memory), pc must be increased by 1 and sc diminished by 1. But to diminish sc by 1, you have to write to secondary memory. In order to avoid this operation, a special field called delta, in the header of the object in main memory, is used to record the changes to sc from the moment the object is loaded into main memory. The global counter c is then equal to pc + sc + delta. Figure 11.13 shows the roles of the three different counters for the same object. The object is referenced by three objects in main memory (pc = 3). It was referenced by six objects in secondary memory (sc = 6), but as delta equals −2, two objects have been transferred to main memory.

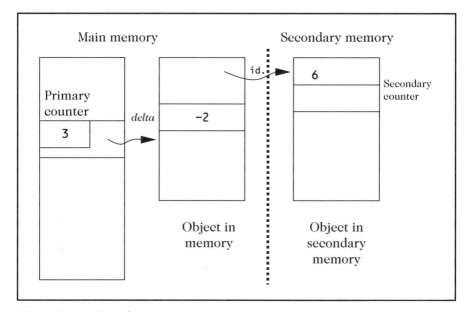

Figure 11.13 The reference counters

The reference counters change in precise circumstances: when a leaf is expanded to a full object, when an object is contracted to a leaf, assignment or de-assignment of an object. When a leaf in expanded to a full object, the object's fields containing long identifiers are converted to short identifiers. For each of the converted objects, the pc counter is increased by 1 and delta decreased by 1. When an object is contracted to a leaf the reverse applies. Assignments and de-assignments can only take place in main memory, therefore only the primary counter is changed. During an assignment operation the counter is increased by 1, during a de-assignment it is decreased by 1.

If an object's primary counter reaches zero, the global counter is calculated. If the global counter equals zero, the object is no longer referenced and it can therefore disappear. If this is not the case, the object is still referenced by objects in secondary memory; it can therefore be withdrawn from main memory but must be preserved in secondary memory. In this latter case, it must be written to secondary memory from its image in main memory. In order to avoid unnecessary writes, a bit in the object's header is set to 0 or 1 to indicate whether the object has been modified or not. This bit is shown in Figure 11.2 for each entry in the table of resident objects. Thus, by quickly going through the table of resident objects you can decide which objects' space in main memory can be recovered.

Up till now, the situation described corresponds to that of objects that exist in secondary memory. During program execution, the Smalltalk interpreter has to create numerous temporary objects. These temporary objects must not be saved to disk. The solution used is to create an object in the object table and to consider it as a persistent object, the only difference being that it does not have a long identifier in its representation. A problem arises when a temporary object has to be converted into a permanent object, because the system must allocate it a long identifier corresponding to its place on the disk and there is not necessarily a correspondence between the value returned when the hashing function is applied to the long identifier and the value of the short identifier. In order to resolve this problem an indirection block is used, as shown in Figure 11.14. The old entry for the temporary object is preserved, using a forward pointer to the new entry. The initial object body is preserved but it is associated with the new entry and the header contains the long identifier allocated by the system.

The designers of LOOM have chosen a complicated architecture: double addressing space with data conversion between main memory and secondary memory, reference counters managed on two levels and the use of follow pointers in both main and secondary memory. The reasons for this choice are as follows. If you compare this solution with a solution that uses paged memory, you will notice that the execution process only uses the resources it needs. A paging mechanism brings a whole page into main memory when only one object is needed. In LOOM, main memory is only used by referenced objects. Measurements have shown that performance depends on the degree of object clustering. If the objects are very dispersed, a paging or virtual memory system tends to collapse under the same conditions.

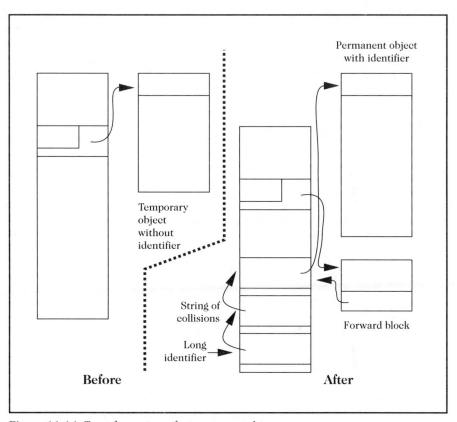

Figure 11.14 Transformation of a temporary object

11.6 Distributed architecture

Figure 11.1, at the start of this chapter, showed the main components in the architecture of database software packages. We indicated that this break-down assumed no hypotheses about the distribution of functions in the case of a distributed machine environment. Database applications are evolving at the same speed as the computing power of terminals. Nowadays, workstations with large central memories and a large amount of computing power are being used in place of traditional terminals. It is these workstations that have made possible the development of the new applications which have emerged from the computer-aided design field (VLSI design, document design, engineering applications, CASE, and so on). Generally, these workstations do not provide significant data storage capacities. Therefore, there must be a dedicated unit for permanently storing data: *the server*. The various hardware configurations encountered are shown in Figure 11.15.

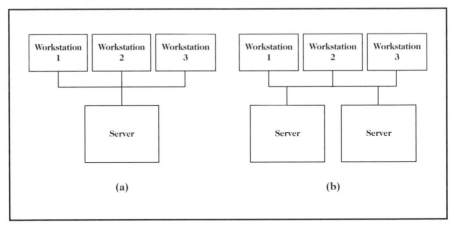

Figure 11.15 Single-server and multi-server configurations

Figure 11.15(a) shows a single-server configuration, whereas Figure 11.15(b) shows a multi-server configuration. Although some systems are studying operating system kernels for multi-server distributed architectures, these have not yet been used in object-oriented database systems. The first systems have used a single-server configuration. Even in a simplified environment, the choices between architectures and the problems that arise are numerous. How do you distribute the functions between the workstation and the server? How do you distribute task execution? How do you provide transaction management? The purpose of this section is to described the main solutions presently in use. Object-oriented systems differ profoundly from relational systems. In the case of a relational system, the breakdown between the application program and the server could probably be done by isolating the sequences of accesses expressed in an SQL language block in the application program, transmitting the request to the server, executing the request on the server and returning the reply.

That solution is not possible in the case of an object-oriented language because the processing statement is encapsulated in the methods and these methods are computational logical units. On the one hand, relational processes are by nature associative and processors are optimized to handle select and join operations. On the other, even if some object-oriented processes are similar to relational ones, a large part of the processing consists of navigating around the database.

At present, there are two main classes of servers in use in the prototypes and products: *object servers* and *page servers*. In object servers, both the workstation and the server understand the notion of an object and the transfer unit between them is an object. In page servers, only the workstation understands the notion of an object and the transfer unit is the page. The O_2 and Orion prototypes and the first versions of Gemstone use object servers, whereas the Encore/ObServer and Exodus prototypes and the new versions of Gemstone and O_2 have adopted page servers.

11.6.1 Object servers

In an architecture with object servers, some of the functions in Figure 11.1 are duplicated on the workstation and the server, as shown in Figure 11.16. When the application program on the workstation needs an object, the search starts in the workstation's object cache. If it fails, the server is asked for the object. The server starts by examining its object cache, then the page frames and, as a last resort, it accesses the disk.

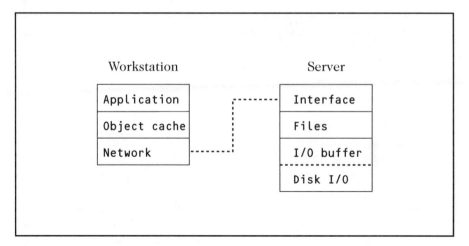

Figure 11.16 Object server architecture

11.6.2 Page servers

In the page server, the unit for transfers between the workstation and the server is the page. Only the workstation can integrate and understand the mechanisms linked to object management. Figure 11.17 shows the distribution of functions between the server and the workstation.

Even though we mentioned the fact that a workstation can have a page cache and an object cache, the object cache is not vital. If there is an object cache, only the objects used by the application program are copied from the pages to the cache. When an object is updated in memory, it must be copied back to the page that contained it in the first place, and that page is not necessarily present in the page cache when the copy has to be made.

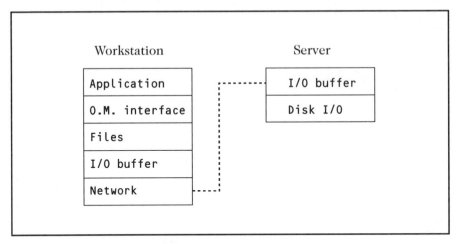

Figure 11.17 Page server architecture

11.6.3 Advantages and disadvantages

To evaluate the advantages and disadvantages of these two architectures you must take the following criteria into account: the number of messages on the network, the distribution of processes between the server and the workstation, the effects on transaction management, the amount of copying and the complexity of the software.

If you consider the fact that on average an object is much smaller than a page (a page contains several objects), the mechanism for transferring objects between the server and the workstation will be invoked much more often in an object server architecture than in a page server architecture. However, the cost of sending a message on a network is not proportionate to the length of the character string transmitted; the costs of sending a 100-byte object and a 4 Kbyte page are roughly the same. Furthermore, if clustering strategies have placed objects that are frequently accessed together on the same page, transferring objects between the server and the workstation wastes all the advantages because they are transferred one by one. Transferring pages is consistent with the clustering mechanism's role and reduces the number of transfers.

One of the main advantages of the object server architecture is to make the workstation and the server fulfil symmetrical roles. In particular, as the server has all the functions for interpreting objects, it can execute the methods, thus relieving the workstation of certain tasks. This aspect is particularly interesting when a method that involves a large number of objects on the server has to be executed. If that method was executed on the workstation it would necessitate the transfer of all the objects from the server to the workstation. This phenomenon is well known in distributed architectures. It is sometimes preferable to transfer processing to the data rather than the other way round. Even if the principle seems simple, the migration of processes from the workstation to the server causes problems in cases where the execution contexts on the workstation and the server are not consistent. An example will help us understand this problem. Let us assume that the processing consists of selecting all the historic buildings whose entrance fee is less than 25F. At the time when this processing is invoked it could happen that new historic buildings have recently been created on the workstation and the server has not yet recorded them. There are two possible solutions for resolving this problem. In the first solution, the processing is executed on the server but the execution context (that is, the new historic buildings) is also transferred. In the second solution, the processing is done in parallel on the server and the workstation and the conflicts are resolved afterwards. Whichever solution is used, the migration of processing is a complicated mechanism in a database environment, and in particular for transaction management and fault recovery. In conclusion, the advantage gained by the distribution of processing is strongly counterbalanced by the technical difficulty of implementing it.

Another advantage the object server has over the page server is that the object server knows exactly what objects are used by the application programs on different workstations. All uses are known centrally. This is a distinct advantage for transaction management. If a locking mechanism is used to allow concurrent transactions, locks can be put on objects and the server knows about them all. In the case of a page server, it is difficult to achieve finer granularity than the page. Locking a page implies limiting concurrent accesses to that page by two workstations that want to access two different objects located on that page.

In an object server, the amount of copying is high. When an application program asks for an object, that object has gone through several layers of software, starting from the disk: first the object is copied into the server's pages frame, then into the server's object cache, then it is taken by the transfer mechanism and copied into the workstation's object cache. In such an architecture there can be up to four successive copies.

With a page server, there is one less copy because the server does not have an object cache. Furthermore, techniques that combine the object cache and the page cache can be implemented on the workstation.

The last important aspect is the evolution of the technology. Workstations are becoming more and more powerful, and therefore they can carry out increasingly complex processing. On the other hand, network technology is also evolving, allowing faster transfers. Nevertheless, the cost of initializing a message transfer will remain high in relation to the transmission time. The combination of these factors seems to indicate that it would be better to carry out even the most complicated tasks on the workstation itself, even if a large volume of data has to be transferred. Therefore this last factor mitigates in favour of the page server.

11.6.4 An example of a distributed architecture

The Encore/ObServer system is an object-oriented system with a server/ workstation type of architecture. The system is divided into two main modules: Encore and ObServer. Encore supports an object-oriented data model. It is responsible for managing the data types and interpreting the language. The ObServer module is the object manager. These two modules communicate according to the principles of client–server tasks by using remote procedure calls. Each client has a copy of the Encore module, responsible for managing the types (as well as its application). ObServer is responsible for managing the storage units during transfer between the server's secondary memory space and a main memory space shared with Encore. It is this object storage and location aspect that we will describe below.

The object storage mechanism takes the hierarchy of composition and the inheritance hierarchy into account. Each object has a unique identifier. Each time an object is accessed, the object's header contains the references to its various components. These constitute a list of pairs in the form (t, p) where t represents the component's type and p is a reference to the component's value. If the components are stored contiguously, p is an offset inside the object. If not, p is an access reference in the server's addressing space. In fact, all these can be considered to be identifiers, the only difference being that certain identifiers correspond to real objects and are interpreted by the language's modules whereas the others are simply access identifiers for the object manager. The object representation adopted by Encore allows data organization to be adapted to the needs of the processes.

Furthermore, ObServer provides an additional facility for improving performance: the clustering of objects in the segments. A segment is the unit for transfers between secondary and main memory. Its size can vary. Encore provides its own file management system, so that it can guarantee that data will be stored contiguously, because Unix does not guarantee the contiguity of pages in a segment. When a client receives a segment, all the objects are copied into a table of objects present in memory and the segment is released. The segment is therefore a one-way communication unit between the server and the workstation. Each client can have their own copy of the same segment.

After these general remarks, we will now discuss the mechanisms in ObServer for accessing objects. Remember that for ObServer an object identifier does not necessarily correspond to a real object but may in certain cases correspond to objects' components. Be that as it may, all these items are referenced by an identifier. ObServer distinguishes between two

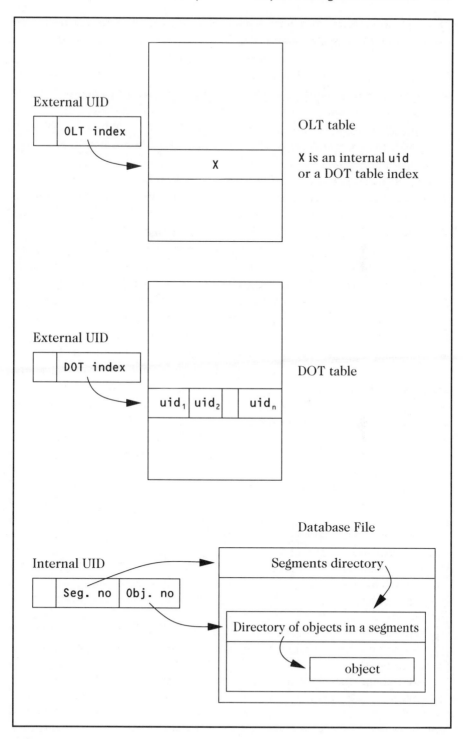

Figure 11.18 Locating objects

types of identifiers: *external identifiers* and *internal identifiers*. The external identifier is a constant which refers to an object in the database. When this identifier is de-referenced you obtain an internal reference which is used by the system to locate the object. The two types of identifier are coded in the same number of bytes. However, an external identifier may correspond to several internal identifiers. This is due to the fact that the system can manage several copies of the same object. When an object is destroyed, the external identifier is not reused but then refers to an empty object.

The correspondences between the external identifiers and the internal identifiers are managed by tables in the following way. The system maintains three tables: the OLT (Object Location Table), the DOT (Duplicate Object Table) and the DBF (Data Base File) as shown in Figure 11.18.

An external identifier is made up of a code and an indice. The code indicates whether the identifier is external or internal and the index corresponds to the entry in the OLT. The corresponding entry contains either an internal identifier or a duplicate object identifier. A duplicate object identifier is made up of a code and an entry in the duplicate object table. The corresponding entry is a set of internal identifiers. An internal identifier is a triplet made up of a code, a segment number and the index for an entry in the segments table. The index corresponds to an object in the segment involved. Figure 11.19 gives a global description of the database; it contains the directory of segments, the directory of objects for each segment and the objects themselves.

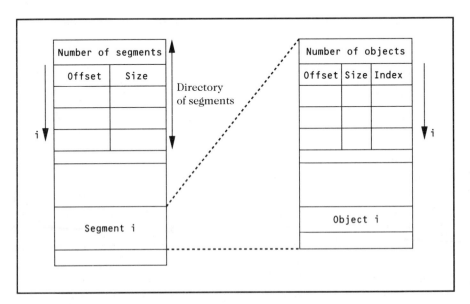

Figure 11.19 Structure of a segment

The directory of segments includes the total number of segments and a table in which each entry corresponds to a segment. An entry includes the size of the segment and an offset in relation to the start of the database. For any given segment, the index of the entry in the table is an identification number which does not change over time.

A segment is organized in a similar way. A segment's directory of objects contains a table used for locating the objects. Each entry in the table contains an offset or a reference to the object, the size of the object and an index field. For the object involved, this index field corresponds exactly to the object's index in the OLT. This field was introduced to facilitate updates when objects are moved.

When a segment is transferred from secondary memory to main memory, a segment table is managed in main memory for each client. This table is used when you want to access a duplicate object. An internal identifier, corresponding to a segment present in this table, will be chosen from the list of internal identifiers.

The architecture of Encore/ObServer clearly illustrates the distribution of functions between the workstations and the server. The server is not capable of interpreting objects. It is only used to manage the strings of characters referenced by an identifier.

Bibliographical notes

In the past few years many efforts have been made to improve database technology. In this chapter, we do not pretend to have presented a complete and exhaustive view of the subject, we simply wished to describe the major changes. In order to understand this subject it is useful to have some knowledge of the basic mechanisms used in operating systems. To acquire this you should refer to the book by Krakowiak ([Kra85]) and a work on the Unix system ([Tan89]).

Essentially, we have concentrated on two points: the global architecture of the object manager and addressing mechanisms with one level or two levels, independently of the representation of objects. The breakdown of the object manager into layers is completely conventional and can be found in several abstracts of technical reports or reviews ([Man89], [Car87b]) and [Sto90]. The distribution of tasks between workstations and servers is an architecture proposed for several systems. The discussion about page servers and object servers comes from work done on the O_2 system ([DFMV90]). In addressing mechanisms, the representation of object identity is the key element. The analysis of the different ways of representing identity is that proposed by [KC86].

The study of addressing mechanisms in databases is a crucial problem for performance. On the one hand, databases have emphasized data structures adapted to disk management and placed restrictions on the size of records and the representation of data items. On the other, programming languages have proposed more complex representations and exploit virtual memory mechanisms to the full, in order to manage the data in main memory. Numerous systems have been designed to resolve this dysfunction. Basically, there are two ways: a single level of representation and addressing or two levels of representation, one for the disk and one for main memory.

The idea of having a single level of addressing probably goes back to the time when the Multics system was being developed ([BCD72]). As we have already said, one of the first uses of the concept of virtual memory for managing permanent data (disk space) was in the Socrate system ([Abr72]). The extension of this mechanism for both permanent and temporary data was made possible by the mechanism for allocating secondary memory in a transaction's virtual addressing space ([ABB*86], [Tev87]). This is the idea that was used in the Bubba ([CFW90], [BAC*90]), Cricket ([SZ90b]) and Mneme ([MS88], [Mos89]) projects. This procedure is different from that which database designers have favoured in the past, where they themselves managed the input/output buffers and the disk space. Discussion about the problems arising from the use of virtual memory can be found in [Sto81], [Tra82], [Sto82], [Tha86] and [Epp89].

Another solution, for a single level of representation, is to have a representation in main memory which is analogous to that on disk and to provide mechanisms that encapsulate the table of resident objects and give access to cursors for navigating around the objects at main memory level. Systems such as AIM ([KDG87]), Damokles ([DLG87]), DASDBS ([PSS*87], [SPSW90]), Exodus ([CDRS86]) and Prima ([HMMS87]) have favoured this approach.

In solutions built on two levels of representation, the data items from disk are converted into a suitable form when they arrive in main memory. This technique seems to have been first introduced by M. Atkinson for the persistent language PS-algol ([ACC81], [ACC83], [CAC*84], [Bro89]). It is also used extensively in Smalltalk implementations ([KK83], [BS83a], [Kae86]). Such systems have been built for persistent programming languages. The study [Mos90] compares the advantages and disadvantages of format conversion and evaluates performance.

Generally, the solutions retained for persistent programming languages do not take into account the management of complex objects in the way it is implemented by object managers for object-oriented database systems. Systems such as E ([RC89]), O_2 ([VBD89]), Orion ([KBB*88], [KGBW90], ODE [AG89]), Encore-ObServer ([SZR86], [HZ87]) and Trellis/Owl ([OBS86]) use disk representation with two levels of representation extensively.

Exercises

1. The new applications, such as CAD, fundamentally change the problems of implementing a database system. What differences are there

between the way a traditional management application interacted with a relational DBMS and the way these new applications interact with an object-oriented system?

2.   Object-oriented managers can be divided into three categories. Name them and give a brief summary of their characteristics.

3.   There are two main types of addressing mechanism used in the new database systems. What is the difference between them and what are their relative advantages and disadvantages?

4.   Describe the six ways that object identity has been implemented and comment on them.

5.   The Virtual Space mechanism used in Socrate is not very adaptable to schema modifications. Why is this? Could you propose modifications and improvements to the space allocation mechanism for schema modification?

6.   What is the function of the PIDLAM in PS-algol?

7.   In PS-algol, when an object is brought into main memory, two strategies can be applied for converting references. What are they and what are their relative disadvantages?

8.   The LOOM system, used in Smalltalk, implements two special types of objects called leaf objects and empty objects. Describe them and their uses.

9.   Explain the difference between object servers and page servers and why new versions of Gemstone and O_2 have migrated to the latter.

10. How is the correspondence between internal and external identifiers managed in ObServer?

12

Data management

Only the set of recipes that always work should be called science.
All the rest is literature.
Paul Valéry
Moral sayings

In the preceding chapter, we were mainly interested in the system's general architecture and main components. We emphasized the interaction between the highest layer of the system (the language) and data access. As we have often remarked, the data manipulated by the new database systems is complex. This means that an object's components may vary in length. Similarly a component may be repeated several times. A complex object is, by nature, an object with a variable length which may exceed the size of a page. The purpose of this chapter is to study data structures and the problems arising from data management with the aim of installing secure, reliable and efficient systems in secondary memory. The problems discussed are:

- Representing different structures;
- Managing very large objects;
- Managing instances of a class;
- Indexing;
- Clustering objects in secondary memory;

- Managing transactions;
- Managing versions.

We will concentrate, in particular, on the first four points, which call for the implementation of original techniques. As far as the last three are concerned, we will limit ourselves to giving a detailed bibliography.

12.1 Data representation

We have seen that in all the various type systems that are used there are two main basic constructors: the set which is used to model collections of data items of the same type, and the tuple which is used to model records with names of attributes. We also frequently found arrays and lists, but the problems they cause are similar to the ones we will describe for sets. We must be able to combine the set and tuple constructors in a random manner. For example, a restaurant can be modelled by a tuple made up of a name, an address, which is a tuple in its own right, and a set of menus; those menus could be tuples made up of the name of a dish and a price.

The description given below of the problem of data representation is not specific to a particular system but applies to a large range of systems. It is equally applicable to the object-oriented models and to the extensions of the relational model, such as the NF2 models described in Chapter 7, for example.

12.1.1 The normalized representation of a structure

In order to study the different forms of representation, we will use a variation on an example already given in the previous chapter. Let us consider the structure of an object in the Restaurant class which is made up of a name, an address, which is itself made up of a road and a town (the town attribute refers to an object in the Town class), and of a menu, which is a set. The menu is a set of dishes. The wine list is modelled by a set of tuples composed of the wine's name, vintage and price.

```
class Restaurant type [
                   name : string(12)
                   address : [
                              road : string(12)
                              town : Town ]
                   dayclosed: string(8)
                   menu: { [
                         name : string(12)
                         price : integer
                         dishes : { string(12) } ] } }
```

```
wines: { [
              name : string(12)
              vintage : integer
              price : integer ] } ]

class Historic_building type [
              name : string(12)
              town : Town
              entrancefee : integer ]

class Town type [
              name: string(12)
              county: string(12) ]
```

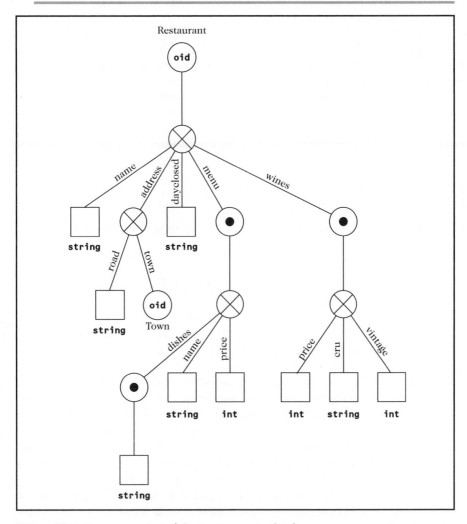

Figure 12.1 Representation of the Restaurant class' type

If you define the structure of the objects in this way, you can then represent the **Restaurant** class' type as a labelled graph (*see* Figure 12.1). This graphic representation uses two types of node. The round nodes designate either a tuple ($\otimes$) or a set ($\odot$). The square nodes designate the atomic types: integers, reals and character strings. The objects are represented by a circle containing the **oid** symbol labelled with the name of the corresponding class.

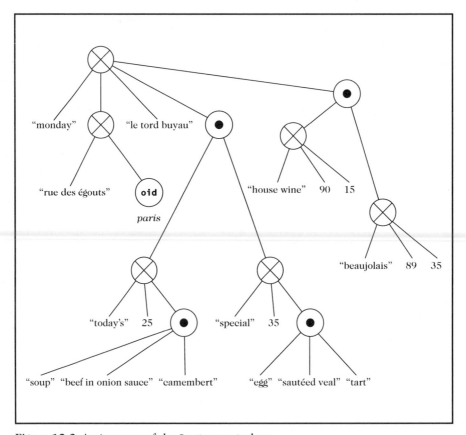

Figure 12.2 An instance of the **Restaurant** class

Figure 12.2 gives a possible instance of an object in the **Restaurant** class. Only the leaves of the tree structure bear information in this figure. Notice that the character string **paris** designates the object's identifier and not its value.

Starting from this representation, you can obtain a *normalized* representation of the object by carrying out a simple transformation. All you have to do is decide on how to implement a tuple and a set. In the case of the tuple, you can opt for an array whose dimensions are equal to the number of attributes, each element containing an internal link to the value of the attribute. For example, the address attribute corresponds to the second element in the array and the link does not point directly to the address' value but to another tuple structure which is used to find the value. There are numerous possible options for implementing the set structure which have all been used to a greater or lesser extent in database systems. We can distinguish three main classes of solutions: arrays of pointers, lists and relational. The array of pointers is a structure which contains an entry for each element in the set. There are many possible variations of implementations based on the list concept: open or closed lists; with chaining in one or both directions; with the elements in the list ordered or unordered, the order being defined on a value. In the relational implementation, as many logical records are constructed as there are elements in the set. Each record is made up of two values, the first identifying the origin of the set and the second identifying an element in the set. Even though this relational implementation is possible, we will not discuss it further because it does not allow direct access to the data.

Figure 12.3 shows a normalized representation of the instance in Figure 12.2, in which the sets are represented as arrays of pointers. A representation is said to be *normalized* if all the data is in the leaves and the other nodes only contain information about the structure and the links.

We can make the following remarks about this representation:

- It corresponds to a maximum level of fragmentation of the structure because each data item can be located independently. This means it provides greater adaptability and possibilities of change when values are updated. However, too great a level of fragmentation is prejudicial to the representation of the data on disk in so far as the different parts of the structure may be distributed in different physical records. For this reason we are going to consider transformations that will decrease the number of fragments and allow us to take other characteristics, such as the size of objects, into account. Therefore, a normalized representation can be used in main memory but cannot be easily accepted in secondary memory.

- In Figure 12.3, we made no hypotheses about the nature of the links between the structure's components. We can consider there to be two types of links: internal links and external links. Generally, the links can be physical addresses, indirect addresses or object identifiers. In the cases of indirect addresses or object identifiers we must create an intermediate directory for translating them. Furthermore, the links can be *internal* or *external*. An internal link can only be interpreted inside a given environment. Thus, the internal links between the different components of a restaurant could only be interpreted locally to that restaurant. On the other hand, the link to a town is an external link. It corresponds to an object identifier and its scope is global within the database. If two types of links are used then there must be a way of differentiating between them, and consequently a different coding must be implemented for each type.

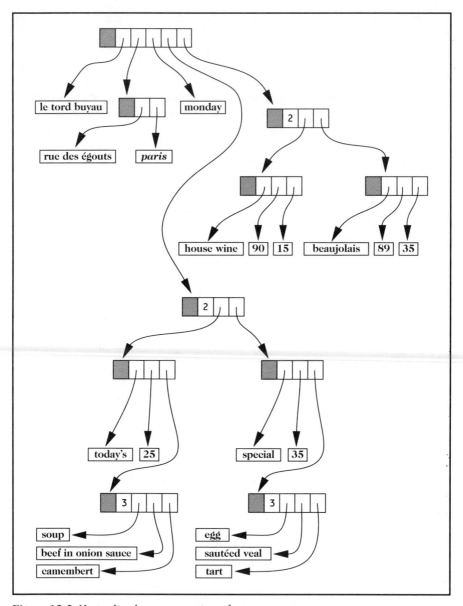

Figure 12.3 Normalized representation of a restaurant

So as to prevent too great a fragmentation of a structure, we must look at ways of bringing back all or some of the data from the leaves to the root. If the representation is such that all the data is at the root, then we have a *flat* or *linear* representation. The possibility of ending up with that result depends upon what decisions are made about the representations of very long strings and sets. Figure 12.4 shows a linear representation of a restaurant.

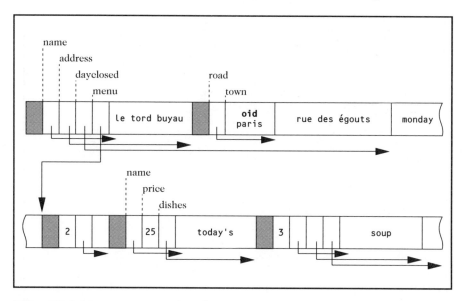

Figure 12.4 Linear representation of a restaurant

The main disadvantage of this representation is that the total length of an object can exceed the length of a page. As a page is the input/output unit, it is important to be able to contain all the data in a set of pages and to find the correct division. One solution that can be used to achieve this is to define two types of objects: *short objects* whose length is less than a page and *long objects* whose size is greater than a page.

Notice that if all the atomic representations are of the same length and the sizes of all the sets are predefined in the database's schema, the linear representation is exactly equivalent to the representation of Socrate's virtual space, seen in the preceding chapter. In this case, every data item has a predetermined place in the virtual space and projection onto the disk space is relatively simple. This solution cannot be applied when certain values are very long or subject to frequent modifications (of size or number of elements).

12.1.2 Calculating the length of an object

The length is calculated by evaluating a recursive function length(n). This function operates on the tree structure representation of an object and assumes the existence of the following functions: the child (n) function returns all the child nodes of a node; the type(n) function returns the type of the node (atom, tuple, set); the header_length function returns the header's length according to the node's type; the function atom_length returns an atom's length according to its type.

```
Function length(n):=
   if type(n) = atom
      then return atom_length(n) + header_length(type(n))
      else
         total_length:= header_length(type(n))
         for all p in child(n) do
            if length(p) > page_size
               then total_length:= total_length + id_size
               else total_length:= total_length + length(p)
            endif
         endfor
   endif
   return total_length
```

This algorithm uses a parameter, id_size, which represents the length of the identifier which is used to locate a long object. The algorithm's principle is to progressively calculate a node's size starting from the leaves of the tree structure. When a node's size reaches the length of a page, its linear representation is replaced by an identifier which points to the representation of a long object.

12.1.3 Representing short and long objects

Depending on their types, short objects are represented in the following ways:

- The tuples are made up of three parts: the header, the fixed-length part and the variable-length part. The tuple's header structure contains information about its type, its total length and the presence of optional attributes, in the form of a bit list. The fixed-length part is made up of entries related to each attribute. The value of an atomic fixed-length attribute is stored here. The value of a variable-length attribute is referred to by an offset and a length. The variable-length part is handled as a linear representation, as long as the total length of this area is shorter than a page. If not, this area is replaced by an indirection pointer to a space that contains the long objects. This space is handled in an independent way.

- The sets are structured in an identical way to the tuples. The header contains the type of the elements in the set, its total length and its cardinality. Then there is a list of offsets, one for each element.

- A fixed-length atom is represented in its basic form. A variable-length atom (a character string, for example) is represented by its length followed by its value.

The long objects are managed in a different way. All the long objects are grouped together in a file. Each long object has a long object identifier. These identifiers are used for accessing the long objects catalogue. Each entry in the catalogue gives the long object's type and additional indications about accessing its components. The basic types have the following representations:

- A long tuple is represented by a sequence whose elements have different lengths.

- A long set is implemented as a B-tree. The B-tree is used as the access structure to the elements in the set. If the elements are objects, their identifiers are used as the key for constructing the B-tree; if the elements are tuple type values, the value of an attribute can be used as a key; in other cases the elements' internal numbers are used as the key. If one of the elements in the set is itself a long object, the data area will contain the long object identifier.

- A long atom is represented by a *sequence* of elements of the same length. The elements in the sequence can be accessed by number. For example, a character string will be represented by a sequence whose elements' length is 1.

The system for representing long objects and short objects can be thought of as a two-level system. The first level allows you to access short objects, whereas the second allows you to access long objects via the intermediary of an additional catalogue. If we compare this procedure with the linear representation, given in the previous section, the latter could well be implemented on a set of contiguous or chained pages (this distinction depends on the strategy for allocating pages on the disk). In that case, part of the data could only be accessed by going through it sequentially. With the two level representation, we can access certain parts of an object efficiently because they are clustered on a page. Access to the very large parts is done in an independent way, using an indexed structure. This structure can be used, when needed, to locate the part that interests the application program.

Figure 12.5 shows a representation of this two-level system. Compare this with Figure 12.4 and notice the changes that have taken place between these two modes of representation. This figure illustrates the notions that have just been described. We have indicated the nature of the different areas: the header, the fixed-length part and the variable-length part. Furthermore, we assumed that there were two long attributes: the restaurant's name and the set of menus. The values of these attributes are accessed by an indirection pointer with a long object identifier. The name attribute is organized as a sequence of characters, whereas the menu attribute is organized as a B-tree whose key is the menu's name.

The length of an object may be changed during updates. If the object is an atomic object the transformation is easy. In the case of a set, the representation may have to be changed from an array of pointers to a B-tree.

When a short object is converted to a long object the area corresponding to the old representation is replaced by a long object identifier. The question of the inverse transformation, when the size of an object decreases, also arises. These conversion operations are naturally costly. Therefore, it is desirable to avoid too frequent structural changes where an object is transformed back and forth from one representation to another. Generally, therefore, once an object is in the long form it does not change back to the short form.

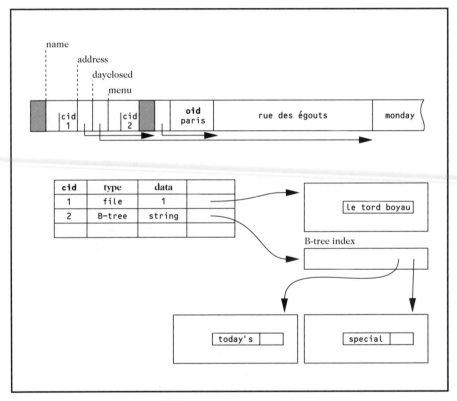

Figure 12.5 Representation of a long object

12.2 Large sets and long strings

In the preceding section, we saw that once an object's size exceeds that of a page we have to implement specific mechanisms. This is why the first database systems were mainly designed to manipulate fields whose length could not exceed 256 bytes. It is only recently that several extensions have been proposed for managing fields whose length can reach several megabytes, or even several gigabytes. The long fields are necessary if databases are to be capable of supporting the new applications. These applications handle data items (such as images or texts) that come in the form of very long character strings. Similarly, the explicit introduction of a set constructor obliges system designers to foresee cases where the cardinality of those sets could reach several million elements.

The problem of storing large volumes of data existed well before database systems. File management systems were designed to satisfy this need. A system like Unix allows users to manage variable-length files by randomly assigning them 512-byte pages. Other file management systems are designed to manage a set of records according to a given organizational method: sequential, direct or indexed. These largely depend (for a fixed type of operation) on the technical choices that have been made. For example, sequential reading of a file is much faster if the pages are consecutive rather than distributed at random on the disk.

Therefore, the simplest idea for handling very long fields in a database system is to use the facilities provided by the file management system. Each long field in the database is seen as a file. Even if it is conceptually possible, this solution has re-entry aspects that considerably limit its efficiency. The data units of a database are themselves managed using the file management system. If one of those data units contains a long field, the file management system would have to be re-invoked. Therefore, it is preferable to provide specific mechanisms for handling long fields. This type of solution has been implemented in several systems. Among these, we can mention the extensions to SQL for System-R and the Starburst project, the WiSS file management system used in the Exodus project and the extensions to Ingres.

The choice of a technical solution must take the following three aspects into account:

- Reading or writing a long field must be similar to reading or writing a simple value from the point of view of the application. In other words, the fact that the field is spread over several pages of the disk must be transparent to the application program.

- You must be able to execute specific operations, such as reading, writing or updating, on all or part of a long field, and also concatenate two fields.

- The disk pages used for managing long fields must not be selected randomly, if you want good performance, and above all too great a fragmentation of data must be avoided.

The basic idea, which has been used in most of the systems, is to see a long field as an uninterpreted sequence of characters. The field's header is a B-tree whose keys are the positions in the sequence, each leaf corresponding to a page containing part of the data. Figure 12.6 shows an example of a long field.

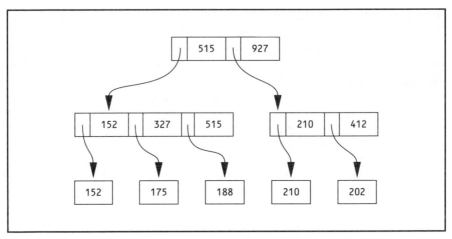

Figure 12.6 Representation of a long field

The root of the tree is made up of pairs (address, key); the address is a pointer to the child node or to a leaf, and the key gives the maximum position in the chain stored in the subtree related to that pointer. The B-tree's root contains the sequence of keys [515, 927]. This means that the first subtree contains the first 515 characters and the second subtree contains the rest of the long field. These keys represent offsets related to the higher level. For example, the character in position 100 in the rightmost leaf corresponds to an offset of 210 + 100 = 310 in relation to the second subtree, and an absolute offset of 515 + 310 = 825.

Let us remember that in a B-tree, if k designates the parameter associated with a node, the root of the tree contains between 2 and $2k + 1$ pairs, and an internal node between k and $2k + 1$ pairs. The loading rate of the leaves is between 0.5 and 1.0. You can easily see, looking at these parameters, that very long objects can be handled. Let us assume that the pointer and the key are each 4 bytes long and that a page is 4096 bytes long. Thus, an internal node can contain a maximum of 512 pairs. With a one-level tree we can therefore reference a maximum of 512 pages, which is about 2 megabytes. With two levels in the tree we can reference a maximum of 262 144 pages, or about 10 gigabytes of data.

The operations associated with this structure are:

- Read n bytes starting from position d.
- Insert n bytes starting from position d.
- Add n bytes to the end.
- Delete n bytes starting from position d.

The algorithms used for these operations are variations on the algorithms for B-trees. However, they differ in several aspects. In the read operation, you not only search for position d, you also read n bytes starting from that position. Similarly for the insert operation, you insert not just one element but a sequence of elements. Consequently, if the sequence cannot be contained in the leaf that corresponds to position d, all the keys related to the borders between the pages necessary for storing the additional bytes must be inserted into the tree. This amounts to inserting a set of keys, not just one key. For the deletion operation, several keys may be globally deleted, which means the tree has to be reorganized. Below, we give the algorithm for a read; you can write the others as an exercise if you wish.

Read algorithm

We will use a to designate the address and c to designate the key in a pair. A node is a sequence of pairs $(a[i], c[i])$ where $i \in [1, 2k + 1]$.

```
start:= d; page:= root; read page;
while page is not a leaf do
    save page number on a stack;
    look for i such that c[i-1] < i ≤ c [i];
    save i on the stack;
    start:= start - c[i-1], page:= a[i];
    read page;
byte d is the start position in the page
traverse the B-tree using the stack to get the n bytes
```

This representation of a long field can easily be adapted in order to handle a set of elements with a large cardinality. The first solution is to see the set as a sequence of bytes, which is the same as the case we have just discussed. Another solution is to assume that each element can be identified either by a key or by an identifier. You then construct a B-tree on that key. This solution is based on the principle that we want to read n bytes from a given position. If this hypothesis is true and the only operations envisaged are reading the complete structure and adding to the end of the object (a write is an addition), the B-tree construction is no longer necessary. Then the critical problem is the allocation of pages so that reading and adding operations are as efficient as possible. On the one hand, it is desirable that the object is distributed over the smallest possible number of contiguous pages and on the other, that disk fragmentation is minimized. Such solutions have been studied, but they are outside the context of this work.

The problems we have described in these last two sections on representational modes for structured data items and the management of large data items are not independent from the problem of object clustering. The aims of clustering techniques involve the way data items are organized on disk and ways of placing an object's components as close as possible to the object itself. In Section 12.5, we will give some indications of the techniques used to cluster objects, mainly in the form of a bibliography.

12.3 **Representing inheritance**

We have just studied the problem of representing data items from the points of view of object structure and size. There is another aspect of the problem of representation, that of the inheritance relationship between classes. When objects are created the class in which they are created is specified. This indication is used by the system to associate the structure corresponding to that class with the object. Also, the inheritance relation indicates the possible specializations of that class. As we saw in Chapter 9, the inheritance relation is not interpreted in the same way in different systems. For some of them, instances of a class are all objects of that class which have been explicitly created. For others, they are all the instances of that class plus the instances of the subclasses. In this section we will discuss the problem of organizing data items so that all the instances of a class can be efficiently accessed, independently of the interpretation of the inheritance relation.

We will use an example to discuss this problem. Figure 12.7 shows an inheritance graph for the classes Where-to-go, Restaurant, Historic_building, Museum and Historic_restaurant. The Historic_restaurant class inherits from the Restaurant and Historic_building classes.

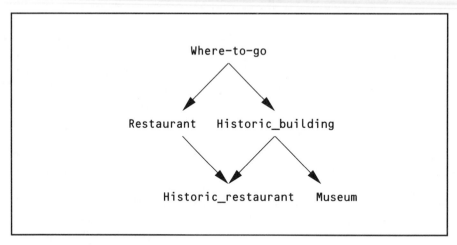

Figure 12.7 Inheritance graph

The tables in Figure 12.8 show a set of instances. Even though we have not defined the structure of each class, you can easily construct it from that table. The instances are grouped according to the class they belong to. Each class has a tuple structure and the attributes all have atomic types. In the table, the first column indicates the object's identifier. When an attribute is not defined for a class, the corresponding space is left blank. The day attribute indicates the closing day of a restaurant. Similarly the date attribute gives the date a historic building was built, whereas the arts attribute gives the museum's speciality. The other attributes are easily understood.

Class	oid	name	town	day	cookery	...
	001	la concorde	paris			...
Where_to_go	002	moulin rouge	paris			...
Restaurant	003	flo	paris	2	alsatian	...
	004	eiffel	paris			...
Historic_building	005	arc-triomphe	paris			...
	006	louvre	paris			...
Museum	007	orsay	paris			...
	008	picasso	paris			...
Historic-restaurant	009	coupole	paris	1	trad.	...
	010	grand vefour	paris	1	modern	...

Class	oid	...	date	arts	to-see
	001	...			
Where_to_go	002	...			
Restaurant	003	...			
	004	...	1890		
Historic_building	005	...	1810		
	006	...	1635	painting chinese art	
Museum	007	...	1915	painting photos	
	008	...	1700	painting	
	009	...	1935		painting
Historic_restaurant	010	...	1799		decor

Figure 12.8 Some instances of classes. (For editing purposes, this table has been broken into two parts to represent all the attributes.)

The distribution of data items in the storage space is in some ways analogous to the clustering problem (which we will look at later) in so far as we try to cluster the objects in the same class in the same storage units or in neighbouring units. Here, we will examine the effect of the inheritance relation on the distribution of objects.

We will discuss four main modes of organizing the storage space:

- Unordered (or universal) with or without class extension.
- According to a horizontal division.
- According to a vertical division.
- According to the AOV[1] technique.

In all of these modes, we will assume that the object has an identifier which can be used by one of the techniques discussed in the previous chapter in order to access it. Furthermore, it is normal to assume that each object has a header where the identifier, the object's type and information useful for storage, such as its length, are recorded.

12.3.1 Unordered organization

In the unordered mode, all the objects are put into the same unit, whatever their class. This assumes that the storage space can handle variable-length objects, as is the case for present-day systems. The data items are stored in the form of a single array of values constructed from all the attributes. The array has an entry for each attribute in the class, and as many rows as there are objects. When an attribute is not defined for an instance of a class, the corresponding value does not exist and a null value must be inserted.

12.3.2 Horizontal division

In a horizontal division, an object is placed in the file for the class to which it belongs. Figure 12.9 shows an illustration of this organization. For the same reason as previously mentioned, if you create an object in the Historic_restaurant class that object is also an instance of all the super-classes of the Historic_restaurant class. You can then decide either to create another copy of the values of attributes that exist in the superclasses or to build an extension. If you duplicate the data in the various classes, access to the data relating to a class will be easier. On the other hand, any updates will have to be propagated to all the copies. If the data is not duplicated, you have to go through all a class' subclasses in order to find the information relating to that class. The table in Figure 12.10 contains the objects in the Where_to_go class in a case where the data is duplicated. You can easily generalize this principle for the other classes.

---

1   A stands for attribute, O for object and V for value.

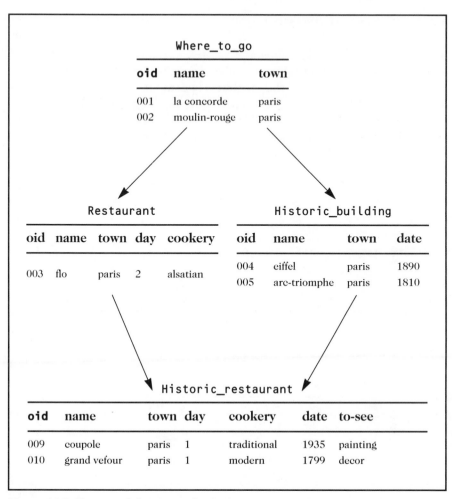

Figure 12.9 Horizontal division without copies

Where_to_go

oid	name	town
001	la concorde	paris
002	moulin rouge	paris
003	flo	paris
...	....	......
009	coupole	paris
010	grand vefour	paris

Figure 12.10 Objects in the Where_to_go class

12.3.3 Vertical division

In vertical division mode the data is fragmented but all the data related to an attribute is preserved. Thus, in each class, the value of the identifier is recorded with the values of the attributes specific to that class. In the case of the `Where_to_go` class, the result is analogous to that illustrated in the table in Figure 12.10. However, the values related to the `Historic_restaurant` and `Historic_building` classes are given in Figures 12.11 and 12.12.

oid	to-see
009	paintings
010	decor

Figure 12.11 Vertical division of historic restaurants

oid	date
004	1890
005	1810
009	1935
010	1810

Figure 12.12 Vertical division of historic buildings

If we assume that the data is stored in the form of relations, all the data related to a class is obtained by doing relational joins on those relations.

12.3.4 AOV

Representation in AOV form is not recent. In the 1970s, it was used in the Tramp and Leap languages in order to code records with different structures in a homogeneous way, which is the precise problem we are trying to resolve. Data is coded in the form of a triplet of values, where the first contains the attribute, the second the object's identifier and the third the value. This method can be seen as being at the intersection between vertical representation and horizontal representation. Each value is referenced by an identifier and an attribute. The table in Figure 12.13 illustrates this form of representation.

This solution was adopted for the implementation of the TAXIS system with the possibility of knowing each object's class and an additional indirection pointer for variable-length values.

oid	attribute	value
001	name	la concorde
001	town	paris
002	name	moulin rouge
002	town	paris
003	name	flo
003	town	paris
003	day	2
003	cookery	alsatian
004	name	eiffel
004	town	paris
004	date	1810
...	....	......
010	name	grand vefour
010	town	paris
010	day	1
010	cookery	modern
010	date	1789
010	to-see	decor

Figure 12.13 A set of objects in AOV representation

12.3.5 Comparisons

Without having analysed these representational modes exhaustively, we can nevertheless draw the following conclusions in terms of space occupied and efficiency of access:

- The space occupied is an indicator linked to the redundancy of data. The horizontal representation method without copies is the least costly. The vertical representation method is more expensive and its cost depends on two factors: the size of the identifier and the depth of the inheritance graph. The identifier is the part that is repeated, and the deeper the inheritance graph the more times it is repeated. The most expensive method is the AOV technique, because both the identifiers and the names of the attributes are repeated.

- The efficiency of access operations is also an essential criterion. It is difficult to judge the effects of a method if you do not know the requirements in advance. Let us assume that the operations are limited to the following: (1) find all the instances of a class, (2) find all the data for a given object, (3) find the value of an object's attribute. In the case of a horizontal representation, the first operation can be carried out efficiently. However, in the case of a vertical representation, you would have to perform the equivalent of several relational joins, if it was a relational implementation. The AOV structure is particularly adapted to the last type of operation.

- In order to speed up accesses to data, database systems use indices. The concept of the index is different in the contexts of object-oriented models and relational models. Even though we look at this problem below, we can already say that horizontal representation without copies is not compatible with indexing. For example, if you want find all the Where-to-go to places starting from Paris, and you construct the index on the Where-to-go table, the reply to the question will be incomplete. In order to get a complete reply, you would have to construct an index on the Where-to-go, Historic_restaurant, Historic_building and Museum classes. These techniques will be described in detail in the next section.

12.4 Indexing

An index is a data structure used to speed up the search for elements that conform to a given criterion. Their use in the optimization of a query language improves performance. The principle is well known: for any query expressed by a user, is there an equivalent expression that costs less in terms of manipulations in main memory and input/output operations? Optimization techniques for relational systems are highly developed and they are mainly based on the use of indices. At present, optimization techniques for object-oriented systems are still being researched. There are two reasons for this. First, the rules for transforming a query into an equivalent expression are much more complex and no one has yet studied an exhaustive set of rules. Also, the models for evaluating access costs will have to be reworked because of the differences from the relational environment. Nevertheless, if we restrict ourselves to very simple situations, we can distinguish between two main classes of strategies that can be applied when searching for objects using their terminal attributes:

1. You consider all the instances of a main class and select those instances, one after the other, in order to examine the values of the class' attributes. This procedure is the equivalent of *forward chaining*.

2. You select the objects that conform to the terminal criteria and then you look for the ones that have them as an attribute value; this is *backward chaining*. Indices help to implement this strategy.

The choice between these two systems, which does not occur in the relational model, is the responsibility of the optimizer. In what follows, we will go over the problems raised above point by point, and then show how they can be resolved.

12.4.1 Problems arising from indexing

The indexing techniques used in relational database systems cannot be directly transposed to object-oriented databases, in spite of the apparent similarities between a class and a relation and an object and a tuple. Each difficulty is caused by one of the aspects of the object model, which we will review in this section.

12.4.1.1 Inheritance and subtyping

We saw that an intuitive way of describing inheritance is to say that objects in a subclass inherit the structure and the behaviour of the objects in the superclass, and can have additional characteristics.

Inheritance limits the comparison between classes and relations. In the relational model, relations are independent of each other, whereas classes are organized into an inheritance hierarchy. In relational systems, building an index on an attribute of a relation is the equivalent of returning, for a value of that attribute, the set of tuples that contain that value. An index built on a class must return the set of corresponding objects not only in that class but also in all the subclasses.

Therefore, the scope of indexing must be extended to the subclasses (*see* Figure 12.7) For example, if we are looking for the Where_to_go places in the town located in department 75, we must examine the restaurants, the historic buildings, the historic restaurants and the museums. An index built on the Restaurant class using the department will be partially redundant *vis-à-vis* an index on the Where_to_go class. Therefore, we can see that searches in an index must be made on two vectors: the class (which gives the range of the index) and the key value of the attribute indexed.

In order to limit the redundancy factor, we can use implementation techniques that take the classes dimension into account. For example, we could partition the instances of the Where_to_go classes into a set of instances that are neither historic buildings nor restaurants, then repeat the process for the restaurants and the historic buildings. Though this solution has the advantage of limiting data redundancy, it fragments an index into sub-indices and searches for a value will have to use several indices.

12.4.1.2 Object composition laws

Objects cannot be perfectly identified with tuples either, because objects are not flat: an attribute's value may just as easily be atomic (**string**, **integer**, **real**, **boolean**) as complex (that is, an object itself or a complex structure). Figure 12.4 shows the composition graph for the Where_to_go class. The town attribute's domain is the Town class. However, the Town class has two atomic attributes: name and dpt (department). Notice that this graph can contain loops, the neighbouring_town attribute for example.

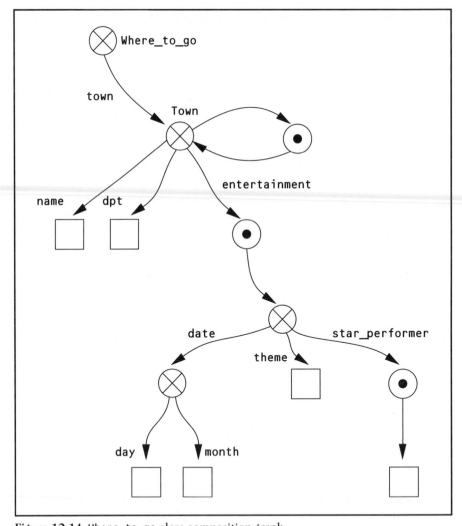

Figure 12.14 Where_to_go class composition graph

An index can be seen as a basic select query: select objects from a class according to a criterion applied to the atomic terminal nodes of the graph.

Relational indexing (corresponding to the first depth level) is badly adapted when the attribute is a complex object. In the object-oriented model, you must index on the attribute composition chain in order to obtain efficient indexing.

There are two strategies for indexing the Where_to_go class on the town's department: link the departments' values directly to the Where_to_go class instance identifiers, or link the departments' values to the towns and the towns to the instances of Where_to_go. The advantages and disadvantages of these two strategies will be looked at later. Subdividing the path throws up the problem of undefined values again, but in a new way: at any point along the path you may come across undefined values, and not just at a terminal node, as in a relational system.

The last important problem is that of sets. The Town class' entertainment attribute is a set of tuples whose star performer attribute is itself a set of character strings. When faced with sets, the solution which consists of fragmenting an index into basic components cannot be used. However, it is possible to design a technique for indexing the Town class using the attribute path: entertainment-*.star_performer-*, where the asterisk indicates that the attributes domain is a set. This index can be used to find the town where a star_performer is performing.

12.4.1.3 Indexing on methods

One of the essential characteristics of object-oriented models is encapsulation: objects can only be manipulated via their interfaces, built out of methods. As we have already seen, a method has a dedicated argument (the receiver of the method) which is an object in the class in which it is defined. It returns an object or a value. For example, let us assume that there is a method, for an object in the Town class, which calculates the area of a town from its radius. The definition of the area method could be written as follows in O_2:

```
add method area: float in Town co2 {
return 3.1415 × (self → radius)^ 2
}
```

You may want to index the objects in the Town class according to their areas. In the same way as a path index is modified when there are updates, an index on a method is modified each time a new town is created or a town's radius is modified.

The case described in the example is simple. Generally, indexing a method is much more complicated. In practice, the body of a method can call other methods and in such a situation it is difficult to know which variables are used in calculating the result. We will not develop this aspect any further because it is still a research area.

12.4.2 Path indices and composite indices

The definitions given in this section are based on the models described in Chapter 7. Given a database schema S for a model with object identity and the associated graph G_S, an *access path* is a path in G_S with the following properties[2]:

1. The path starts at a node that is a class;

2. The path ends at a node that is either a class or an atom;

3. The path does not contain two successive unlabelled arcs, which means that structures such as sets of sets are not allowed.

A path of length n is written $t_0.a_1.a_2...a_n$ where t_0 is the name of the start class, and a_i is the name of an attribute or the symbol $*$ indicating an arc relating to a set. The constraints imposed on the definition of an access path are based on the fact that the path is used for indexing. The path starts with a class because we want to build the index on the set of instances of a class. The path ends with an atom or a class because the index's keys must be simple elements. If the terminal node is a class then the key will be the identifier of an object in that class. If the terminal node is an atom, the key is the atom's value (**integer**, **real**, **string**).

An access path is *mono-valued* if all the arcs in the path are attributes, and *multi-valued* if not. Therefore, an access path can be seen as a mono- or multi-valued function associating the terminal node's values with the instances of the start node. Here are a few examples of access paths: the `Where_to_go . town . name` path is mono-valued and 2 long. The `Where_to_go . town . neighbouring_town . * . neighbouring_town . *` path is 6 long. In this path, the `neighbouring_town` is used twice, meaning that we are looking for the neighbouring towns 2 removed. The `Town . entertainment . * . star_performer. *` path associates a town with the star performers who are performing in an entertainment in that town.

Given that a graph has been built from a schema S, with any path we can associate type expressions that conform to the following relationships:

---

if a_i is an attribute symbol then
$\mathbf{T}(t_{i-1}) = [...., a_i : t_i,....]$ if t_{i-1} is a class
$t_{i-1} = [...., a_i : t_i,....]$ if t_{i-1} is not a class.

if a_i is a set symbol ($*$) then
$\mathbf{T}(t_{i-1}) = \{t_i\}$ if t_{i-1} is a class
$t_{i-1} = \{t_i\}$ if t_{i-1} is not a class.

---

2 Type definitions are those given in Chapter 7 and the **T** application gives a type.

For example, with the `Town . entertainment . * . star_performer . *` path we associate the following types: t_0= `Town`, $\mathrm{T}(t_0)$ = [..., `entertainment` : t_1,..], t_1 = {t_2}, t_2= [..., `star_performer`: t_3,..], t_3 = {t_4}, t_4 = `string`.

So as to reduce the length of access path expressions, we can incorporate the * symbol into the preceding attribute. For the `Town . entertainment . * . star_performer . *` path we get `Town . entertainment-* . star_performer-*`. In this way the `entertainment-*` and `star_performer-* `attributes are attributes whose domain is a set.

A *total instance* of an access path $t_0.a_1.a_2...a_n$ related to an instance I of a schema S is a sequence of non-null elements $< v_0, v_1, ..., v_n >$ such that:

1. for any i, v_i is an instance of type t_i,

2. $v_i = v_{i-1}.a_i$ if a_i is an attribute symbol, or $v_i \in v_{i-1}$ if a_i is the set symbol (*).

Figure 12.15 shows some instances associated with the schema in Figure 12.14. For simplicity's sake, we have not given complete values. We have limited ourselves to those values that are useful for the examples related to the access path.

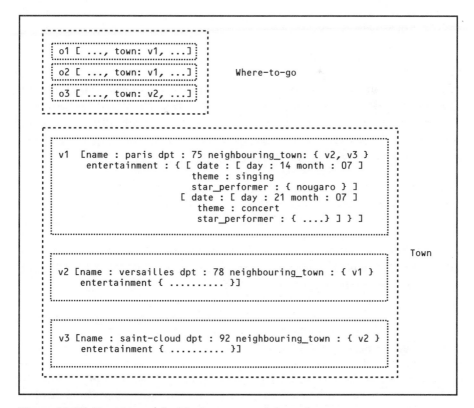

Figure 12.15 Instances of the `Where_to_go` and `Town` classes

For the `Where_to_go . town . entertainment . * . star_performer . *` access path, the following sequence of elements is an instance of the access path:

$v_0 = o1,$

$v_1 = v1,$

$v_2 = \{\ [\ date : [\ day : 14\ month : 07\ ]$

theme : singing `star_performer` : { nougaro }]]

[date : [day : 21 month : 07]

theme : concert `star_performer` : { ....}] },

$v_3 = [\ date : [\ day : 14\ month : 07\ ]$

theme : singing `star_performer` : { nougaro }],

$v_4 = \{\ nougaro\ \},$

$v_5 = nougaro,$

In order to define indices in an object-oriented model we use the concept of an access path extension. The *extension*

$$[\![t_0.a_1.a_2...a_n]\!]$$

of an access path $t_0.a_1.a_2...a_n$ is the set of instances of that path. We can define two types of index using this: composite indices and path indices.

A *composite index* on a path $t_0.a_1.a_2...a_n$ is a multi-valued function, written INC, whose argument is of type t_n (the end of the path) and whose result is of type $\{t_0\}$ (set of the start of path type), that is, its definition is:

$$\text{INC}\ (v_n) = \{v_0 \mid \exists v_1, ..., v_{n-1} < v_0\ v_1, ..., v_n > \in [\![t_0.a_1.a_2...a_n]\!]$$

A *path index* on a path is a multi-valued function, written INH, whose argument is of type t_n (the end of the path) and whose result is a set of instances of the path, that is, its definition is:

$$\text{INH}\ (v_n) = \{< v_0,\ v_i, ..., v_n > \mid\ < v_0\ v_1, ..., v_n > \in [\![t_0.a_1.a_2...a_n]\!]$$

In the case of the `Where_to_go . town . dept` path and for the instances in Figure 12.15, the composite index and the path index take the following values:

INC(75) = { o1, o2 }, INC(78) = { o3 }
INH(75) = { <o1, v1, 75>, <o2, v1, 75> }, INH(78) = { <o3, v2, 78> }.

A composite index only preserves the terminal values of the path, whereas a path index preserves all the values associated with the path. The path index is richer in terms of quantity of information than the composite index. In particular, the path index allows certain queries, which involve the evaluation of predicates on the classes in the path, to be handled efficiently. Let us consider the following query: 'Select the Where_to_go to places in department 75 such that there is at least one entertainment in the town'. If we have a composite index on the Where_to_go . town . dept path we start by finding the Where_to_go places in department 75, and then, using a forward chaining strategy, in each case we search for the town and check whether there is an entertainment. But if we have a path index, we can obtain the towns involved directly by simply looking up the index; all we have to do then, in order to satisfy the query, is to look for the entertainment. A path index is particularly useful when you have nested queries.

12.4.3 Implementing the indices

12.3.4.1 Composite index

The traditional technique for storing an index is to use a B-tree. If the index was built from a class, the elements at the leaf nodes are the identifiers of the objects in the class. The logical structure of a record in the index for a key value must contain all the information about the evaluation of the INC function for that value. This includes: the key value v, the total length of the record, the number of elements and the list of objects related to INC(v). Figure 12.16 illustrates this structure.

key	length of the key	length of the record	number of elements	o1 o2 ..... ok

Figure 12.16 Logical structure of a record

There are several possible solutions to the problem of storing the list $o_1, o_2, ..., o_k$. The simplest is to order them according to the values of the identifiers. Remember, however, that the objects $o_1, o_2, ..., o_k$ are instances of a class, therefore they can also be instances of a subclass. Therefore, it may be useful to fragment the list $o_1, o_2, ..., o_k$ according to the subclasses of the main class. Queries in the form: `select the historic buildings in department 78`, can be handled by using the index on the Where-to-go class with the path `Where_to_go . town . dept`. If the list of objects $o_1, o_2, ..., o_k$ is partitioned into sublists relating to historic buildings, restaurants, historic restaurants and museums, the reply to the query is obtained easily using the index. However, an index on the `Historic_building` class with the path `Historic_building . town . dept` only returns a partial reply to queries in the form `select the Where_to_go places in department 78`.

12.4.3.2 Path index

Let us consider a path index built on the path $t_0. a_1. a_2... a_n$ with the types $t_0, t_1, t_2, ..., t_n$. If the types from t_i to t_k ($i > 0$ and $k < n$) are not classes, the sequence of values $v_i, ..., v_k$ is redundant because v_{i+1} is a component of v_i and so forth. On the other hand, if types $t_0, t_1, t_2, ...t_{n-1}$ are classes, the sequence of values $v_0, v_1, v_2, ..., v_{n-1}$ is solely composed of distinct identifiers. In this way, the sequence can be represented easily. As an exercise, you might like to look for solutions for coding an instance of an access path $< v_0, v_1, v_2, ..., v_{n-1} >$ when some v_i are values and not object identifiers. The structure of a record is given in Figure 12.17. In this figure you can see the list of all the path instances for a given key value that have the same terminal value v_n.

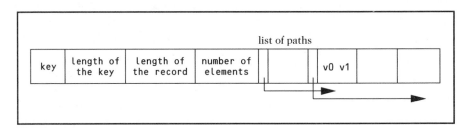

Figure 12.17 Representation of a path index

12.4.3.3 Multi-index

In the sections above, we have seen two techniques for representing composite indices and path indices. There is another solution, which can be applied to both types of index, which is to consider that any path with a length n can be subdivided into paths with a length of 1. In this way, an index is no longer seen as a single structure but as the result of the combination of several indices; this is called a *multi-index*. For example, the `Where_to_go . town . dept` path can be decomposed into two indices: the first index, whose key will be the department value, will return a Town type object; the second index's key will be a `Town` type object and it will return objects of the `Where_to_go` type. The combination of these two indices gives an equivalent result to a composite or path index.

Generally, if we consider an access path $t_0 . a_1 . a_2 ... a_n$ with types t_0, t_1, t_2, ..., t_n, attribute a_i can be interpreted as a function from t_{i-1} to t_i. Building an index for attribute a_i is the same thing as constructing the inverse function from t_i to t_{i-1}.

In cases where the types t_0, t_1, t_2, ..., t_n are classes and t_n is an atomic type, each attribute a_i can be interpreted as a binary relation R_i built on $t_{i-1} \times t_i$. This relation contains the graph of the function from t_{i-1} to t_i. Figure 12.18 shows the values of the two relations R_1 and R_2 for the `Where-to-go . town . dept` path.

R_1		R_2	
Where_to_go	Town	Town	Integer
o1	v1	v1	75
o2	v1	v2	78
o3	v2		

Figure 12.18 Relational representation of a multi-index

If we use ⋈ to denote the product of two relations, the extension of an access path can be built using the equation:

$$[\![t_0 . a_1 . a_2 ... a_n]\!] = R_1 \bowtie ... \bowtie R_n$$

Multi-indices have the advantage of allowing indices to be shared by several access paths. If the user has decided to prioritize the two access paths `Where_to_go . town . dept` and `Where_to_go . town . name`, the index on the `town` attribute can be shared. This solution is an alternative to the ones previously described because the information manipulated by the other two types of index can be found by joining relations. In particular, we saw that a path index is useful when the query involved the evaluation of predicates on the objects in the path. This advantage is not lost with a multi-index because, during the successive combinations, the objects in the intermediate classes are found via the successive joins. Nevertheless, a path or composite index is a data structure where the information is already calculated, whereas with a multi-index the information has to be recalculated every time it is used. A complete discussion of the relative merits and drawbacks of these different types of index is beyond the scope of this book.

12.4.4 Updating an index

The state of a database can be represented by an object graph. In order to simplify the description of this graph, we will assume that all the types in the schema are classes or atomic types. This graph is the instantiation of the database schema graph. The nodes in the graph correspond to the objects and the arcs represent the laws of composition between objects. Therefore, the arcs are labelled by attribute or set symbols. There are four large classes of modifications: creating a node, deleting a node, creating an arc and deleting an arc.

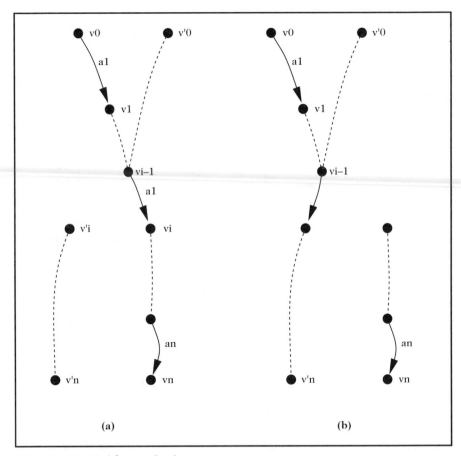

(a)   (b)

Figure 12.19 Modifying a database

The first two modifications have limited implications for indices. They only involve those indices where the access path has length 1 and it is built over the atomic values; traditional solutions are adapted for these. However, the last two modifications have important consequences for composite or path indices. Let us consider the operation that involves replacing the value

v_i of attribute a_i of object v_{i-1} by a new value v'_i, and let us assume that attribute a_i is part of path $t_0. a_1. a_2... a_n$. Graphs (a) and (b) in Figure 12.19 show the state of the database before and after the modification. In the figure, we have represented instance $< v_0, v_1, ..., v_{i-1}, v_i, ..., v_n >$ of the access path in order to show the changes. The deletion of arc (v_{i-1}, v_i) cuts off the paths going from v_0 to v_i, whereas the creation of arc (v_{i-1}, v'_i) re-creates these paths.

We will use the following notations:

- $\delta_C(v_0, v_n)$ is a path from object v_0 to object v_n according to access path $C = t_0. a_1. a_2... a_n$.
- $V_C^+(v_i) = \{v_n \mid v_n : t_n \wedge \delta_{CA}(v_i, v_n)\}$ represents the set of terminal objects of the access path starting from v_i.
- $V_C^-(v_{i-1}) = \{v_0 \mid v_0 : t_0 \wedge \delta_{CA}(v_0, v_{i-1})\}$ represents the set of start objects of the access path to v_{i-1}.

When the access path is implicit, we will used the simplified notations δ, V^+, V^-.

12.4.4.1 Updating a composite index

We defined a composite index as a function that takes a key v_n of type t_n and returns all the objects in class t_0. Therefore, such an index is a binary relation made up of a set of pairs (v_0, v_n). Any basic modification of the database can have consequences for this relation. Adding an arc consists of inserting the pairs $V^-(v_{i-1}) \times V^+(v'_i)$ into the relation. Similarly, deleting an arc (v_{i-1}, v_i) consists of deleting the pairs $V^-(v_{i-1}) \times V^+(v_i)$ from the relation.

Therefore, the execution of the instruction $v_{i-1}.a_i := v'_i$ should carry out two basic operations on the index. Carrying out two successive steps is costly and leads to useless operations. The procedure below describes a much more efficient strategy.

1. Calculate $V^+(v_i)$ and $V^+(v'_i)$.
2. (a) If $V^+(v_i) = V^+(v'_i)$ then no update.
   (b) If $V^+(v_i) \subset V^+(v'_i)$ calculate $\Delta = V^+(v'_i) - V^+(v_i)$ and insert the pairs $V^-(v_{i-1}) \times \Delta$ in the binary relation.
   (c) If $V^+(v_i) \supset V^+(v'_i)$ calculate $\Delta = V^+(v'_i) - V^+(v_i)$ and delete the pairs $V^-(v_{i-1}) \times \Delta$ in the binary relation.
   (d) In all other cases calculate $\Delta_1 = V^+(v'_i) - (V^+(v_i) \cap V^+(v'_i))$ and $\Delta_2 = V^+(v_i) - (V^+(v_i) \cap V^+(v'_i))$, then insert $V^-(v_{i-1}) \times \Delta_1$ and delete $V^-(v_{i-1}) \times \Delta_2$.

This procedure implies the calculation of the set $V^-(v_{i-1})$, that is, traversing the paths by backward chaining. This can only be done cheaply if the inverse references are stored. This is a major inconvenience of using a composite index.

12.4.4.2 Updating a path index

If $< v_0, v_1, ..., v_{i-1}, v_i, ..., v_n >$ is an instance of an access path in which arc (v_{i-1}, v_i) is replaced by (v_{i-1}, v'_i), the update of the path index can be done in the following way:

1. In each key v_n of $V^+(v_i)$ delete the path instances in the form $< v_0, ..., v_{i-1} > .\delta(v_{i-1}, v_n)$ and record the sequence $< v_0, ..., v_{i-1} >$ in the temporary relation S.
2. In each key v'_n of $V^+(v'_i)$ insert the path instances $S(< v_0, ..., v_{i-1} >)$ $< v_{i-1}, v'_i > .\delta(v'_i, v'_n >$.

In the first part of the algorithm, we build a temporary relation S which contains all the sequences in the form $< v_0, ..., v_{i-1} >$ that terminate in v_{i-1}. In the second part, we generate the sequences using this temporary relation. Notice that, in contrast to the procedure for a composite index, no backward chaining operation is necessary; a path index contains all the information about the path and not just the extremities.

12.5 Clustering, transactions and versions

This section describes the main problems arising from three database functions: the clustering of data, transaction management and version management. From the point of view of databases, these functions are not new and the hierarchical, network and relational systems proposed technical solutions. It is useful to survey the direction research is taking in the context of the new database technologies. At present, there have not been sufficient experiments on the models, algorithmic techniques and practical solutions for us to be able to arrive at any concrete conclusions. For this reason, in this part we shall explain the motivations and give the most representative bibliographical references.

12.5.1 Clustering

Data clustering is a technique for placing the data on disk in such a way as to minimize physical disk accesses to the records when processes are executed. The cost of reading records is an important factor in the evaluation of performance. Consequently, any technique that aims to minimize it improves the system's overall performance. A simple example will help us understand this problem. Let us assume that an object is made up of objects o_1, o_2 and o_3. If the three components are in three different records then it takes three disk accesses to read the whole object. A clustering strategy consists of placing the three components in the smallest possible number of records. One factor that limits clustering is object sharing. If an object is shared by several parents, it can only be placed near to one parent, unless it is duplicated near each parent, in which case the consistency of the copies will have to be managed.

M. Scholnick ([Sch77b]) proposed an optimal way of partitioning a hierarchical schema into subschemas for the hierarchical model. The optimization criterion is based on the frequency of data accesses. Similarly, most relational systems now provide the command **cluster** which can be used to cluster several relations' tuples in the same record according to a common attribute value. This technique, allied to the use of a clustering index, makes join operations on relations much more efficient.

Object-oriented databases pose new problems whose origins are analogous to those of the problems described for indexing, that is: objects have complex structures and can be composed of objects; objects are instances of classes and classes are organized according to an inheritance hierarchy; the objects may have very varied lengths. Before looking at the solutions that have been adopted for the new database systems, let us remind ourselves of some of the general principles of clustering algorithms.

The aim of a clustering algorithm is to place objects that are used at the same time as close together on disk as possible. Here is the list of the main problems encountered when designing a clustering algorithm:

- *Static or dynamic clustering.*
  In *static* clustering, the objects are placed when they are created and they are not reorganized when they are updated. *Dynamic* clustering can take place at any time, and the system adapts to the changes. In an environment where write operations are more numerous than read operations, dynamic clustering is much more interesting. The principles of the first dynamic algorithms were proposed by Yu ([Yu74], [YSLT81]).

- *The main types of algorithms.*
  The problem of clustering can be seen as a graph partitioning problem. The nodes of the graph are the objects and the arcs are the references between the objects. This problem is NP-complete ([YCLS85]). This is why heuristic algorithms that look for a quasi-optimal solution are implemented. The general principle is to look at the relative positions of the objects handled during a process. The positions of the objects accessed simultaneously will be brought closer together whereas the others will be moved away, ([Sta84], [SPO89]). The main difficulty with adaptive systems is the stability of the system; too frequent reorganizations decrease performance.

- *Input parameters to the algorithm.*
  The essential parameter is the frequency of accesses to objects. This information must be stored with each object and updated at certain times to take changes in the database into account. This solution can be expensive if there are frequent modifications. One alternative is to record only the frequency of accesses between types of objects. This data is then stored in the types catalogue and not for each object.

Most object-oriented systems have developed a clustering strategy. In Orion ([KBC*88], [KGBW90]), a multi-class segment is a set of pages used to cluster composite objects in the Orion sense of the term. In ObServer ([HZ87]), the objects are clustered in segments. A segment is made up of an object and its sub-objects, as in a hierarchical structure, and can contain all the objects of the same type. In O_2 ([BD90], [Ben90b], [Ben90a]), the concept of a placement tree is used both to define the way in which the components of a complex object are clustered and for clustering the objects in a class in the same segment. This strategy is transparent to the programmer and the *placement trees* can be modified without the programs having to be recompiled. Only the system's lower layers are involved. In the PRIMA project ([HMMS87], [SS89a]), the concept of a *molecule* is the logical unit for clustering of complex objects. In systems such as Cactis ([HK89]) and ODE ([AG89]), clustering techniques have also been implemented. Finally, let us remember that one possible strategy for the clustering of complex objects is structuring them into long objects and short objects, which we described in Section 12.1.3. This description is based on the work of [KCF88]. It also draws on the work of [DPS86] on the physical organization of data carried out at the University of Darmstadt as part of the DASDBS project.

12.5.2 Transaction management

The notion of the transaction was introduced into database systems in order to handle the problems of concurrent data accesses and fault recovery (software or hardware). Numerous systems have been proposed and, during the development phase of relational systems, fundamental results were obtained ([EGLT76], [Gra78]). An important example is the protocol called *two-phase locking*, which is one of the most widely used. A synthesis of the abundant literature on this subject can be found in [Pap86] and [BHG87].

In the hierarchical, network and relational systems, the models describe a transaction as a sequence of reads and writes. Furthermore, a transaction is an atomic unit of processing. This means that its effects are either entirely reflected in the state of the database or not at all. A transaction that executes and terminates normally is *validated*; a transaction that does not terminate is *aborted*. A transaction management system must guarantee the following properties:

- If a transaction is validated, all its effects must be known by other transactions that are executing concurrently.

- If a transaction aborts, no operation carried out by that transaction is known to other transactions.

- If several transactions are executing concurrently, the overall effect is the same as if they were executing *serially*, and if there is a fault the system can be recovered.

With the new database systems the question is to decide whether transaction management should be based on new models. It is obvious that these systems can reuse the technology developed previously and continue to consider a transaction as a set of reads and writes. However, it would be better to go further, that is, to look for a greater degree of concurrent execution by exploiting the information contained in the database schema. In particular, the knowledge about the operations that can be carried out on a particular data type can be used. For example, the operation for inserting an object into a set can be executed concurrently by two transactions both applying that operation to the same set. This is because, according to the semantics of sets, the order of insertion operations is not significant. With a traditional locking mechanism, this would not be possible because there would be a write conflict. The use of abstract data types for defining new transaction management mechanisms has been the subject of several research projects ([Kor83], [SS85], [Wei87], [Her87]).

We saw that object-oriented systems are used in applications that very often include design tasks. In such environments, transactions can last hours, even days. It is unacceptable that a transaction that lasts a long time should block a transaction that lasts a short time. Similarly, if such a transaction is aborted, the work done must not be lost. These facts lead to new problems and, consequently, new directions. Among those being explored let us mention:

- Models with nested transactions ([LMWF88], [BBG89]): a nested transaction corresponds to the subdivision of a transaction into a tree of sub-transactions, each sub-transaction being itself susceptible to subdivision.

- Models with public and private databases ([BKK85]): in this approach, a long transaction can only be executed on a private database, after an exit check from the public database to the private database. In the opposite direction, at the end of the long transaction there is an entry check to the public database.

- Models with versions ([Rot90]): this type of model interacts with the notion of a version in a database. A long transaction is modelled as a sequence of short transactions which act on versions of the database objects. The next section will describe the basic notions concerning the concept of version. As the versions of an object are independent of each other, access conflicts are very rare.

12.5.3 Version management

Non-traditional database applications, like computer-aided design, software engineering or office automation, require that successive states of an object over time are preserved. The set of these states makes up the set of *versions* of an object. These versions can be ordered according to a partial order which expresses the successive derivations of a version and is called the *versions tree*. The interactions between version management, object identity and an object's type are new problems for researchers. In an object-oriented model, an object o can reference an object o'. If the object o has several versions, the reference can be *static* or *dynamic*. A static reference identifies a single version, whereas a dynamic reference is interpreted when the program is executed. A dynamic reference can be interpreted as a query about the set of versions. A related problem is that of the *consistency of versions* and maintaining it through *consistent configurations*.

The models used for describing these concepts are far from being settled. The research is too recent for them to have been sufficiently tried out. Another problem is knowing whether all the versions of the same object are of the same type or derived types. The articles [KL84], [KCB86], [Zdo86] and [Bla90] are among the most interesting propositions.

In the models based on object versions, a phenomenon of daisy-chained version creations occurs when composite objects are implemented. The complexity of this phenomenon, called *percolation*, has been studied ([AJ89], [KL89]), and means for limiting it have been proposed ([KC90]). Another approach is to define versions of the database in place of object versions ([CJ90]). The versions of the database are also created by derivation, but a system of stamps is used to avoid storing redundant versions of an object that already exists in two different versions in the database.

Bibliographical notes

The purpose of the chapter was to show how data management has been modified by the introduction of new concepts. Mainly, we have dealt with four themes: the representation of complex objects, the management of very large objects, the management of instances of a class and indexing.

The idea of representing a complex object using a tree structure is not new and probably goes back to the hierarchical data model. The underlying model is that of labelled trees or trees with values that form a lattice. The use of this lattice with the set and tuple operators is described in [BK86] and an analogous model is expounded in [KV84]. The same principle figures in [AB84] and [AK89]. We showed how a way of physically organizing the data can be derived from this abstract representation. The IMS hierarchical database system ([IBM78]) implemented most of the possible solutions.

Systems with complex objects have proposed different representational modes ([LP83], [DKA*86], [DPS86], [KCB88], [Wei89]). The data representation that mixes short objects and long objects is directly derived from the model in [KCF88].

The management of very long objects and the associated algorithmic technique is taken from that proposed by the Exodus project ([CDRS86]). It is closely related to the ordered relation notion used in Ingres ([Sto83]). These solutions allow indexed accesses to all or part of a long object. In the case of sequential accesses, the technique developed in the context of the Starburst project ([LL89]) is the most appropriate.

Indexing techniques have been widely used in database systems in order to improve access performance and their development was accelerated by the discovery of B-trees by Bayer and McCreight ([BM72], [Com78]).

The indexing model we have described is a synthesis of the work of [BK89] and [KM90]. It can be applied in the context of object-oriented models and in models with complex objects.

Join index techniques have been developed for models with complex objects ([VKC86], [Val87]). The work on Gemstone and Orion was among the first for object-oriented systems. In Gemstone ([MS86]), path indices are implemented as combinations of basic indices, which allows a basic index to be shared by several path indices. The Orion system proposed path indices and composite indices. Comparative studies on these structures were carried out in [KL89].

The use of indices in the optimization techniques for query languages was the basis for most of the heuristics developed for relational systems ([Sel79]). Optimization remains an open question for the new database systems ([KM90], [JWKL90]).

Exercises

1. Show ways in which a tuple and a set can be represented using arrays, pointers and relations.

2. Explain the concept of maximum fragmentation and why this is undesirable.

3. Objects can be divided into short objects and long objects. How do the ways they are represented vary?

4. Describe the B-tree implementation of a long field.

5. Discuss the relative merits of the random, horizontal, vertical and AOV modes of representation.

6. What two aspects of the object-oriented model make indexing such a database different from indexing a relational database and why?

7. How would you distinguish between a composite index and a path index?

8. Describe the principles and advantages of multi-indices.

9. Clustering strategies can be static or dynamic. What is the difference between them?

10. Why are traditional transaction management techniques badly adapted to the new database systems and what solutions have been proposed?

General bibliography

[AB84]   S. Abiteboul and N. Bidoit. Non First Normal Form Relations: an Algebra Allowing Restructuring. *ACM PODS International Conference*, 1984

[AB86]   S. Abiteboul and N. Bidoit. Non First Normal Form Relations: an Algebra Allowing Restructuring. *Journal of Computer and Systems Sciences,* December 1986.

[AB87a]   S. Abiteboul and C. Beeri. On the Power of Languages for the Manipulation of Complex Objects. *International Workshop on Theory and Applications of Nested Relations and Complex Objects,* 1987.

[AB87b]   M. Atkinson and P. Buneman. Types and Persistence in Database programming Languages. *AMC Computing Surveys,* June 1987.

[ABB*86]   M. Accetta, R. Baron, W. Bolosky, D. Golub, R. Rashid, A. Tevanian, and M. Young. Mach: A New Kernel Foundation for Unix Development. *Summer Usenix International Conference,* June 1986.

[Abr72]   J.-R. Abrial. *Projet Socrate.* Technical report, Université de Grenoble, 1972.

[Abr74]   J.-R. Abrial. Data Semantics. *Data Base Management,* 1974.

[ABW86]   K. Apt, H. Blair, and A. Walker. *Towards a Theory of Declarative Knowledge.* Technical report no. RC 11681, IBM Research, 1986.

[ACC81]   M. Atkinson, K. Chisholm, and W. Cockshott. PS-algol: an Algol with a Persistent Heap. *ACM SIGPLAN Notices,* 17(7), July 1981.

[ACC83]   M. Atkinson, K. Chisholm, and W. Cockshott. CMS – A Chunk Management System. *Software Practice and Experience,* 13(3), 1983.

[ACO85]   A. Albano, L. Cardelli, and R. Orsini. Galileo: A Strongly Typed, Interactive Conceptual Language. *ACM Transactions on Database Systems,* 10(2), June 1985.

[AG88]   S. Abiteboul and S. Grumbach. Col: a Logic-Based Language for Complex Objects. *EDBT International Conference,* 1988. ACM Transactions on Database Systems 16 (1), 1991.

[AG89]   R. Agrawal and N. Gehani. ODE, Object Database and Environment: The Language and the Data Model. *ACM SIGMOD International Conference,* June 1989.

[AGVW89]   S. Abiteboul, S. Grumbach, A. Voisard, and E. Waller. An Extensible Rule-based Language with Complex Objects and Data-functions. *DBPL-II Workshop,* June 1989.

[AH87]   S. Abiteboul and R. Hull. IFO: A Formal Semantic Database Model. *ACM Transactions on Database Systems*, 12(4), December 1987.

[AHD90]   T. Andrews, C. Harris, and J. Duhl. *The Ontos Object Database.* Technical report, Ontologic Inc., Burlington, MA, 01803, 1990.

[AJ89]   R. Agrawal and H. Jagadish. On Correctly Configuring Versioned Objects. *VLDB International Conference*, August 1989.

[AK89]   S. Abiteboul and P. Kanellakis. Object Identity as a Query Language Primitive. *ACM SIGMOD International Conference*, June 1989, still to appear in JACM.

[Ari86]   G. Ariav. Temporally Oriented Data Models. *ACM Transactions on Database Systems*, 11(4), December 1986.

[ASL89]   A. Alashqur, S. Su, and H. Lam. OQL: A Query Language for Manipulating Object-Oriented Databases. *VLDB International Conference*, 1989.

[Atk90]   M. Atkinson. Private discussion. February 1990.

[Bac78]   J. Backus. Can Programming be Liberated from the Von Neumann Style? A Functional Style and its Algebra of Programs. *Communications of the ACM*, 21(8), 1978.

[BAC*90]   H. Boral, W. Alexander, L. Clay, G. Copeland, M. Franklin, B. Hart, M. Smith, and P. Valduriez. Prototyping Bubba, A Highly Parallel Database System. *IEEE Transaction on Knowledge and Data Engineering*, 2(1), March 1990.

[Bar90]   G. Barbedette. LispO_2: A Persistent Object-Oriented Lisp. *EDBT International Conference*, March 1990.

[Bar91]   G. Barbedette. *Itinéraire d'un langage orienté-objet persistant*. Doctoral thesis, Université de Paris-Sud, 1991.

[Bat86]   D. Batory. GENESIS: A Project to Develop an Extensible Database Management System. *International Workshop on Object-Oriented Database Systems*, September 1986.

[BBG*88]   D. Batory, J. Barnett, J. Garza, K. Smith, K. Tsukuda, B. Twichell, and T. Wise. GENESIS: An Extensible Database Management System. *IEEE Transactions on Software Engineering*, 14(11), 1988.

[BBG89]   C. Beeri, P. Bernstein, and N. Goodman. A Model for Concurrency in Nested Transaction Systems. *Journal of the ACM*, 36(2), April 1989.

[BCD72]   A. Bensoussan, C. Clingen, and R. Daley. The Multics
           Virtual Memory: Concepts and Design. *Communications of
           the ACM*, 15(5), 1972.

[BCD89]   F. Bancilhon, S. Cluet, and C. Delobel. Query Languages for
           Object-Oriented Database Systems: The O_2 Proposal. *DBPL-
           II Workshop*, June 1989.

[BD90]   V. Benzaken and C. Delobel. Enhancing Performance in a
           Persistent Object Store: Clustering Strategies in O_2. *Inter-
           national Workshop on Persistent Object Systems*, September
           1990.

[BDMN73]   G. Birtwistle, O. Dahl, B. Myhrhaug, and K. Nygaard.
           Simula, Begin. Petrocelli Charter, 1973.

[BDPT90]   P. Borras, A. Doucet, P. Pfeffer, and D. Tallot. OOPE: The O_2
           Programming Environment. January 1990. Unpublished
           report.

[Bee88]   D. Beech. A Foundation for Evolution from Relational to
           Object Databases. *EDBT International Conference*, March
           1988.

[Ben89]   V. Benzaken. Regroupement d'objets sur disque dans un
           système de bases de données orienté-objet. *Cinquièmes
           Journées Bases de données avancées,* September 1989.

[Ben90a]   V. Benzaken. An Evaluation Model for Clustering Strategies
           in the O_2 Object-Oriented Database System. *ICDT
           International Conference*, December 1990.

[Ben90b]   V. Benzaken. *Regroupement d'objets sur disque dans un
           système de bases de données orienté-objet.* Doctoral thesis,
           Université de Paris-Sud, 1990.

[BF79]   P. Buneman and R. Frankel. FQL – A Functional Query
           Language. *ACM SIGMOD International Conference*, May
           1979.

[BFN82]   P. Buneman, R. Frankel, and R. Nikhil. An Implementation
           Technique for Database Query Languages. *ACM Transactions
           on Database Systems*, 7(2), June 1982.

[BHG87]   P. Bernstein, V. Hadzilacos, and N. Goodman. *Concurrency Control and Recovery in Database Systems*. Addison-Wesley, 1987.

[BK86]   F. Bancilhon and S. Khoshafian. A Calculus for Complex Objects. *ACM PODS International Conference*, March 1986.

[BK87]   J. Banerjee and W. Kim. Semantics and Implementation of Schema Evolution in Objects. *ACM SIGMOD International Conference*, 1987.

[BK89]   E. Bertino and W. Kim. Indexing Techniques for Queries on Nested Objects. *IEEE Transaction on Knowledge and Data Engineering*, 1(2), 1989.

[BK90]   C. Beeri and Y. Kornatzky. Algebraic Optimization of Object-Oriented Query Languages. *ICDT International Conference*, December 1990.

[BKK85]   F. Bancilhon, W. Kim, and H. Korth. A Model for CAD Transactions. *VLDB International Conference*, August 1985.

[Bla90]   D. Blakeman. Version and Variant Control for a Commercial Application of Persistence. *Workshop on Persistent Object Systems*, September 1990.

[BLW88]   D. Batory, T. Leung, and T. Wise. Implementation Concepts for an Extensible Data Model and Data Language. *ACM Transactions on Database Systems*, 13(3), 1988.

[BM72]   R. Bayer and McCreight. Organization and Maintenance of Large Order Indexes. *ActaInformatica*, 1, 1972.

[BNR*87]   C. Beeri, S. Naqvi, R. Ramakrishan, O. Schmueli, and S. Tsur. Sets and Negation in a Logic and Database Language (LDL1). *ACM PODS International Conference*, 1987.

[Bor85]   A. Borgida. Features of Languages for the Flexible Handling of Exceptions in Information Systems. *ACM Transactions on Database Systems*, 10(4), December 1985.

[Bro89]   A. Brown. *Persistent Stores*. Technical report no. PPRR-71-89, University of St Andrews and Glasgow, 1989.

[BRS82]   F. Bancilhon, P. Richard, and M. Scholl. On line Processing
             of Compacted Relations. *VLDB International Conference*,
             September 1982.

[BS81]   F. Bancilhon and N. Spyratos. Update Semantics of
             Relational Views. *ACM Transactions on Database Systems*,
             6(4), December 1981.

[BS83a]   S. Ballard and S. Shirron. The Design Implementation of
             VAX/Smalltalk-80. G. Kranser, editor, *In Smalltalk-80: Bits
             of History, Words of Advice*, Addison-Wesley, 1983.

[BS83b]   D. Bobrow and M. Stefik. *The LOOPS Manual: a Data and
             Object-Oriented Programming System for InterLisp.* Xerox
             Palo Alto Research Center, 1983.

[BW79]   D. Bobrow and T. Winograd. KRL, Another Perspective.
             Cognitive Science, 3(1), June 1979.

[CAC*84]   W. Cockshott, M. Atkinson, K. Chisholm, P. Bailey, and R.
             Morrison. POMS: a Persistent Object Management System.
             Software Practice and Experience, 14(1), 1984.

[Car84a]   L. Cardelli. A Semantics of Multiple Inheritance. *Semantics
             of Data Types*, Springer-Verlag, 1984.

[Car84b]   L. Cardelli. *Amber.* Technical report, ATT Bell, 1984.

[Car87a]   L. Cardelli. Basic Polymorphic Type Checking. *Science of
             Computer Programming*, 1987.

[Car87b]   M. Carey, editor. *Special Issue on Extensible Database
             Systems*. IEEE Transaction on Knowledge and Data
             Engineering, 1987.

[Car88]   L. Cardelli. Structural Subtyping and the Notion of Power
             Type. *ACM POPL International Conference*, 1988.

[CD74]   H. Tardieu, C. Deheneffe, J.-L. Hainaut. The Individual
             Model. *International Workshop on Data Structure Models
             for Information Systems*, May 1974.

[CDLR90]   S. Cluet, C. Delobel, C. Lécluse, and P. Richard. RELOOP, an Algebra Based Query Language for an Object-Oriented Database System. *Data and Knowledge Engineering*, 5, 1990.

[CDRS86]   M. Carey, D. DeWitt, J. Richardson, and E. Shekita. Object and File Management in the EXODUS Extensible Database System. *VLDB International Conference*, 1986.

[CDV88]   M. Carey, D. DeWitt, and S. Vandenberg. A Data Model and Query Language for EXODUS. *ACM SIGMOD International Conference*, May 1988.

[CFW90]   G. Copeland, M. Franklin, and G. Weikum. Uniform Object Management. *EDBT International Conference*, March 1990.

[CGK*90]   D. Chimenti, R. Gamboa, R. Krishnamurthy, S. Naqvi, S. Tsur, and C. Zaniolo. The LDL System Prototype. *IEEE Transaction on Knowledge and Data Engineering*, 2(1), March 1990.

[CH85]   A. Chandra and D. Harel. Horn Clause Queries and Generalizations. *Journal of Logic Programming*, 1, 1985.

[Cha76]   D. Chamberlin. SEQUEL 2: A Uniformed Approach to Data Definition, Manipulation and Control. *IBM Journal of Research and Development*, 20(6), 1976.

[Cha81]   D. Chamberlin. A History and Evaluation of System R. *Communications of the ACM*, 24(10), 1981.

[Che76]   P. Chen. The Entity-Relationship Model-Toward a Unified View of Data. *ACM Transactions on Database Systems*, 1(1), March 1976.

[Chi68]   D. Childs. Feasibility of a Set-Theoretic Data Structure – a General Structure Based on a Reconstituted Definition of Relation. *IFIP International Conference*, North Holland, 1968.

[Chi84]   T. Chikayama. Unique Features of ESP. *Fifth Generation Computer Systems Conference*, 1984.

[CJ90]   W. Cellary and G. Jomier. Consistency of Versions in Object-Oriented Databases. *VLDB International Conference*, August 1990.

[Cle86]   J. Cleaveland. *An Introduction to Data Types*. Addison-Wesley, 1986.

[CM84]   G. Copeland and D. Maier. Making Smalltalk a Database System. *ACM SIGMOD International Conference*, June 1984.

[Cod70]   E. Codd. A Relational Data Model for Large Shared Data Banks. *Communications of the ACM*, 13(6), June 1970.

[Cod79]   E. Codd. Extending the Relational Model to Capture More Meaning. *ACM Transactions on Database Systems*, 4(4), December 1979.

[Col82]   A. Colmerauer. *Prolog II: Reference Manual and Theoretical Model*. Technical report, Faculté des Sciences de Luminy, 1982.

[Com79]   D. Comer. The Ubiquitous B-tree. *ACM Computing Surveys*, 11(2), June 1979.

[Cox86]   B. Cox. *Object-Oriented Programming: An Evolutionary Approach*. Addison-Wesley, 1986.

[CW85]   L. Cardelli and P. Wegner. On Understanding Types, Data Abstraction and Polymorphism. *ACM Computing Surveys*, 17(4), 1985.

[DA82]   C. Delobel and M. Adiba. *Bases de Données et Systèmes Relationnels*. Dunod, 1982.

[Dat86]   C. Date. *An Introduction to Database Systems*. Addison-Wesley, 1986.

[DB82]   U. Dayal and P. Bernstein. On the Correct Translation of Update Operations in Relational Views. *ACM Transactions on Database Systems*, 7(3), September 1982.

[Dep83]   Department of Defense. *Ada Reference Manual*. U.S. Department of Defense, January 1983.

[Deu90]   O. Deux. The Story of O_2. *IEEE Transaction on Knowledge and Data Engineering*, 2(1), March 1990.

[DFMV90]   D. DeWitt, P. Futtersack, D. Maier, and F. Velez. A Study of Three Alternative Workstation-Server Architectures for Object-Oriented Database Systems. *VLDB International Conference*, August 1990.

[DGL87]   K. Dittrich, W. Gotthard, and P. Lockemann. DAMOKLES: The Database Systems for the UNIBASE Software Engineering Environment. *IEEE Transaction on Knowledge and Data Engineering*, 10(1), 1987.

[DHD72]   O. Dahl, C. Hoare, and E. Dijkstra. *Structured Programming*. Academic Press, 1972.

[DKA*86]   P. Dadam, K. Kuespert, F. Andersen, H. Blangen, R. Erbe, J. Guenauer, V. Lum, P. Pistor, and G. Walch. A DBMS Prototype to Support Extended NF2 Relations: an Integrated View on Flat Tables and Hierarchies. *ACM SIGMOD International Conference*, 1986.

[DN66]   O. Dahl and K. Nygaard. Simula – an Algol-based Simulation Language. *Communications of the ACM*, 9(9), 1966.

[DP89]   A. Doucet and P. Pfeffer. A Debugger for O_2, an Object-Oriented Database Language. *TOOLS International Conference*, November 1989.

[DP90]   A. Doucet and P. Pfeffer. Using a Database System to Implement a Debugger. *IFIP Working Conference on Database Semantic*, Windermere, UK, July 1990.

[DPS86]   U. Deppisch, H. Paul, and H. Schek. A Storage System for Complex Objects. *Workshop on Object-Oriented Database Systems*, September 1986.

[DT88]   S. Danforth and C. Tomlinson. Type Theories and Object-Oriented Programming. *ACM Computing Surveys*, 20(1), 1988.

[EGLT76]   L. Eswaran, J. Gray, R. Lorie, and I. Traiger. The notion of Consistency and Predicate Locks in a Database System. *Communications of the ACM*, 19(11), November 1976.

[Epp89]   J. Eppinger. *Virtual Memory Management for Transaction Processing Systems*. Technical report no. TR 89-115, University of Carnegie Mellon, Computer Science Dpt., 1989.

[FGJM85]   K. Futatsugi, J. Gogen, J.-P. Jouannaud, and J. Messeger. Principles of OBJ2. *ACM POPL International Conference*, 1985.

[FT83]   P. Fischer and S. Thomas. Operators for Non First Normal Form Relations. *International Computer Software Applications Conference*, 1983.

[GG77]   D. Gies and N. Gehani. Some Ideas on Data Types in High Level Languages. *Communications of the ACM*, 20(6), 1977.

[GM88]   G. Graefe and D. Maier. *Query Optimization in Object-Oriented Database Systems: the REVELATION Project*. Technical report no. CS/E 88-025, Oregon Graduate Center, 1988.

[GR83]   A. Goldberg and D. Robson. *Smalltalk80: The Language*. Addison-Wesley, 1983.

[Gra78]   J. Gray. *Notes on Database Operating Systems*. Technical report no. RJ 2188, IBM San Jose, 1978.

[Gro71]   Database Task Group. *CODASYL DBTG Report*. Technical report, ACM, 1971.

[Gro75]   Database Task Group. Study Group on Database Management Systems: Interim Report. *FDT*, 7(2), 1975.

[GT79]   J. Gogen and J. Tardo. *An Introduction to OBJ: a Language for Writing and Testing Software Specifications*. North Holland, 1979.

[GV85]   G. Gardarin and P. Valduriez. *Bases de Données Relationnelles – Analyse and Comparaison de Systèmes*. Eyrolles, 1985.

[GV90]   G. Gardarin and P. Valduriez. *ESQL: An extended SQL with Object and Deductive Capabilities*. Technical report no. 1185, INRIA, 1990.

[Har86]   R. Harper. *Introduction to Standard ML*. Technical report, University of Edinburgh, 1986.

[HCM*90]   L. Haas, W. Chang, G. Lohman, J. McPherson, G. Lapis, B. Lindsay, H. Piranesh, M. Carey, and E. Shekita. Starburst Mid-Flight: As the Dust Clears. *IEEE Transaction on Knowledge and Data Engineering*, 2(1), March 1990.

[Her87]   M. Herlithy. Extending Multiversions Time-Stamp Protocols to Exploit Type Information. *IEEE Transactions on Computers*, 36(4), April 1987.

[HK87]   R. Hull and R. King. Semantic Database Modelling: Survey, Applications and Research Issues. *ACM Computing Surveys*, 19(3), September 1987.

[HK89]   S. Hudson and R. King. Cactis: A Self-Adaptative Concurrent Implementation of an Object-Oriented Database Management System. *ACM Transactions on Database Systems*, 14(3), September 1989.

[HM83]   M. Hammer and D. McLeod. Database Description with SDM: A Semantic Database Model. *ACM Transactions on Database Systems*, 6(3), September 1983.

[HMMS87]   T. Härder, K. Meyer-Wegner, K. Mitschang, and A. Sikeler. PRIMA: ADBMS Prototype Supporting Engineering Applications. *VLDB International Conference*, 1987.

[Hoo84]   J. Hook. Understanding Russel – a First Attempt. *Semantics of Data Types*, Springer-Verlag, 1984.

[Hul84]   J.-M. Hullot. *Programmer en CEYX version 15*. Technical report, INRIA, 1984.

[HY84]   R. Hull and C. Yap. The Format Model: A Theory of Database Organisation. *Journal of the ACM*, 31(3), July 1984.

[HZ87]   M. Hornick and S. Zdonik. A Shared Segmented Memory System for an Object-Oriented Database. *ACM Transactions on Office Information Systems*, 5(1), January 1987.

[IBM78]   IBM. *Information Management System/ Virtual Sorage (IMS/VS)*. IBM, 1978.

[IBM81]   IBM. *SQL Data Systems Concepts and Facilities*. IBM, 1981.

[Ich79]   J. Ichbiah. Rationale of the Design of the Programming Language ADA. *ACM SIGPLAN Notices*, 14(6), 1979.

[JS82]   B. Jaeschke and H. Schek. Remarks on the Algebra of Non First Normal Form Relations. *ACM PODS International Conference*, 1982.

[JWKL90]   B. Jeng, D. Woelk, W. Kim, and W. Lee. Query Processing in Distributed ORION. *EDBT International Conference*, March 1990.

[Kae86]   T. Kaehler. Virtual Memory on a Narrow Machine for an Object-Oriented Language. *OOPSLA International Conference*, September 1986.

[KBB*88]   W. Kim, N. Ballou, J. Banerjee, H. Chou, J. Garza, and D. Woelk. Integrating an Object-Oriented Programming System with a Database System. *OOPSLA International Conference*, 1988.

[KBC*88]   W. Kim, J. Banerjee, H. Chou, J. Garza, and D. Woelk. Composite Object Support in an Object-Oriented Database System. *ACM SIGMOD International Conference*, May 1988.

[KC86]   S. Khoshafian and G. Copeland. Object Identity. *OOPSLA International Conference*, September 1986.

[KC90]   R. Katz and E. Chang. Managing Change in a Computer-Aided Design Database. S. Zdonik and D. Maier, editor, *Readings in Object-Oriented Database Systems*, Morgan-Kaufmann, 1990.

[KCB86]   R. Katz, E. Chang, and J. Bhateja. Versions Modeling Concepts for Computer-Aided Design Databases. *ACM SIGMOD International Conference*, May 1986.

[KCB88]   W. Kim, H. Chou, and J. Banerjee. Operations and Implementation of Complex Objects. *IEEE Transactions on Software Engineering*, 14(7), 1988.

[KCF88]   S. Khoshafian, M. Carey, and M. Franklin. *Storage Management for Persistent Complex Objects*. Technical report no. ACA-ST-118-88, MCC, April 1988.

[KDG87]   K. Kuespert, P. Daddam, and J. Guenauer. Cooperative Object Buffer Management in the Advanced Information Management Prototype. *VLDB International Conference*, 1987.

[KdMS89]   J. Kiernan, C. de Maindreville, and E. Simon. The Design and Implementation of an Extensible Deductive Database System. *SIGMOD Records*, September 1989.

[Kel85]   A. Keller. Algorithms for Translating View Updates into Database Updates for Views Involving Projections, Selections and Joins. *ACM PODS International Conference*, 1985.

[Ken78]   W. Kent. *Data and Reality*. North Holland, 1978.

[KGBW90]   W. Kim, F. Garza, N. Ballou, and D. Woelk. Architecture of the Orion Next-generation Database System. *IEEE Transaction on Knowledge and Data Engineering*, 2(1), March 1990.

[Kie89]   J. Kiernan. *Intégration des types abstraits de données dans un SGBD relationnel déductif*. Doctoral thesis, Université de Paris VI, September 1989.

[Kim82]   W. Kim. On Optimizing an SQL-like Nested Query. *ACM Transactions on Database Systems*, 7(3), September 1982.

[Kim89]   W. Kim. A Model of Queries for Object-Oriented Databases. *VLDB International Conference*, 1989.

[Kin84]   R. King. Sembase: A Semantic DBMS. *International Workshop on Expert Database Systems*, October 1984.

[KK83]   T. Kaehler and G. Krasner. LOOM Large Object-Oriented Memory for Smalltalk-80 Systems. G. Krasner, editor, *In Smalltalk-80: Bits of History, Words of Advice*, Addison-Wesley, 1983.

[KL84]   R. Katz and T. Lehman. Database Support for Versions and
              Alternatives of Large Design Files. *IEEE Transactions on
              Software Engineering*, 10(2), March 1984.

[KL89[W. Kim and F. Lochovsky, editors. *Object-Oriented Concepts,
              Databases, and Applications*. ACM Press, Addison-Wesley,
              1989.

[KM85]   R. King and D. McLeod. Semantic Database Models. *Data-
              base Design*, 1985.

[KM90]   A. Kemper and G. Moerkotte. Advance Query Processing in
              Object Bases Using Access Support Relations. *VLDB
              International Conference*, August 1990.

[Kor83]   H. Korth. Locking Primitives in a Database System. *Journal
              of the ACM*, 30(1), January 1983.

[KP76]   L.Kerschberg and J. Pacheco. *A Functional Database
              Model*. Technical report, University of Rio de Janeiro, 1976.

[KP88]   P. Kolaitis and C. Papadimitriou. Why not Negation by
              Fixpoint? *ACM PODS International Conference*, 1988.

[KPM84]   G. Khan, D. Plotkin, and D. MacQueen. *Semantics of Data
              Types*. Springer-Verlag, 1984.

[Kra85]   S. Krakowiak. *Principes des Systèmes d'Exploitation des
              Ordinateurs*. Dunod, 1985.

[KRS88]   H. Korth, M. Roth, and A. Siberschatz. Extended Algebra
              and Calculus for N1NF Relational Databases. *ACM
              Transactions on Database Systems*, 13(4), December 1988.

[Kup85]   G. Kuper. *The Logical Data Model: a New Approach to
              Database Logic*. Doctoral thesis, Stanford University,
              September 1985.

[Kup87]   G. Kuper. Logic Programming with Sets. *ACM PODS Inter-
              national Conference*, 1987.

[KV84]   G. Kuper and M. Vardi. A New Approach to Database Logic.
              ACM PODS International Conference, 1984.

[Lie86]   R. Lieberman. Using Prototypical Objects to Implement Shared Behavior in Object-Oriented Systems. *OOPSLA International Conference*, September 1986.

[Lip81]   W. Lipski. On Databases with Incomplete Information. *Journal of the ACM*, 28(1), 1981.

[LL89]   T. Lehman and B. Lindsay. The Starburst Long Field Manager. *VLDB International Conference*, 1989.

[LMWF88]   N. Lynch, M. Merrit, W. Weihl, and A. Fekete. *A Theory of Atomic Transactions*. Technical report no. MIT/LCS/TM-362, MIT, 1988.

[LP76]   M. Lacroix and A. Pirotte. Generalized Joins. *SIGMOD Records*, 8(3), 1976.

[LP83]   R. Lorie and W. Plouffe. Complex Objects and their Use in Design Transactions. *IEEE Databases for Engineering Design Applications*, May 1983.

[LR88]   C. Lécluse and P. Richard. Modeling Inheritance and Genericity in Object-Oriented Databases. *ICDT International Conference*, August, 1988.

[LR89a]   C. Lécluse and P. Richard. A Uniform Way of Manipulating Objects and Structured Values in Object-Oriented Databases. *International Workshop on Database Programming Languages*, June 1989.

[LR89b]   C. Lécluse and P. Richard. Langages Orienté-Objet et Bases de Données: l'expérience O_2. *Cinquiémes Journées Bases de Données Avancées*, September 1989.

[LR89c]   C. Lécluse and P. Richard. Modeling Complex Structures in Object-Oriented Databases. *ACM PODS International Conference*, March 1989.

[LR89d]   C. Lécluse and P. Richard. The O_2 Database Programming Language. *VLDB International Conference*, August 1989.

[LR90]   C. Lécluse and P. Richard. *Data Base Schemas and Types Systems for DBPLs, a Definition and its Applications.* Technical report, GIP Altaïr, June 1990.

[LRV88]   C. Lécluse and P. Richard, and F. Velez. O_2, an Object-Oriented Data Model. *ACM SIGMOD International Conference*, May 1988.

[LS79]   B. Liskov and A. Snyder. Exception Handling in CLU. *IEEE Transactions On Software Engineering*, SE-5(6), November 1979.

[LZ74]   B. Liskov and S. Zilles. Programming with Abstract Data Types. *ACM SIGPLAN Notices*, 9(4), 1974.

[Mak77]   A. Makinouchi. A Consideration on Normal Form of Not-Necessarily-Normalized Relation in the Relational Model of Data. *VLDB International Conference*, 1977.

[Man89]   F. Manola. *Object Model Capabilities for Distributed Object Management.* Technical report no. TM-0149-06-89-165, GTE Laboratories, 1989.

[Mat83]   D. Matthews. *Programming Language Design with Polymorphism.* Doctoral thesis, Cambridge University, 1983.

[MBC*88a]   R. Morrison, A. Brown, R. Carrick, R. Connor, A. Dearle, and M. Atkinson. *The Napier Type System.* Technical report no. PPRR-69-88, Glasgow and St Andrews Universities, 1988.

[MBC88b]   R. Morrison, F. Brown, and R. Connor. *The Napier88 Reference Manual.* Technical report no. PPRR-77-89, Glasgow and St Andrews Universities, 1988.

[Mey85]   B. Meyer. *EIFFEL: a Language for Software Engineering.* Technical report no. TRC85-15, University of California, November 1985.

[Mey88]   B. Meyer. *Object-Oriented Software Construction.* Computer Science, Prentice Hall, 1988.

[Mey90]   B. Meyer. *Conception et Programmation par Objets.* InterEditions, 1990.

[MH88]   J. Mitchel and R. Harper. The Essence of ML. *ACM POPL International Conference*, January 1988.

[Mil78]   R. Milner. A Theory of Type Polymorphism in Programming. *Journal of Computer and Systems Sciences*, 17, 1978.

[Min75]   M. Minsky. *A Framework for Representing Knowledge.* McGraw-Hill, 1975.

[Mit84]   J. Mitchel. Type Inference and Type Containment. *Semantics of Data Types*, Springer-Verlag, 1984.

[Mit 86]   J. Mitchel. Representation Independence and Data Abstraction. *ACM POPL International Conference*, 1986.

[MNC*89]   G. Masini, A. Napoli, D. Colnet, D. Léonard, and K. Tombre. *Les Langages à Objets.* InterEditions, 1989.

[Mor79]   R. Morrison. *S-algol Reference Manual.* Technical report no. 79/1, St Andrews University, 1979.

[Mos89]   J. Moss. Addressing Large Distributed Collections of Persistent Objects: The Mneme Project's Approach. *International Workshop on Database Programming Languages*, June 1989.

[Mos90]   J. Moss. *Working with Persistent Objects: To Swizzle or Not to Swizzle.* Technical report no. 90-38, University of Massachussetts, 1990.

[MP84]   J. Mitchel and G. Plotkin. Abstract Types have Existential Types. *ACM POPL International Conference*, 1984.

[MS86]   D. Maier and J. Stein. Indexing in an Object-Oriented DBMS. *Workshop on Object-Oriented Database Systems*, September 1986.

[MS88]   J. Moss and S. Sinofski. Managing Persistent Data with Mneme: Designing a Reliable, Shared Object Interface. *In Advances in Object-Oriented Database Systems*, Springer-Verlag, 1988.

[MW80]   D. Moon and D. Weinreb. *Flavors: Message Passing in the Lisp Machine.* Technical report no. 602, MIT, 1980.

[Naq86]   S. Naqvi. A Logic for Negation in Database Systems. J. Minker, editor, *Workshop on Foundations of Deductive and Logic Programming*, 1986.

[NT89]   S. Naqvi and S. Tsur. *A Logical Language for Data and Knowledge Bases.* Computer Science Press, 1989.

[OBS86]   P. O'Brien, B. Bullis, and C. Schaffert. Persistent and Shared Objects in Trellis/Owl. *International Workshop on Object-Oriented Database Systems*, 1986.

[Osb88]   S. Osborn. Identity, Equality and Query Optimization. K. Dittrich, editor, *Advances in Object-Oriented Database Systems*, Springer-Verlag, 1988.

[OT86]   S. Osborn and T. Treleaven. The Design of Relational Database Systems with Abstract Types as Domains. *ACM Transactions on Database Systems*, 11(3), September 86.

[PA86]   P. Pistor and F. Andersen. *Principles for Designing a Generalized NF2 Data Model with an SQL-type Language Interface.* Technical report, IBM-Heidelberg, 1986.

[Pap86]   C. Papadimitriou. *The Theory of Database Concurrency Control.* Computer Science Press, 1986.

[PCP89]   D. Plateau, R. Cazalens, and B. Poyet. *A Customizable Abstract I/O Server for Complex Object Edition.* Technical report, GIP Altaïr, 1989.

[Pfe91]   P. Pfeffer. *Débogage en environnement orienté-objet persistant.* Doctoral thesis, Université de Paris-Sud, Orsay, 1991.

[PM88]   J. Peckham and F. Maryanski. Semantic Data Model. *ACM Computing Surveys*, 20(3), September 1988.

[PSS*87]   H. Paul, H. Schek, M. Scholl, G. Weikum, and U. Deppisch. Architecture and Implementation of the Darmstadt Database Kernel System. *ACM SIGMOD International Conference*, 1987.

[RC89]   J. Richardson and M. Carey. Implementing Persistence in E Language. *International Workshop on Persistent Objects Systems*, 1989.

[Rei86]   R. Reiter. A Sound and Sometimes Complete Query Evaluation Algorithm for Relational Databases with Null Values. *Journal of the ACM*, 33(2), 1986.

[RH89]   D. Stemple, R. Hull, and R. Morrison. *International Workshop on Database Programming Languages*. Morgan Kaufmann, 1989.

[Rot90]   K. Rotzell. Transactions and Versionning in an OODBMS. *OODBT Workshop*, October 1990.

[SA86]   R. Snodgrass and I. Ahn. Temporal Data Bases. *Computer*, 19(9), 1986.

[SCB*86]   G. Schaffert, T. Cooper, B. Bullis, M. Kilian, and C. Wilpot. An Introduction to Trellis/Owl. *OOPSLA International Conference*, September 1986.

[Sch 77a]   J. Schmidt. Some High Level Language Constructs for Data of Type Relation. *ACM Transactions on Database Systems*, 2(3), September 1977.

[Sch77b]   M. Schonilck. A Clustering Algorithm for Hierarchical Structures. *ACM Transactions on Database Systems*, 2(2), 1977.

[Sch83]   U. Schiel. An Abstract Introduction to the Temporal Hierarchic Data Model THM. *VLDB International Conference*, 1983.

[Sco76]   D. Scott. Data Types as Lattices. *SIAM Journal on Computing*, September, 1976.

[Sel79]   P. Selinger. Access Path Selection in a Relational Database Management System. *ACM SIGMOD International Conference*, June 1979.

[SFL80]   J. Smith, S. Fox, and T. Landers. *Reference Manual for ADAPLEX*. Technical report, Computer Corporation of America, 1980.

[Shi81]   D. Shipman. The Functional Data Model and the Data Language Daplex. *ACM Transactions on Database Systems*, 6(1), March 1981.

[SM80]   J. Schmidt and M. Mall. *Pascal/ R Report*. Technical report no. 66, Fachbereich Informatik, University of Hamburg, July 1980.

[SO91]   D. Straube and M. Özsu. Queries and Query Processing in
            Object-Oriented Database Systems. *ACM Transactions on
            Office Information Systems,* 1991.

[SPO89]   P. Scheuermann, Y. Park, and E. Omiecinski. Heuristic
            Reorganization of Clustered Files. *FODO International
            Conference,* December 1989.

[SPSW90]   H. Schek, H. Paul, M. Scholl, and G. Weikum. The DASDBS
            Project: Objectives, Experiences, and Future Prospects.
            IEEE Transaction on Knowledge and Data Engineering,
            2(1), March 1990.

[SRH90]   M. Stonebraker, L. Rowe, and Hirohama. The Implementation
            of POSTGRES. *IEEE Transaction on Knowledge and Data
            Engineering,* 2(1), March 1990.

[SS85]   P. Schwartz and A. Spector. Synchronizing Shared Abstract
            Data Types. *ACM Transactions on Computer Systems,* 2(3),
            August 1985.

[SS89]   H. Schoning and A. Sikeler. Cluster Mechanisms Supporting
            the Dynamic Construction of Complex Objects. *FODO
            International Conference,* June 1989.

[Sta84]   J. Stamos. Static Grouping of Small Objects to Enhance
            Performance of a Paged Virtual Memory. *ACM Transactions
            on Computer Systems,* 2(2), May 1984.

[Sto81]   M. Stonebraker. Operating Support for Database Management.
            Communications of the ACM, 24(7), 1981.

[Sto82]   M. Stonebraker. Virtual Memory Management for Database
            Systems. *ACM Operating System Review,* 18(2), 1982.

[Sto83]   M. Stonebraker. Document Processing in a Relational Data-
            base System. *Transactions on Office Information Systems,*
            8(2), April 1983.

[Sto90]   M. Stonebraker, editor. *Special Issue on Database Prototype
            Systems.* IEEE Transaction on Knowledge and Data Engi-
            neering, 1990.

[Str89]   B. Stroustrup. *Le Langage C++.* InterEditions, 1989.

[Su83]   S. Su. SAM*: A Semantic Association Model for Corporate and Scientific Statistical Databases. *International Conference on Information Science*, 1983.

[SWKH84]   M. Stonebraker, M. Wong, E. Kreps, and G. Held. The Design and Implementation of Ingres. *ACM Transactions on Database Systems*, 9(3), September 1984.

[SZ89]   G. Shaw and S. Zdonik. An Object-Oriented Query Algebra. *Data Engineering*, 12(3), September 1989.

[SZ90a]   G. Shaw and S. Zdonik. A Query Algebra for Object-Oriented Databases. *6th International Conf. on Data Engineering*, February 1990.

[SZ90b]   E. Shekita and M. Zwilling. Cricket: A Mapped, Persistent Object Store. *International Workshop on Persistent Object Systems*, September 1990.

[SZR86]   A. Skarra, S. Zdonik, and S. Reiss. An Object Server for an Object-Oriented Database System. *International Workshop on Object-Oriented Database Systems*, 1986.

[Tan89]   A. Tanenbaum. *Les Systèmes d'exploitation. Conception et Mise en Oeuvre*. InterEditions, 1989.

[Tev87]   A. Tevanian. A Unix Interface for Shared Memory and Memory Mapped Files under Mach. *Summer Usenix International Conference*, June 1987.

[TF86]   S. Thomas and P. Fisher. *Nested Relational Structures. Advances in Computing Research*, JAI Press, 1986.

[Tha86]   S. Thatte. Persistent Memory: A Storage Architecture for Object-Oriented Database Systems. *International Workshop on Object-Oriented Database Systems*, 1986.

[Tra82]   I. Traiger. Virtual Memory Management for Database Systems. *ACM Operating Systems Review*, 16(4), 1982.

[TZ84]   S. Tsur and C. Zaniolo. An Implementation of GEM Supporting a Semantic Data Model on a Relational Backend. *ACM SIGMOD International Conference*, 1984.

[Ull85]   J. Ullman. Implementation of Logical Query Languages for Databases. *ACM SIGMOD International Conference*, June 1985.

[Ull89]   J. Ullman. *Principles of data and Knowledge Base Systems.* Computer Science Press, 1989.

[VAB*86]   J. Verso, S. Abiteboul, F. Bancilhon, N. Bidoit, V. Delebarre, S. Gamerman, J.-M. Laubin, M. Mainguenaud, T. Mostardi, P. Pauthe, D. Plateau, P. Richard, M. Scholl, and A. Verroust. *VERSO: a Database Machine Based on non 1NF Relations.* Springer-Verlag, 1986.

[Val87]   P. Valduriez. Join Indices. *ACM Transactions on Database Systems*, 12(2), June 1987.

[VBD89]   F. Velez, G. Bernard, and V. Darnis. The O_2 Object Manager: an Overview. *VLDB International Conference*, August 1989.

[VD90]   S. Vandenberg and D. DeWitt. *An Algebra for Complex Objects with Arrays and Identity.* Technical report no. 918, University of Wisconsin, 1990.

[VKC86]   P. Valduriez, S. Khoshafian, and G. Copeland. Implementation Techniques of Complex Objects. *VLDB International Conference*, August 1986.

[Weg77]   P. Wegbreit. *ACM Conference on Data: Abstraction, Definition and Structure.* ACM, 1977.

[Weg90]   P. Wegner. Object-Oriented Systems. July 1990. Unpublished report.

[Wei87]   W. Weihl. Commutativity-Based Concurrency Control for Abstract Data Types. *IEEE Transactions on Software Engineering*, 13(1), January 1987.

[Wei89]   G. Weikum. Set-Oriented Disk Access to Large Complex Objects. *International Conference on Data Engineering*, 1989.

[WLH90]   K. Wilkinson, P. Lyngbæk and W. Hasan. The Iris Architecture and Implementation. *IEEE Transaction on Knowledge and Data Engineering*, 2(1), March 1990.

[WSSH88]   P. Wilms, P. Schwarz, H. Schek, and L. Haas. *Incorporating Data Types in an Extensible Database Architecture.* Technical report no. RJ 6405, IBM, 1988.

[YCLS85]   C. Yu, M. Cheing, K. Lam, and M. Siu. Adaptative Record Clustering. *ACM Transactions on Database Systems*, 10(2), June 1985.

[YSLT81]   C. Yu, M. Siu, K. Lam, and F. Tai. Adaptative Clustering Schemes: General Framework. *IEEE Computer Software and Application Conference*, November 1981.

[Yu74]   C. Yu. A Clustering Technique Based on User Queries. *Journal of American Society for Information Sciences*, 1974.

[Zan83]   C. Zaniolo. The Database Language GEM. *ACM SIGMOD International Conference*, 1983.

[Zdo86]   S. Zdonik. Version Management in an Object-Oriented Database. *International Workshop on Advanced Programming Environments*, 1986.

[ZM90]   S. Zdonik and D. Maier, editors. *Readings in Object-Oriented Database Systems.* Database Management Systems, Morgen Kaufmann, 1990.

Index

379